A World of Lost Innocence

A World of Lost Innocence:
The Fiction of Elizabeth Bowen

By

Nicola Darwood

CAMBRIDGE
SCHOLARS
P U B L I S H I N G

A World of Lost Innocence:
The Fiction of Elizabeth Bowen,
by Nicola Darwood

This book first published 2012

Cambridge Scholars Publishing

12 Back Chapman Street, Newcastle upon Tyne, NE6 2XX, UK

British Library Cataloguing in Publication Data
A catalogue record for this book is available from the British Library

ISBN (10): 1-4438-3909-4, ISBN (13): 978-1-4438-3909-9

DEDICATION

This book could not have been written without the friendship and assistance of a number of people. I am especially indebted to Julia Briggs whose encouragement, enthusiasm and criticism was invaluable. My thanks also go to Jane Dowson for her timely advice, and to Gary Day and Sarah Brown for their involvement in the early days. However, this book would not have been possible without the love and support from my friends and family, especially Steve, Emma and Rachel.

CONTENTS

ACKNOWLEDGEMENTS

I am grateful to Curtis Brown Group Ltd on behalf of the Estate of Elizabeth Bowen for granting permission to quote from Bowen's published and unpublished material, to the Harry Ransom Centre, The University of Texas at Austin for permission to quote from *Anna* and to Durham University Library for permission to quote from correspondence from Elizabeth Bowen to William Plomer.

INTRODUCTION

It is, according to Elizabeth Bowen, "not only our fate but our business to lose innocence, and once we have lost that it is futile to attempt to picnic in Eden" (Bowen 1946, 264). This book charts Bowen's employment of the motif of innocence as a recurrent theme in her novels and short stories, and notes the transition from innocence to experience which plays a significant role in the epistemological journey faced by Bowen's characters so that they do not remain "incurable strangers to the world" (*DH*, 106), a journey often precipitated by a moment of recognition. Bowen's treatment of innocence is not simply one of a binary opposition between "innocence" and "experience"; Bowen's manipulation of the narrative and her complex use of syntax subverts such a reading as she avoids the conventional trope to be found in earlier fiction such as Blake's *Songs of Innocence and Experience* and *Auguries of Innocence*, the *bildingsroman* novel or the nineteenth century realist novel. The endings of Bowen's novels also complicate this reading as they fail to provide the closure associated with earlier teleological novels; by denying the reader such a closure, Bowen's fiction resists the notion that she is enforcing any moral judgement about innocence and its loss on her readers.

Innocence has, of course, been a pervasive theme in story-telling since stories from the Old Testament were told and retold around fires and from the pulpit. As a literary concept, the origin of ideas of innocence can be found in the story of the fall of Adam and Eve and their consequent expulsion from Eden, ideas later built on by, for example, the novels of Henry James and, ultimately so far as this book is concerned, the fiction of Elizabeth Bowen. However, over the centuries, social rules have changed and, with these changes, society's perceptions of the meaning of innocence have also altered. This is particularly apparent when one considers changing attitudes to childhood and innocence from the Middle Ages to the nineteenth century: from an era where there was little recognition of childhood as a distinctive state, to one of the romantic idealisation of the child, an idealisation disrupted by Freud's violent and sexualised picture of childhood. As a writer in the twentieth century, Bowen would have necessarily absorbed these changing perceptions. Writing over five decades (her first book of short stories, *Encounters*, was published in 1923 and her last complete novel, *Eva Trout, or Changing Scenes* in 1968), her novels and short stories were published during a period in which notions of innocence were themselves continually destabilized by cultural, intellectual, national and international events. Bowen's proposition that it is "futile to attempt to picnic in Eden" once innocence is lost raises the question as to whether loss of innocence is equally vital for both the individual and society. Of equal importance is the transition from innocence to experience in the epistemological journey faced by Bowen's characters and the role of recognition in that journey, together with the part that the increasingly complex narrative plays in Bowen's fiction. The narration of these journeys, however, unsettles the notion of moral certainties prevalent in realist or *bildingsroman* fiction and so I address two central concerns: the innocence of the characters within the texts, and the epistemological journey of the reader.

Deriving from the Latin word "nocens",[1] "innocence" is defined by the Oxford English Dictionary as "[t]he quality or fact of being innocent"; the definition continues, innocence is "[f]reedom from sin, guilt, or moral wrong in general; the state of being untainted with, evil; moral purity [...] Freedom from specific guilt [...] Freedom from cunning or artifice, guilelessness, artlessness, simplicity". The dictionary further defines the term "innocent" in relation to a person as "[d]oing no evil; free from moral wrong, sin, or guilt [...] pure, unpolluted [...] Having or showing the simplicity, ignorance, artlessness, or unsuspecting nature of a child or one ignorant of the world" (995-996).[2] These parts of speech–the noun and the adjective–thus provide a point of departure for a discussion of innocence. From the original meaning of word as not causing harm, one usage of the word "innocence" is associated with a person's state before sexual intercourse; questions of childhood innocence are irrevocably tied to notions of sexuality and morality for, from one point of view (both in Bowen's fiction and in society), childhood innocence is lost once there is an awareness of sexuality, an awareness that can also highlight issues of morality.

In 1999, Hermione Lee noted "I think there is more to be said about sex in Bowen—repression, danger, ambivalence" (1999, 4): certainly coming to terms with sexuality is one of the major contributory factors on the journey from innocence to experience and Bowen's concern with the ending of innocence in young girls and women is a favourite theme throughout her fiction (though, of course, treated from a variety of angles), its loss arising from a transition which is often associated in Bowen's fiction with moments of recognition. Drawing on Terence Cave's work, I borrow Aristotle's concept of *anagnôrisis* (recognition) to analyse its role in the journey from innocence to knowledge, from childhood to adulthood.

Recognition of one's own sexuality is an important part of this process and it is in this context that the impact of Freudian notions of sexuality is apparent in Bowen's work; social perceptions of innocence, particularly childhood innocence, changed irrevocably after Freud's publication of his theories and, although Henry James' literary influence can also be seen in Bowen's fiction, her novels were all written in a post-Freudian context. In *English Novelists* Bowen acknowledges the importance of sexuality and class as themes in fiction:

> One cannot deny that, with the nineteenth century, a sort of fog did begin, in the English novel, to obscure vital aspects of life. It became more difficult to write greatly because it became less possible to write truly. There was facetiousness on the subject of class, squeamishness on the subject of sex (1942b, 32).

Such a stance echoes her belief that human interest is needed in a novel, in particular the psychological conflict that occurs between two people (ibid, 13).

Discussing the role of violence in relation to innocence, Frederick Karl notes that "the innocent and the good suffer for the crass casuality of the guilty and the evil" (1964, 107) and that "even the author's sense of good and evil will tend to merge them one into another; the conflict will become resolved less in clear colours than in various shades of darks-and-whites, in muted greys" (ibid, 108). He continues his argument:

> we find, also, that the innocent, good person is very often the cause of evil and guilt that is manifest in his antagonist. Frequently, the good person is drawn to the evil one, for good and evil in this scheme lie within the framework of what are considered "normal" human relationships; and humiliation becomes the sole vehicle of evil action. (Ibid.)

This particular aspect of Karl's reading of Bowen's fiction echoes the narratorial comment in *The Death of the Heart*: "[i]n love, the sweetness and violence [the innocent] have to offer involves a thousand betrayals for the less innocent" (*The Death of the Heart*, 106). In Bowen's fictional world violence and chaos often occur as a result of the actions of a character who might be regarded as "innocent", for example Portia Quayne (*The Death of the Heart*), Emmeline Summers (*To the North*), or Jeremy, Eva Trout's son (*Eva Trout, or Changing Scenes*), while the impact of death has a large part to play in the transition from a state of innocence to its loss. Violence, chaos and death occur as a culmination, or as Eva Trout's guardian, Constantine Ormeau, puts it, a "concatenation" (*ET*, 267) of events, which may act as the antithesis to the state of innocence depicted throughout Bowen's novels and in many of her short stories.

My approach in this book owes much to the work of various critics, specifically the work of Hermione Lee. Lee's approach to Bowen's work (*Elizabeth Bowen*, originally published in 1981), which highlights the importance of Bowen's life in relation to her fiction, provides a model for this book in which biographical detail, including material obtained from previously unpublished letters, is used to help to establish the context for the novels and selected short stories. Although many of Bowen's letters have been published in *The Mulberry Tree* (edited by Lee) and in Victoria Glendinning's edited collection of the letters and diaries of Bowen and Charles Ritchie (*Love's Civil War: Elizabeth Bowen & Charles Ritchie: Letters and diaries from the love affair of a lifetime*: 2008), there remain a number of letters that have yet to be published and some of these can be found in the libraries of Manchester University and Durham University. These letters, written to L.P. Hartley and William Plomer respectively, discuss Bowen's thoughts about her life, her novels and the novels of others. A number of her letters to L.P. Hartley specifically refer to the time in which she wrote *The Little Girls* and describe her feelings of loss and melancholy following the death of her husband, Alan Cameron, emotions that can be read into Dinah's distress as she discovers that the coffer is empty when, for her, "the game's collapsed. We saw there was nothing *there*" and she asks the question "So where am I now?" (*LG*, 163). Conversely, Bowen's correspondence with William Plomer provides both an understanding of how she saw her own work, particularly in relation to *The Death of the Heart*, *The Little Girls* and *Eva Trout, or Changing Scenes*, and the importance to Bowen of Plomer's approval of her writing.[3]

Lee's approach is not unique in the study of Bowen's fiction, nor was it the only model I used when writing this book. Phyllis Lassner (*Elizabeth Bowen*, 1990) provides biographical details of Bowen's life before turning her attention to Bowen's fiction through the application of feminist theory, an approach used by Lis Christensen (*Elizabeth Bowen: The Later Fiction*, 2001). Maud Ellmann also applies this model in her study, *Elizabeth Bowen: The Shadow Across the Page* (2003), indeed Ellmann's stated desire is to show how Bowen's "fiction literally houses her experience" (2003, 8). Andrew Bennett and Nicholas Royle's reading of Bowen's novels (*Elizabeth Bowen and the Dissolution of the Novel*, 1995) provided another framework which I found useful when deciding on my approach. Their identification of a single motif in each novel, which is then used as a springboard for a discussion of that particular text, provided the impetus for my work in which the common thread of the notion of innocence is utilised in an exploration both of this theme and the narrative strategies employed by Bowen. However, whilst adopting certain elements of these studies I have not consciously adopted their theoretical approaches, although in common with all these critics I have drawn on a close textual analysis of the texts and appropriated aspects of historical, structuralist and psychoanalytic theories in my reading of Bowen's fiction. Whilst I primarily utilise elements of narratological and Lacanian theory I would not, of course, suggest that this is the only valid approach to Bowen's fiction; these are just two theoretical tools that can be applied to Bowen's fiction. I haven't, for example, followed Renée Hoogland's study (*Elizabeth Bowen: A Reputation in Writing*, 1994) in which she reads Bowen's fiction through a feminist lesbian theoretical perspective, a reading which appears to preclude other valid interpretations of Bowen's work. Lee, in her introduction to the second edition of *Elizabeth Bowen*, suggests that Hoogland's approach "seems a flattening, intractable model for Bowen's slippery and complex fictions" (1999, 11); my hope is that my methodological approach avoids providing an "intractable" and reductive reading of Bowen's fiction.

Karl argues that "the large issues of the day, whether treated directly as in the sociological novel, or indirectly as in the psychological novel which generalizes on the sociologist's particulars, will not be present in Miss Bowen's canon" (1964, 111), but his view has since been contradicted by more recent critics, notably Phyllis Lassner. She notes that Bowen's novels are concerned with the major issues of the period, and she cites, in particular, *The House in Paris* where she observes that Bowen deals directly with the question of Jewishness in a post-Nuremberg Law setting. Lassner shows that Bowen highlights Nazi anti-Semitic attitudes through her characterisation of Max Ebhert as victim (1998, 203-204). Allan Hepburn's collection of Bowen's essays (*People, Places, Things: Essays by Elizabeth Bowen*, 2008) provides added illumination to Bowen's thoughts throughout the twentieth century. Although many of the essays concentrate on the "lighter side" of Bowen, others speak of her impressions of the Paris Peace Conference in 1946, of Hungary, Prague and, of course, Ireland—each essay providing an insight to the work of the Conference or her fascination with the post-war complexities faced by people in Europe. Her eye for detail can also be seen in her fiction and I would argue that the larger issues of the twentieth century are reflected in Bowen's novels and that an analysis of their cultural context adds to our understanding of Bowen's continued and developing use of innocence throughout her *oeuvre*. Individual chapters therefore investigate the cultural context of the particular novels and short stories under consideration as an introduction to the changing treatment of innocence. Such an approach extends to a consideration of changing cultural consciousness over the five decades of Bowen's fiction, as well as to Bowen's own responses to cultural changes and political events.

This structure also provides an opportunity to observe the development of specific aspects of innocence as well as the wider development of Bowen's style as I would argue that Bowen's treatment of individual character and of innocence as a central theme, whilst comparatively superficial in her earliest short stories and novels, became more elaborate through her more complex narrative structure and characterisation in her later fiction.   By drawing selectively on the theories of narratology of Shlomith Rimmon-Kenan, Gérard Genette and others, and Terence Cave's study of recognition (classical *anagnôrisis*), the role of the unfolding narrative itself is examined in the development of Bowen's representation of innocence. Bowen's narratives deliberately manipulate the reader's own journey from innocence to experience during the process of reading and thus individual chapters also examine this journey by interrogating the narration of the novels. Bowen's views on questions of innocence can be read in the authorial comments to be found throughout her novels: Jennifer Breen argues that "although the world of a novel is not an embodiment of the author's beliefs about her actual world, a fictional world often implies a world-view that can be deduced from the way the behaviour of the characters is constructed in that fictional world" (1990, 11) and such a view is particularly useful when considering Bowen's own responses to notions of innocence.

Her representation of innocence and experience is not simply one of binary opposites and her choice of narrative strategies further complicates such a simplistic trope; this is particularly so in relation to the roles of the narrator and the narrative and the authorial manipulation of the reader's epistemological journey. In this book I identify a number of ways in which Bowen manipulates the narrative: the manipulation of time, the changing focalisation (or point of view) of the narrative, the use of authorial voice and the open endings of her novels, each one having an effect on the reader's comprehension of the text as they often delay understanding or confuse the reader's perceptions of the characters' journey from innocence to experience.

Bowen's manipulation of time within her novels is probably the easiest one to recognise. Whilst there is such manipulation in her earlier novels, specifically moments when the reader is informed about events that have taken place before the narration of the "present" and particular episodes when the narration appears to move forward by a considerable period of time, *The House in Paris* is the first novel in which the manipulation of time is particularly apparent. The tripartite structure of the novel and its non-linear narrative provides the opportunity to discuss not just the "present" but also the "past" and, in doing so, the structure also allows the narrator to present the narrative from varying points of view. A similar strategy is used in *The Little Girls* where the past is framed by the narration of contemporary events; such manipulation, of course, has the potential to further confuse the reader.

Bowen believed that the manipulation of time in the narrative was an important factor in fiction, stating that "[t]he either concentration or even or uneven spacing-out of events along time is important." (1945b, 258). As is discussed in chapter six, this a narrative tool she used to great effect in her ninth novel where the longest chapter in the novel, running to just over thirty seven pages, narrates the events of just one day. In his work, Genette discusses the "isochronism of a narrative", which he defines as "*steadiness in speed*" (1972, 87). He continues,

> The isochronous narrative [...] would thus be here a narrative with unchanging speed, without accelerations or slowdowns, here the relationship duration-of-story/length-of-narrative would remain steady. It is doubtless unnecessary to specify that such a narrative does not exist, and cannot exist except as a laboratory experiment: at any level of aesthetic elaboration at all, it is hard to imagine the existence of a narrative that would admit of no variation in speed – and even this banal observation is somewhat important: a narrative can do without anachronies, but not without *anisochronies*, or, if one prefers (as one probably does), effects of *rhythm*. (Ibid, 88)

Building on and providing a further explanation of Genette's work, Rimmon-Kenan states that "we can discern two forms of modification [to the narrative speed]: acceleration and deceleration. The effect of acceleration is produced by devoting a short segment of the text to a long period of the story [...]. The effect of deceleration is produced by the opposite procedure" (1983, 53), an effect particularly seen in the final chapter of *The Little Girls*. She concludes her explanation by stating that "the pace [of the narrative] is accelerated through a textual 'condensation' or 'compression' of a given story-period into a relatively short statement of its main features" (ibid).

Throughout Bowen's fiction the variable and multiple viewpoint of the narration is important, becoming particularly evident in *The House in Paris*. Genette highlights the role of "focalisation" or point of view of the narrative, an element which Rimmon-Kenan defines as "the angle of vision through which the story is filtered in the text" (1983, 43). Such a manipulation manifests itself in a variety of ways from, for example, Matchett's explanation to Portia of the events leading to the divorce of Thomas Quayne's parents which is at variance with the version offered to St. Quentin by Anna (*The Death of the Heart*) to the use of diaries and letters as a narrative tool in many of Bowen's novels. Bowen's use of letters, which further manipulates the reader's understanding of the text, can be seen particularly in *A World of Love* where Guy's letters are interpreted and then re-interpreted by the main protagonists, each reading either adding to the reader's comprehension or, conversely, leading the reader to doubt the veracity of the text. Bowen takes this strategy further in *Eva Trout, or Changing Scenes* as the reader is confronted by letters which never reach their intended destination. Indeed, Professor Holman's letter, which forms the central section of that novel, is written with the knowledge that it might never reach Eva; providing a subjective view of Eva, the letter adds to the reader's understanding of her character as it discusses Eva's own presentation of her character to the professor on their flight to America.

The use of authorial voice in Bowen's fiction manifests itself in direct addresses to the reader about, for example, the nature of innocence, the chaos that the innocent can cause and the role of innocence in society, such addresses appearing to embody Bowen's own thoughts about these specific issues. Susan Snaider Lanser argues that

> [a]s a narratological term, "voice" attends to the specific forms of textual practice and avoids the essential tendencies of its more casual feminist images. As a political term, "voice" rescues textual study from a formalist isolation that often treats literary events as if they were inconsequential to human history. When these two approaches to "voice" converge in what Mikhail Bakhtin has called a "sociological poetics" it becomes possible to see narrative technique not simply as a product of ideology but as an ideology itself: narrative voice, situated at the juncture or "social position and literary practice", embodies the social, economic and literary conditions under which it has been produced. (1992, 5)

Lanser is concerned with one specific aspect of narration which has a bearing on the fiction of Elizabeth Bowen, "the distinction between private voice (narration toward a narratee who is a fictional character) and public voice (narration directed toward a narratee "outside" the fiction who is analogous to the historical reader)" (1992, 15) and such a distinction is important in relation to the direct addresses to the reader in Bowen's fiction. Lanser adds that a major element of authorial status [is] a distinction between narrators who engage exclusively in acts of representation – that is, who simply predicate the words and actions of fictional characters – and those who undertake "extrarepresentational" acts: reflections, judgements, generalizations about the world "beyond" the fiction, direct addresses to the narratee, comments on the narrative process, allusions to other writers and texts. (ibid, 16-17)

This becomes important in a work where the authorial voice is frequently heard. Rimmon-Kenan highlights the problems of an approach which is over-simplistic and distinguishes between the author, the implied author, the narrator and the narratee, cautioning against identifying the views of the implied author with those of the actual author for

the two need not be, and in fact are often not, identical. An author may embody in a work ideas, beliefs, emotions other than or even quite opposed to those he has in real life; he may also embody different ideas, beliefs and emotions in different works. (1983, 89)

It remains, of course, impossible to state categorically that any direct narratorial addresses found in Bowen's fiction represent her own opinions; however, they often convey similar messages to the reader and so, in this respect, her work does not demonstrate the variation that Rimmon-Kenan notes in other works of fiction.

The question of viewpoint or focalisation of the narration leads directly to the issue of a gendered approach to narrative: Margaret Homans, for example, suggests that

[i]n recent years there has been an unusual consensus, amongst feminist critics who consider themselves to be doing narrative theory, about the problems posed by conventional sequential narrative for representing women. Starting from a psychoanalytic and/or structuralist premise, virtually all these critics take it as axiomatic that the structure of narrative itself is gendered and that narrative structure is cognate with social structure. (1994, 5)

Homans cites Nancy K. Millar's assertion that "a variety of eighteenth- and nineteenth-century women writers critique the standard, teleological novelistic plots of courtship that offer women marriage or death as outcomes" (ibid) and suggests that the teleological novel can be seen as a male construct (ibid, 7). However, Homans also observes that "[t]hose who write about the twentieth century sometimes note that the feminist break with convention [from the accepted outcomes of a teleological novel] overlaps with the goals of modernism" (ibid, 6). Whilst Bowen would not have considered herself a feminist, it can be argued that though

she continued, in the main, to use the masculine-gendered teleological
narrative, Bowen chose not to provide closure with the ending of her
novels, and thus followed in the footsteps of feminist writers such as
Virginia Woolf (although of course Bowen would not have made such a
claim herself). The question of the acquisition of knowledge, the
epistemological journey experienced both by the character and the reader
of her novels is of particular importance in Bowen's fiction. Epistemology,
"the theory of knowledge", can be defined by asking three questions: what
is knowledge, what can we know and how do we know what we know?
Linked to the reader's journey is the desire to know, "the satisfaction of
epistemophilia" (Bennett and 1995b, 57), the desire which impels the
reader to continue reading the text. Peter Brooks interrogates the
importance of the "function of the end" of a text (1984, 92) and states that

> Barthes makes explicit an assumption common to much thought about
> narrative when he claims that meaning (in the "classical" or "readable"
> text) resides in full predication, completion of the codes in a "plenitude" of
> signification, which makes the "passion for meaning" ultimately desire for
> the end. It is at the end – for Barthes as for Aristotle – that recognition
> brings its illumination, which then can shed retrospective light. The
> function of the end, whether considered syntactically (as in Todorov or
> Barthes) or ethically (as in Aristotle) or as formal or cosmological closure
> (as by Barbara H. Smith or Frank Kermode), continues to fascinate and to
> baffle. (Ibid)

However, as Bennett and Royle observe, some texts (and they
specifically cite Virginia Woolf's story "The Mark on the Wall")
deliberately withhold the answers sought by the reader, denying the reader
the satisfaction associated with the denouement of a murderer unmasked, a
marriage, or the death of the hero (1995b, 57); Bowen too often denies the
reader the satisfaction associated with full knowledge, since she leaves
many questions unanswered, questions that could be vital in the reader's
journey from innocence to experience.

All these narrative techniques result in texts which effectively
deconstruct conventional approaches to innocence, both for Bowen's
protagonists and for her readers. Her syntactical choices, which show
some similarities to the syntax of Henry James, add to her complex
treatment of the notion of innocence as many of her sentences resist a
simplistic reading[4] and the reader has to read and re-read some paragraphs
in order to understand the complexities of both the syntax and the subject
matter. The manipulation of the narrative adds further to the complexities
of her texts as does Bowen's use of authorial voice in her fiction and the

lack of closure found in her novels, a lack which adds to the argument that Bowen resists forcing moral judgements on her reader. Such a resistance arises, perhaps, from her own unconventional views on marriage, reflected by her own marriage and late sexual development (the treatment of sexuality in her novels of the thirties and forties particularly corresponds to the apotheosis of her own sexuality[5]); thus it could be argued that her avant-garde approach to conventional morality arises from her own sexual experiences and complicated lifestyle. Indeed, there is no suggestion in her fiction that a conventional relationship, that is marriage between man and woman, was the only acceptable existence for her protagonists. However, as much of her work can also be read in a Modernist context, it could also be suggested that her resistance to the conventional trope to be found in realist fiction, particularly seen in the light of the lack of closure to be found in the final pages of her novels could, in fact, result from a desire to encourage her readers to participate in a journey of uncertainties.

While I draw upon narratological theory throughout this book, one particular concept from Aristotle's *Poetics* has also been used as part of the theoretical framework, that of *anagnôrisis* or recognition, a narrative tool that is fundamental in creating a transition from innocence to experience, from childhood to adulthood. Throughout Bowen's novels it is possible to identify specific moments within the plot which would appear to have a momentous effect on the protagonist. Lois' realisation of the possibility of an adult sexual relationship (*The Last September*), for example, provides the impetus which thrusts her out of her innocent existence into a world of adult experience. Conversely, in *The House in Paris* Karen's sudden jolt of recognition of the possibility of her aunt's impending death brings the recognition of the inevitability of her own mortality. Terence Cave's *Recognitions: A Study in Poetics* (1998) provides the starting point for a discussion of *anagnôrisis*. He traces the literary history of the term by first defining it:

> Recognition (*anagnôrisis*) is unquestionably the least respectable term in Aristotelean poetics [...]
>
> Recognition is a scandal. The word may seem excessive, but it is appropriate even in its most ordinary, vulgar sense, since recognition plots are frequently *about* scandal – incest, adultery, murder in the dark, goings-on that the characters ought to know about but usually don't until it's too late. [...] In Aristotle's definition anagnorisis[6] brings about a shift from ignorance to knowledge; it is the moment at which the characters understand their predicament fully for the first time, the moment that resolves a sequence of unexplained and often implausible occurrences, it makes the world (and the text) intelligible. Yet it is also a shift *into* the

implausible: the secret unfolded lies beyond the realm of common experience. (1998, 1-2)

Cave explores two aspects of *anagnôrisis*: the first he describes as "the supposedly trivial nature of the recognition scene as a contrivance" (ibid, 2), scenes which often lead to laughter, associated with the discovery of items within a plot such as "the birthmark, the scar, the casket, the handbag", items which are "local and accidental details on which recognition seems to depend, yet which seem unworthy of serious attention" (ibid). Cave's second "face of recognition" is

> a scandal [...] that takes us directly to what is most crucial to our sense of the literary, to the capacity of fictions to astonish us, upset us, change our perceptions in ways inaccessible to other uses of language. Recognition delivers a shock (ibid).

Bowen's fiction often demonstrates the use of this latter narrative ploy; *anagnôrisis* provides those pivotal moments in the plot when recognition, whether partial or complete, changes a character's understanding of the world in which s/he lives, although often such a change is brought about through a series of smaller recognitions which, when considered with hindsight by the reader, can be seen to have cumulatively effected this change. Cave adopts F.L. Lucas's definition of *anagnôrisis* as "the realization of the truth, the opening of the eyes, the sudden lightening flash in the darkness [...] This flash of revelation may appear, as Aristotle points out, either before it is too late, or after [...]" (Lucas 1928, 95).[7] Lucas continues "[...] Or the flash may come after the catastrophe, serving only to reveal it and complete it, as when Œdipus discovers his guilt" (ibid). While Terence Cave uses the notion of "recognition" both in relation to a revelation of identity and the discovery of facts (that is *anagnôrisis*),[8] Lucas is uneasy with the word "recognition" as a definition for *anagnôrisis*:

> "Recognition" is a mistranslation. We associate the word too closely with the narrow sense of discovering a person's identity ; where *anagnorisis* may equally well signify the discovery of things unknown before, and applies alike to the recognition of Imogen by Posthumus and the realisation by Othello of the true facts of the situation. "Realisation" indeed would be a possible translation of the word. (1928, 95)

Bowen's use of *anagnôrisis* is patently influenced by Henry James's practice but while Bowen never formally acknowledged her use of this device in her fiction, her brief survey of the English novel, *English*

Novelists (published in 1942 and which discusses fiction from the seventeenth century to the novels of Virginia Woolf), indicates that the recognition which arises from the impact of the actions of one character on another is an important element in English fiction. She states that the novelists of the eighteenth century used character and plot, but

> a third was needed, to merge these two. What was this? – interest in human relationships. The tract in which men and men, or women and men, affect, act on and conflict with each other was still waiting to be explored. It had been accepted that it is from a man's character that his actions spring. One had now to see the effect that one man or woman, by acting in character, had on the action or character of another. It had, too, to be seen that human behaviour seldom follows a set course (or course planned in the head), being often deflected by accidents. The nature and cause of accidents that deflect behaviour might be called the stuff of the novel. Most often, these are psychological: conflicting desires between two people are more important than a tempest or a coach being overturned. (1942b, 13)

This is, of course, particularly apposite to her own fiction, for whilst Bowen's novels may be considered within their own historical context, their plots are predominantly concerned with the "conflicting desires between two people".

There is a growing body of criticism of Bowen's fiction and much has informed my own reading of her work but, as already mentioned, the study which has had the greatest influence on my book has been Hermione Lee's *Elizabeth Bowen* (originally published in 1981 and revised in 1999). This offers an interpretation of Bowen's work interpolated with biographical information and probably provides the most useful starting point for any study of Bowen. Lee's appreciation of Bowen's fiction is evident from her opening comment: "Elizabeth Bowen is one of the greatest writers of fiction in this language and in this century. She wrote ten novels, at least five of which are masterpieces" (1999, 1). However, Lee is also critical about Bowen's writing, specifically her criticism of her contemporaries, stating that when Bowen wrote about writers she admired (and Lee cites her work on Virginia Woolf in particular) she could be "indulgent and flowery", and, in relation to E. M. Forster, "over-effusive" (ibid, 217).[9] Lee's study is a particularly valuable contribution to Bowen criticism, its biographical details and individual discussions providing both essential background reading and a model for this book. Other studies (particularly those of Bennett and Royle, Lassner, Ellmann and Coates) have all played an important part in my reading of Bowen's fiction.

As Lee notes in her introduction to the second edition of *Elizabeth Bowen*, in the eighteen years between the publication of the first and second editions, Bowen's fiction began to attract attention from critics in a variety of fields including Anglo-Irish studies and feminist criticism. More recently, there has been a further surge in the critical reception of Bowen's fiction; indeed, an edition of *Modern Fiction Studies* (published in the summer of 2007) focuses entirely on Bowen's fiction. No longer gathering dust on university bookshelves, Bowen's work has begun to attract an increasing amount of critical attention, a revival probably led by Lee's work and one added to by Andrew Bennett and Nicholas Royle's groundbreaking study *Elizabeth Bowen and the Dissolution of the Novel* (1995). Bennett and Royle's premise for their work, according to Ann Wordsworth, is that rather than providing an "old-fashioned [...] single-author study of a "minor" figure whose work is most often read as a charming but dated embodiment of traditional literary and social studies" (1995, viii), they will offer a "process of dissolution, of 'loosening, fading away, breaking up, unsolving' " (ibid) and their work has provided the springboard for later studies.

Maud Ellmann's *Elizabeth Bowen: The Shadow Across the Page* (2003) acknowledges the debt she owes to Bennett and Royle's study; she states that their work is "[t]he most important influence" on her own study (2003, 17). Her book takes their analysis a step further, providing close readings explicitly based on theories of psychoanalysis and deconstruction. Her account is particularly concerned with identity and sexuality and each chapter examines these themes as they function in specific novels and with particular foci.

John Coates' study of the role of society in Bowen's fiction (*Social Discontinuity in the Novels of Elizabeth Bowen: The Conservative Quest*: 1998) considers, amongst other issues, the stability of marriage compared with the disorder that arises when social conventions are rejected, "the dichotomy between stasis and mobility" (1998a, 291) in eight of Bowen's novels,[10] he pays particular attention to the theme of innocence in *To the North* and *A World of Love*. Eschewing "contemporary critical practices" (ibid, 4), Coates's close readings of these two novels highlight specific instances where a discussion of innocence is of importance and his exploration of innocence, morality, sexuality and the corruption of the innocent in these two particular novels is particularly useful. However, his reluctance to engage with "contemporary critical practices" in his account combined with the lack of reference to the novels' historical moments, and the limited scope of his discussion of the theme of innocence, leave many areas unexplored. Despite not doing so himself, he notes that Heather Bryant Jordan's study[11] places "Bowen in a specific cultural and historical context" (ibid, 245); approving this methodology, Coates states it is probably most useful to place Bowen within the context of her own times, to look at the response her fiction records to the cataclysmic public events about which she knew, the decline of the Anglo-Irish, the First World War, the disintegrations of the 1930s, the return of war in 1939-45 (ibid)

Whilst not consciously following Coates's advice, I have utilised such an approach in order to gain a better understanding of Bowen's responses to the momentous cultural changes in the five decades in which she wrote her novels. Such contextualisation is aided by two book-length biographical studies by Patricia Craig (1986) and Victoria Glendinning (1977); of these, the latter is particularly useful, providing a detailed account of Bowen's life. However, this latter study is strangely reticent about Bowen's sexual relationships with Glendinning's refusal to name Humphrey House as Bowen's first lover being the most striking omission. The diaries of Charles Ritchie offer further biographical information, detailing meetings with and his feelings for Bowen. These are, of course, highly subjective but nevertheless his diaries, which chart his relationship with Bowen from their first meeting in 1941 until her death in 1974, provide a wealth of biographical information about Bowen, recording both her thoughts about every day occurrences to, for example, the pleasure she gained from *Eva Trout, or Changing Scenes* (1983, 85).

Of the articles and book chapters that address the theme of innocence in Bowen's fiction, only those by Frederick Karl, Paul Parish and Robert Coles are specifically relevant to this book. Karl's discussion of innocence in his chapter on Bowen, "The World of Elizabeth Bowen" (1964) provides a useful exploration of the relation between violence and innocence and, as will be seen from this introduction, his reading of Bowen's fiction leads him to suggest that "good" and "evil" are not always represented as binary opposites (1964, 108). Parish's article, "The Loss of Eden: Four Novels of Elizabeth Bowen" (1973), provides another of the few discussions of innocence in Bowen's fiction but only examines four novels, *The Last September, The House in Paris, The Death of the Heart* and *Eva Trout, or Changing Scenes.* There are some similarities between Parish's article and Harriet Blodgett's overtly Christian interpretation of Bowen's novels which argues that the presence of God is to be found in all Bowen's fiction (*Patterns of Reality: Elizabeth Bowen's Novels*, 1975). Both Parish and Blodgett discuss Bowen's use of the myth of Eden and Parish suggests that Bowen's use unites "the elements of nature, love and idealism" in scenes reminiscent of the Biblical story of the Fall of Man (1973, 86). Coles' study, *Irony in the Mind's Life: Essays on Novels by James Agee, Elizabeth Bowen and George Eliot* (1974), discusses the issue of Portia's possible innocence in *The Death of the Heart* and he questions whether she should be seen as an innocent victim or as a cruel, revengeful and spiteful figure (1974, 14).

The earliest account of Bowen's fiction of any length is Jocelyn Brooke's monograph *Elizabeth Bowen* (1952), written for the British Council. It is concerned (necessarily, given its date of publication) with Bowen's earlier fiction. Brooke highlights various aspects of Bowen's fiction and comments on her impressionistic technique, comparing her with Virginia Woolf in this respect. Bowen was apparently delighted with Brooke's appraisal of her work: "I was not only impressed; I learnt a lot from it. It gives me at once a base and a point of departure from which to go on" (Bowen, quoted in Glendinning 1977, 196-197). No further studies were published for 23 years until Edwin Kenney produced his monograph *Elizabeth Bowen* (1975) which offers a brief critique of Bowen's novels and short stories. Kenney suggests that all of Bowen's novels deal with the loss of innocence and goes on to explore this loss specifically in his reading of *To the North*, *The House in Paris* and *The Death of the Heart*. His readings focus however on the loss of childhood innocence, and fail to develop the issue of sexuality, or the role of the narrator. Building on Brooke's and Kenney's studies, Allan Austin's *Elizabeth Bowen* (1989) is a general overview of Bowen's novels which notes Bowen's fascination with "the journey of youth to adulthood with all its attendant hazards" (1989, 4). Austin finds Bowen's language

> impressionistic. Calculated to reverberate, the prose nicely conveys the ambiguities and imponderables of experience that underscore her vision. In approaching her material as more of an x-ray than a camera, she projects essences. (Ibid, 10)

Phyllis Lassner's two major studies of Bowen's fiction, *Elizabeth Bowen* (1990) and *Elizabeth Bowen: A Study of the Shorter Fiction* (1991) provide a feminist reading of Bowen's work. The earlier study concentrates on six of her novels[12] and begins with a brief biography which highlights the losses that Bowen suffered, experiences that later contributed to events within her novels. The later study, as its title suggests, is concerned with Bowen's short stories, and discusses various issues such as loss, sexuality and the comedy of manners. This account also includes extracts from Bowen's own prefaces to her volumes of short stories and reviews and provides an overview of earlier critical studies of Bowen's work. The most comprehensive study of Bowen's short stories, this provides a wealth of information about this form of Bowen's fiction.

In *How Will the Heart Endure: Elizabeth Bowen and the Landscape of War* (1992) Heather Bryant Jordan discusses how war influenced Bowen's writing and contends that Bowen used fiction as a device to disassociate herself from the horrors of war but, at the same time, always sought to provide links between her writing and the external world. A different approach is offered by Renée Hoogland's *Elizabeth Bowen: A Reputation in Writing* (1994) where a lesbian/feminist reading of Bowen's fiction is adopted, providing both biographical information and a detailed close reading of Bowen's novels. These three studies, (Lassner, Hoogland and Jordan) all provide useful explorations of the gender issues which need to be considered in any discussion of Bowen's work and they invite a feminist approach both to her fiction and to her position as a woman writer during the first half of the twentieth century.

Neil Corcoran's *Elizabeth Bowen: The Enforced Return* (2004), although not focussing specifically on the representation of innocence in Bowen's fiction, provides an illuminating study of her fiction. He notes that "Bowen is a writer deeply impressed by the ambitions of High Modernism, even if, until the final two novels, she never entirely loses touch with classic realism" (2004, 4): Bowen is discussed increasingly in relation to the Modernist movement—and "Intermodernism"—and the narrative strategies discussed in this book would appear to support such a reading. Stating that his book is organised around three specific themes, "Ireland, childhood and war" (2004, 11), Corcoran has also been influenced by Bennett and Royle's work: he refers to the "dissolution" of the plot of *The Last September*, and to their work on *The House in Paris*, amongst other novels (ibid, 87). Corcoran's book provides a thematic discussion of Bowen's fiction, tracing similarities and differences through, for example, *The Last September* to *A World of Love* in a continuing discussion of Anglo-Irish history before he turns his attention to the treatment of childhood in Bowen's fiction in the second part of his book. This section discusses *The House in Paris*, *The Death of the Heart* and *Eva Trout, or Changing Scenes* as Corcoran interrogates the themes of childhood, identity and sexuality. The last part of his book discusses the theme of war in relation to *The Heat of the Day* and Bowen's wartime short stories, *The Demon Lover and Other Stories.*

The field of Bowen studies has been greatly enhanced by Eibhear Walshe's edited collection of essays in *Elizabeth Bowen* (2009) and Allan Hepburn's three publications: *The Bazaar and Other Stories* (2008), a collection of previously uncollected short stories; *People, Places, Things* (2008), essays which range from her thoughts about teenagers to the proceedings of the 1946 Paris Peace Conference; and *Listening In* (2010) in which Hepburn draws together some of Bowen's broadcasts, speeches and interviews. In the introductions to these collections, Hepburn provides a new reading of Bowen, one which highlights her own views about the process of writing and of collecting impressions of the world around her.

As will be seen from this review of the pertinent secondary material, while there is a growing body of criticism of Bowen's fiction, and although much ground has been covered, there remain gaps in these critical discussions. Drawing on the range of existing criticism, I hope that I have built on the work of critics such as Lee, Bennett and Royle, Lassner, Christensen, Ellmann and Corcoran and offer a different approach to Bowen's fiction, one which is concerned with her continued preoccupation with the nature and meaning of innocence and which foregrounds the psychological conflicts experienced by her protagonists. This book focuses specifically on the notion of innocence throughout Bowen's novels, examining the subject not only across the range of her work, but also in relation to her unfolding narrative structures through the application of narratological theory, and especially the process by which the readers learn what happens in parallel to, yet very differently from, the characters within her fiction.

Notes

[1] Eric Partridge notes that the definition of this word is "harmful" (1966, 442); its antonym, "innocence" should therefore be defined as "not causing harm".

[2] Second edition (2000).

[3] My transcriptions of relevant unpublished material and an extract from her unpublished manuscript *Anna* can be found in the appendix.

[4] A prime example can be found in *A World of Love* where "mush for the chickens, if nothing else, was never not in the course of cooking" (*A World of Love*, 21)

[5] See chapters three, four and five specifically.

[6] Cave prefers to use this term as if it were English, unitalicised and without the accent over the second "o".

[7] Quoted in Cave (1998, 184).

[8] See, for example, Cave's discussion of Henry James's *The Ambassadors* (1998, 428/463).

[9] This comment relates, of course, to Bowen's critical essays and introductions, rather than her fiction.

[10] Coates does not include *The Hotel* nor *Eva Trout, or Changing Scenes* in his discussion, although he does include the latter in his conclusion where he considers some recent critical approaches to Bowen's fiction.

[11] Discussed below.

[12] Whilst Lassner's study concentrates on *The Last September, Friends and Relations, To the North, The House in Paris, The Death of the Heart* and *The Heat*

of the Day, some mention is also made of Bowen's four other novels (*The Hotel, The Little Girls, A World of Love* and *Eva Trout, or Changing Scenes*).

CHAPTER ONE

INNOCENCE AND VIOLENCE:
THE LAST SEPTEMBER

Bowen states in *The Death of the Heart* (1938) that "[i]n love, the sweetness and violence [the innocent] have to offer involves a thousand betrayals for the less innocent" (*DH*, 106). In Bowen's fictional world violence and chaos often occur as a result of the actions of the innocent and the use of these themes is not to be found solely in *The Last September*. With its violent backdrop however, the novel provides a useful starting point in any discussion about the use of violence in Bowen's fiction; it is a novel which sets the innocence of the main protagonist, Lois Farquar and, arguably, the possible innocence of the Anglo-Irish, within the context of the actual political violence which raged in Ireland during September 1920.

Of course, *The Last September* was not Bowen's first novel. Having published two volumes of short stories, *Encounters* (1923) and *Ann Lee's and Other Stories* (1926), respectively, Bowen published her first novel, *The Hotel*,[1] in 1927. Whilst arguably derivative of E. M. Forster's two novels *A Room with a View* (1908) and *Where Angels Fear to Tread* (1905), nevertheless *The Hotel* introduces one of Bowen's main themes, that of a young, innocent protagonist attempting to cross the divide between adolescence and adulthood. The novel is set in the insular world of a hotel on the Riviera, a novel in which the "outer world is barely recognized" (Atkins 1977, 59), and it tells the story of Sydney Warren as she meets the Reverend James Milton. Sydney is staying in the hotel as a guest of her cousin, Tessa, and her family firmly holds the belief that spending the winter on the Riviera will be of huge benefit to Sydney:

> It had appeared an inspired solution of the Sydney problem. The girl passed too many of these examinations, was on the verge of a breakdown and railed so bitterly at the prospect of a year's forced idleness that the breakdown seemed nearer than ever. Now an ideal winter had offered itself: sunshine, a pleasant social round. Sydney could be out of doors all

day long; she might distinguish herself in tennis tournaments; she might get engaged" (*H*, 20).

It seems that Sydney will fulfil her family's prophecy as she becomes engaged to marry James but a precarious journey through twisting roads which leads Sydney to believe, and possibly to hope, that they will not survive the journey jolts her into a recognition that marriage to James would be a mistake, that it would be "quite impossible" (*H*, 181). When James presses her for an explanation Sydney replies

> [...] I suppose it was the shock of being alive – oh, how can I explain to you? I had no idea we were as real as this. I'd never realized it mattered so much [...] You and me – how could we every have thought of it? It was just a dream. It seemed simple. (*H*, 181-182)

Sydney's moment of *anagnôrisis* is one which is repeated in Bowen's later novels where events force her characters into episodes of recognition which will drastically affect their lives, often effecting the transition from childhood to adulthood, from innocence to experience. As Brooke suggested, *The Hotel* is a novel in which

> one recognizes a hint of that theme which, in her later and more highly wrought novels, will become on of Miss Bowen's chief preoccupations: I mean the predicament of the "innocent heart" pitted against the forces of insensibility and misunderstanding, the victim of its own immaturity (1952, 12-13).

It is not just Bowen's use of recognition or the theme of "the innocent heart" which finds repetition in her later fiction as certain character types can also be found in subsequent novels. In Mrs. Kerr, for example, one can find similarities with other dominant characters such as Lady Naylor, Lady Elfrida, Lady Latterly and, the epitome of the older manipulative woman, Madame Fisher. Ronald Kerr's characteristics can be seen as the prototype for future "cads" such as Markie and Eddie and certain of Colonel Duperrier's traits can also be seen in Major Brutt. Bowen's use of comedy in her later novels can also be traced back to *The Hotel*: James Milton's misuse of the Honourable Mrs. and Miss Pinkerton's bathroom is a prime example of Bowen's satirical view of the English abroad and one which is also found in her description of the English in *The Last September*. Of course, one of the striking similarities can be found in the characters of Sydney and Lois Farquar as the two young women struggle to find their own place in society.

Published in 1929, *The Last September* is unique in Bowen's *oeuvre* in being completely retrospective. In the preface to the 1952 edition, Bowen recorded her desire to write a novel in which "the reader must look, must be conscious of looking, backward – down a backward perspective of eight years". This technique is different from her treatment of time in *The Hotel* in which she "wanted readers to contemplate what could appear to be the immediate moment" (1952, 96), a device she employs in the majority of her novels. The novel, Nicola Humble suggests, taps "into a middle-class nostalgia for a largely fantisized past" (2001, 62) and, to ensure that her readers were aware of the retrospective nature of the novel, the narrator emphasises the passing of time through the description of Lois in the second paragraph of the novel for "[i]n those days girls wore crisp white skirts and transparent blouses clotted with white flowers; ribbons, threaded through with a view to appearance, appeared over their shoulders." (*LS*, 7)[2]

"Fiction within the texture of history"

Whilst Bowen states that the novel is "at many, many removes from autobiography" (1952, 96), it is possible to identify elements in *The Last September* which reflect Bowen's own life as well as references to historical events: one critic, John Coates, considers the novel "strongly autobiographical", an aspect which "seems to enforce attention to the Anglo-Irish predicament" (1990, 205). A number of episodes in the novel would seem to substantiate Coates' reading, for although Bowen was not continuously present in Ireland during the period 1918-1921,[3] she did return to Bowen's Court for holidays, and must have led a comparable life to that of Lois during these periods. At the height of the arson attacks by the IRA in 1921, Bowen was in Italy with her Aunt Edie, recovering from a broken engagement to John Anderson, a lieutenant in the British Army.[4] Her father wrote to tell her that three of their neighbours' houses had been burnt by the Irish (Glendinning 1977, 39-40). In his letter he expressed his concern for his own house, fearing "that as things are now, there can be only one other development. You must be prepared for the next news and be brave. I will write at once." (Bowen 1942a, 440). Henry Bowen's letter must have made a lasting impression on Bowen: her fears that her home too would become one of the "blackened shells with wind whistling through them" (1951b, 136) emerge in *The Last September* and are recorded in the preface:

I *was* the child of the house from which Danielstown derives. Bowen's Court survived – nevertheless, so often in my mind's eye did I see it burning that the terrible last event in *The Last September* is more real than anything I have lived through (1952, 100).

Bowen also draws on this period in Irish history in her short story "The Back Drawing-Room" (1926)[5] in which a ghost story is told by an unnamed guest at a gathering in England. Evoking the violence which was rife in Ireland during the early nineteen twenties, the speaker tells the assembled guests, including a young woman called Lois, of his discovery of a sobbing woman in a house which, on first glance, he believed to have been deserted. On his return to the house in which he was staying, he is astounded to be told by his hosts that arsonists had destroyed the house two years previously (*CS*, 199-210).

Minor details in *The Last September* echo events in Bowen's life: Lady Naylor suggests that Lois should attend art school, a decision also made by Bowen; both share a preference for sitting on the steps of their respective houses at night time,[6] and both become romantically involved with British soldiers. In her 1952 preface, Bowen states:

[i]n 'real' life, my girlhood summers in County Cork, in the house called Danielstown in the story, had been, though touched by romantic pleasure, mainly times of impatience, frivolity, or lassitude. I asked myself *what* should I be, and when? (1952, 96)

echoing a sense shared by both Lois and her cousin Laurence that they are participants rather than observers, an aspect of the novel discussed further below.[7]

Whilst the novel may well contain autobiographical detail, Bowen also commented that the book was "fiction with the texture of history" (ibid, 98). In the novel the "texture of history" is expressly that of the division in Ireland in 1920 with its accompanying violence, and is a constant throughout *The Last September*. The violence of the political struggle between the Irish and the English, the continuing awareness of potential violence and the violence of nature itself all act as a backdrop to Lois' story and that of the other characters in the novel, their actions often played out in what could be perceived as a comedy of manners.

Reviewing two volumes of history in *The New Statesman and Nation* in 1939[8], Bowen stated the

past of Ireland is an uneasy subject: controversial, bloody and bitter, with no trappings, few uninterruptedly pleasant prospects down which the eye can run […] When the Englishman looks at Ireland, something happens which is quite unbearable – the bottom drops out of his sense of right and wrong. That *méfiance*[9] holds good in a generation: few Englishmen who served in His Majesty's Army in Ireland in those years that just preceded the Treaty care to be reminded of that country again.

So, ignorance of Irish history, in the English and most of the Anglo-Irish, has not been seen as a blot on culture – till now [...] Her entity as a country, her continuous, underlying existence, her conditions were very little known of [...] Her native – as opposed to the Anglo-Irish – culture was, before the height of the Gaelic movement, ignored. (1939, 173)

According to some, the revival of Gaelic culture helped to provide in part a catalyst for the growing division between Ireland, England and the Anglo-Irish, a division which led to the Easter Rising of 1916.[10] The events of that Easter, which irrevocably changed the history of Ireland, are memorably portrayed in Yeats' poem "Easter 1916" in which, through the four stanzas of the poem, he compares the emotions of the different groups who were involved in the uprising. Kiberd believes the poem to be "the foundational poem of the emerging Irish nation-state [... in which] the Irishman is still a child." (1996, 114). This notion of the Irishman as a child can also be applied to the Anglo-Irish characters in *The Last September*, an often childlike body of people who appear to remain generally ignorant (or innocent) of political issues throughout 1920. The childlike nature of the Anglo-Irish is often highlighted by Bowen; speaking of their isolation she suggests that it "is possible that Anglo-Irish people, like children, do not know how much they miss. Their existences, like those of only children, are singular, independent and secretive." (1942a, 20). Such an isolated existence could, to a certain extent, explain the apparent political stance of the Anglo-Irish and the violent political situation in Ireland during 1920, whilst acting as a backdrop to the novel, can also be seen to highlight the political ambivalence (either through innocence or ignorance) of many of the characters.[11]

As the breakdown of society progressed and the violence escalated there were growing and realistic fears of reprisals: one such fear was associated with the many relationships between Irish girls and English soldiers. Mr Thompson, the father of Livvy, Lois' friend, fears the actions of the I.R.A. should they find out that Livvy has been consorting with David Armstrong, a second lieutenant in the British army. Mr. Thompson has a deep-seated distrust of the soldiers and, as Livvy tells Lois, "[h]e says I'll get the house burnt over his head with my goings-on" (*LS*, 110). Such a fear would not have been groundless; Curtis reports a military attack on a creamery in County Tipperary following an incident when

Irishmen had cut off the hair of an eighteen-year-old girl for the crime of "walking out" with an English soldier (1994, 336). A comparable incident is noted by Sir Richard who "was delighted when he heard from the postman [...] how three young women in the Clonmore direction had had their hair cut off by masked men for walking out with the soldiers." (*LS*, 61). Although the Irish were, on this occasion, guilty merely of cutting off the girls' hair, reprisals of a more violent nature were feared by many.

The fighting between the British and the Irish became more vicious (and uncontrollable) with the introduction of a new force nicknamed the "Black and Tans", a group of soldiers formed to assist the officers of the Royal Irish Constabulary (R.I.C.). Drawn from British ex-servicemen who had been unable to settle down to civilian life following the end of World War 1, the "Black and Tans" were notorious for their viciousness and lawlessness; they terrified the locals and increased the Irish hatred so that many came to hate all things British (Mackay 1996, 160). The introduction of the "Black and Tans" was, according to Bowen, Britain's first step in acknowledging the situation in Ireland and it was, for her, the "wrong one" (1951b, 135). Fear of the "Black and Tans" pervaded all sections of Irish society a fear which even permeates Sir Richard's dreams in which he "rode round the country on a motor-bicycle from which he could not detach himself. His friends cut him; he discovered he was a Black and Tan." (*LS*, 107). Lois and Livvy share Sir Richard's dislike and fear of the "Black and Tans": travelling back from tea at Mrs. Fogarty's house in Clonmore, they hear a lorry approaching:

> Black and Tans, fortified inwardly against the weather, were shouting and singing and now and then firing shots. The voices, kept low by the rain, the grin of wheels on the rocky road, tunnelled through the close air with a particular horror. To meet in this narrow way would be worse than a dream [...] They heard the lorry grind past the mouth of the boreen[12] with apprehension, feeling exposed and hunted. (*LS*, 75)

With the Troubles as the context for the novel, it is not surprising that there are constant undertones of violence and destruction[13]; whilst these can often be seen in direct contrast to the frivolous, childlike behaviour of the Anglo-Irish and are also expressed in terms of the violence of nature. The wind, for example, blows down three of the ash trees along the approach to the house (*LS*, 8), thus destroying part of the demesne which is seen as a barrier keeping potential marauders at bay:

> The screen of trees that reached like an arm from behind the house –
> embracing the lawns, banks and terraces in mild ascent – had darkened,

deepening into a forest. Like splintered darkness, branches pierced the faltering dusk of leaves. Evening drenched the trees; the beeches were soundless cataracts. Behind the trees, pressing in from the open and empty countryside like an invasion, the orange bright sky crept and smouldered. (*LS*, 22)

The brightness of the orange sky is an omen, its flame-like colour foretelling the time when Danielstown will be burnt, executed, its flames lighting up the evening sky and when a "fearful scarlet ate up the hard spring darkness; [...] It seemed, looking from east to west at the sky tall with scarlet, that the country itself was burning" (*LS*, 206). Whilst the demesne might be considered as protector, it also threatens; the countryside outside the boundary is bright and colourful, whilst the trees of the demesne are "exhaling darkness" (*LS*, 67). It is the darkness of those trees surrounding Danielstown that makes it seem "a very reservoir of obscurity" (ibid), an image which, once again, serves to highlight the isolation of those who live in Danielstown. The notion of natural violence is sustained by the frequent references to the rain which remains a destructive force throughout the novel, never a force for good; the rain destroys Sir Richard's crops (*LS*, 79), it washes away the remains of the tennis party at Danielstown where "[s]omething had now been wiped away from the place with implied finality" (*LS*, 87), there is "a cold apprehension of rain in the beeches, the tinkling and knocking of water beyond the wall" (*LS*, 85) and rain, like the smouldering sky, is used to foretell the impending changes for "it had never rained like this before" (*LS*, 104).

A small, but significant, rôle is played by the rooks, their presence impinging on daily life. Bowen's use of rooks as a disruptive force can be seen as an analogy for, and a harbinger of, the impending changes for the Anglo-Irish. Francie, for example, cannot stay in the room she had long thought of as hers for, as Lady Naylor tells her, "[t]he rooks on that side of the house disturbed so many people; we've changed the rooms round" (*LS*, 16).[14] In addition to the menacing presence of the rooks, Bowen employs the symbolism of the contrast between dark and light to emphasise the perceived safety within the house compared to the violence which exists just outside the demesne of Danielstown. The gathering storm clouds in *The Last September* (both literal and metaphorical) are highlighted by, and contrast with, Bowen's treatment of light, particularly the light which appears to follow Lois.

Dark had so gained the trees that Lois, turning back from the window, was surprised at how light the room was. Day, still coming in from the fields by the south windows, was stored in the mirrors, in the sheen of the wallpaper, so that the room still shone. (*LS*, 22-23)

The effective contrast between light and dark is also used to foreground Gerald's growing attachment to Lois. Returning to Danielstown the day after the tennis party, Gerald is aware of Lois' absence by the lack of colour and light; it "became a dream – parasols with their coloured sunshine" (*LS*, 87) wiped out by the rain—for Gerald darkness has replaced the light that he perceives to surround Lois.

The location of *The Last September* within a context of violence (both natural and man-made), with its contrasting social events and social comedy, provides a narrative in which it is possible to question the political nature of the characters. The very meaning of being Anglo-Irish appears to be rife with ambiguity[15] and it is not possible to apply just one definition to such a body of people, as they could not be considered a homogenous group.[16] William Heath's exploration of the meaning of the term "Anglo-Irish" echoes Bowen's description of the houses of the Anglo-Irish as "isolated by something much more lasting than the physical fact of space: the isolation is innate; it is an affair of origin" (Bowen 1942a, 20). He sees that particular body of people as being isolated, "cut off from the native Catholic Irish by nationality, religion, social and political position" and views Lois' position as the epitome of such isolation (1961, 34). It therefore becomes problematic to provide a definition of "Anglo-Irishness" that could be widely accepted, a problem which also arises when Bowen's own Anglo-Irish roots are examined. Certainly Jack Lane has trouble reconciling Bowen's claim to Irish descent with his own interpretation of Bowen's Irish credentials:

> The Bowen Family undoubtedly had a physical connection with the area – a predatory connection. […] On the other hand, the *Anthology* was meant to reflect the cultural heritage of local people down the generations – and Elizabeth Bowen was certainly not part of that. Her literary outlook, the themes of her books, and her characters derived from another culture. (1999a, 5)[17]

An interview by "The Bellman" appearing in *The Bell* in 1942 provides a stark contrast to Lane's very negative opinion of Bowen.[18] Commenting on "The Bellman's" statement that there were people who did not consider Bowen "an Irish writer at all" Bowen stated:

> I consider myself as an Irish novelist […] As long as I can remember I've been extremely conscious of being Irish – even when I was writing about such very un-Irish things as suburban life in Paris or the English seaside.

> All my life I've been going backwards and forwards between Ireland and
> England and the Continent, but that has never robbed me of the strong
> feeling of my nationality. (Bowen, quoted by "The Bellman" 1942, 425)

Whilst Bowen might claim to be more Irish than English, Hermione
Lee contests that Bowen lived "the most Anglicised kind of Anglo-Irish
life" (1999, 45), a sentiment shared by Brian Fallon who refers to Bowen's
career as being "thoroughly London-orientated" but also notes that she
"retained a certain detachment about England and things English, the sure
mark of the émigré writer" (1999, 177-178). Nevertheless, Bowen's
statement highlights the ambiguity inherent in being Anglo-Irish, in
"living on both sides of the hyphen" (Kenney 1975, 19). In the preface to
The Last September Bowen states that

> [d]uring the Troubles, the position of such Anglo-Irish land-owning
> families as the Naylors, of Danielstown, was not only ambiguous but was
> more nearly heart-breaking than they cared to show. Inherited loyalty (or at
> least, adherence) to Britain – where their sons were schooled, in whose
> wars their sons had for generations fought, and to which they owed their
> "Ascendancy" lands and powers – pulled them one way; their own
> temperamental Irishness the other. (1952, 98-99)

The Anglo-Irish in *The Last September*, whilst, to some extent, cut off
from the local populace, also appear remote within their own world. They
are, for example, isolated individuals as they sit down to dinner on the first
evening of Hugo and Francie Montmorency's visit:

> Spaced out accurately round the enormous table – whereon, in what was
> left of the light, damask birds and roses had an unearthly shimmer – each
> so enisled and distant that a remark at random, falling short of a neighbour,
> seemed a cry of appeal, the six, in spite of an emphasis of speech and
> gesture they unconsciously heightened, dwindled personally (*LS*, 24).

Bowen also uses this theme of isolation in her short story "The Visitor"
(1926)[19] in which a young boy, Roger, is sent to stay with neighbours
while his mother dies; he is "alone, enisled with tragedy" (*CS*, 124) and
also in "Making Arrangements" (1925)[20] where a letter is "enisled [...],
lonely, gleaming and defiant on the silver salver on to which Margery [the
protagonist's wife] had so often flung her gloves (*CS*, 171). Bowen's use
of the unusual word "enisled" has resonances of Matthew Arnold's poem
'To Marguerite, in Returning a Volume of the Letters of Orbis'. The first
stanza of this poem suggests that man lives in isolation despite close
proximity to others.

This echoes the growing isolation of the Anglo-Irish typified in *The Last September* which, together with the contemporary attempts to destroy their way of life, can be seen as the result of their exploitation of the local populace. Their continued ambivalence, whether arising from a lack of recognition of their isolation or from their inability to accept responsibility for their tenants, is apparent in the novel where Anglo-Irish characters regularly take the side of the Irish against that of the English, emphasising the "Irish" element of their identity, even though they would not be recognised as such by the local Irish populace. The ambivalence portrayed by Bowen highlights Lassner and Derdiger's thesis that in the novel

> Bowen complicates and modernizes the traditional Gothic genre in several ways. First, *The Last September* does not portray a simple clash between the civilised and the primitive. Rather, these concepts are shown to be unclear and unstable, with the Anglo-Irish Ascendancy residing in the gap between colonizer and colonized [...] in effect, this liminal space complicates Anglo-Ireland's self proclaimed national identity as the civilized and its identification of the Irish as primitive [...] Anglo-Ireland is subverted by the colonised below. The Ascendancy is also destablized by the actual colonial power above, that is, the power that considers itself to be authentically civilised. This power, in its political, social and cultural permutations, would be the English who criticize and mock Anglo-Irish society in hyperexpressive, yet outdated assumptions of colonial power and stability. (2009, 196)

Sir Richard, for example, is worried that Lois might tell Gerald Lesworth, a soldier in the British Army and Lois' future fiancé, about the cache of guns hidden by the Irish in the grounds. His dismay is highly apparent when Peter Connor, an Irishman, is arrested by Gerald. In response to the announcement of the news the following takes place:

> 'I'm sorry to hear that,' said Sir Richard, flushing severely. 'His mother is dying. However, I suppose you must do your duty. We must remember to send up now and inquire for Mrs Michael Connor. We'll send some grapes. The poor woman – it seems too bad.' He went off sighing, into the library.
>   Gerald was horrified. His duty, so bright and abstract, had come suddenly under the shadowy claw of the persona. 'I had no idea,' he exclaimed to Laurence, 'these people were friends of yours.' (*LS*, 91-92).

Gerald's horror serves to highlight further the ambiguity of Sir Richard's position. Although theoretically protected by the British soldiers, Sir Richard's sympathy, in this instance, lies with the Irishman. Foster however argues that rather than Sir Richard's dismay at Connor's arrest resulting from the ambiguity inherent in being Anglo-Irish or from sympathy with his tenants, it results from the fact that for Sir Richard "the concepts of war and civilisation appear alien, unsubtle, possibly uncivilised" (1993, 106). Such a position could lead the reader to consider Sir Richard in a more positive light for it might show him more as a conscientious objector or pacifist (one of the factions of society identified by Kiberd in his reading of "Easter 1916"), rather than one who has no understanding for the situation in which he finds himself: of course it should also be recognised that for the Anglo-Irish, the British army also felt like invaders, rather than fellow-countrymen.

The violence of both man and nature are contrasted sharply with the more light-hearted episodes in the novel such as the Naylors' tennis party, the tea party at Mrs. Fogarty's house or the dance at the Rolfes' house, a juxtaposition which highlights the political attitudes of the Anglo-Irish, particularly in relation to their opinions of the Irish, the British Army and the British in general. The approval of some of the Anglo-Irish (particularly that of Sir Richard, Lois and Laurence) of their Irish neighbours is somewhat negated by their inability to show any real engagement with the local Irish community. This lack could arguably arise from their isolated existences in the "Big Houses", although conversely Buckland suggests that many "loved Ireland and the Irish and regarded themselves as Irish." He also suggests that other Anglo-Irish shared "a disposition to favour the British connection" (1972, xxiii) but this sentiment is not shared by some of the novel's Anglo-Irish characters who can be seen to dislike the English as a race. Such an attitude is typified by the behaviour of Lady Naylor who scorns the English, particularly those who live in suburban bungalows in Surrey, her attitude, according to Bowen, "a marked Anglo-Irish trait" (1952, 99). This particular stance is highlighted by Bowen's use of humour in the novel. Speaking of Gerald Lesworth's lack of relations, Lady Naylor says to Myra Montmorency:

> No, *he* of course is quite charming, but he seems to have no relations. One cannot trace him. His mother, he says, lives in Surrey, and of course you do know, don't you, what Surrey *is*? It says nothing, absolutely; part of it is opposite the Thames Embankment. Practically nobody who lives in Surrey ever seems to have been heard of, and if one does hear of them they have never heard of anybody else who lives in Surrey. Really altogether, I think all English people very difficult to trace. They are so pleasant and civil, but I do often wonder if they are not a little shallow […] Of course, I don't say Gerald Lesworth's people are in *trade* […] No, I should say they were just villa-ry (*LS*, 58).[21]

There can be no doubt that Lady Naylor exhibits acute snobbery about the suburban English; following Gerald's recital of an article in the *Morning Post*, the narrator states "[a]s Lady Naylor said at the time, no one would dream of taking the *Morning Post* seriously, it was so anti-Irish", continuing that "it was extraordinary how no amount of experience shook these young Englishmen up. Their minds remained cutting books" (*LS*, 95). Dislike of the English is not, however, just the preserve of Lady Naylor. Mrs. Carey considers the English "common". When Betty Vermont (a soldier's wife) exclaims at the Naylors' tennis party "[y]our scrumptious Irish teas make a perfect piggy-wig of me", Mrs. Carey, sitting next to her,

> thought of Mrs Vermont as 'a little person' and feared she detected in her a tendency, common to most English people, to talk about her inside. She often wondered if the War had not made everybody from England a little commoner (*LS*, 46).

A perceived obsession with food is not, of course, solely a trait of the English, nor a trait of all the English in Ireland; Lois is surprised that Laurence, for example, despite his ethereal looks, "should spend so much time when he was not being intellectual in talking and apparently thinking about food." She compares this with Gerald's attitude to food: "[s]oldiers did not talk about food, they ate it." (*LS*, 9)

Whilst humour is used in the comparison between the Anglo-Irish and the English, it is also used to highlight the perceived negative aspects of a character's nature. The soldiers' wives for example are shown in a particularly comic light; the party at the Rolfes' house and the ill-timed, ill-judged and intrusive visit by Mrs. Vermont and Mrs. Rolfe to Danielstown, the Naylors' house, are prime examples of Bowen's social satire, but the use of humour and satire is by no means restricted to the negative portrayal of the English; Laurence too is occasionally subject to the narrator's use of such devices and the flippant remarks of Laurence to Marda about a recent raid add to the satirical effect of the novel:

> Castle Trent was raided for arms last night. Of course, they didn't find any. They think the thing was entirely amateur, nothing to do with the I.R.A. at all. They took away some boots. The Trents think one of the raiders was a gardener's cousin from Balldarra who hates the family. He left a quite unnecessary message behind with a skull and crossbones; he sounds to me rather a silly man. I am hoping perhaps they will come here tonight. We have two assegais and a stiletto that Uncle Richard uses for a paper-knife. (*LS*, 102-3)

Lee sees Bowen's use of satire "as 'a form of elegy' for the declining status of the Anglo-Irish" (1999, 55), believing that the satire helps to illustrate their ambivalence, impotence and eventual demise and the use of humour adds to the inherent ambiguity and ambivalence when Laurence's political stance is considered. The employment of humour can suggest two contrasting readings of his character. It could, for example, be argued that Laurence's flippancy hides an understanding of the political turmoil in Ireland. Conversely he could be, as Hugo Montmorency believes, merely "the undergraduate of today" (*LS*, 44), superficially regarding the fighting and violence as entertainment, without giving any thought to the horrific implications of the events of 1920.[22]

Whilst it is apparent that many of the Anglo-Irish characters in *The Last September* are ambivalent in their views about the war, often despising the protectorate role of the British and yet failing to engage fully with the native Irish people, it is necessary to question whether this ambivalence is due to ignorance, innocence or pragmatism. It is possible, for example, to perceive Sir Richard in two contrasting ways: as a conscientious objector, abhorring the savage and uncivilised nature of the war between the Irish and the English, or as a man who lacks any real understanding of the conflict, enveloped in his own isolated existence, cushioned and protected by the demesne of Danielstown from the harsh realities of Irish life in 1920.

The position of the younger inhabitants of Danielstown is equally ambiguous. It would be relatively easy to argue that the younger inhabitants of Danielstown should be considered innocents in political matters. However, it is important to acknowledge that Lois, Livvy and Laurence (as well, of course, as the older characters) have only recently seen the cessation of the First World War, their experiences of this perhaps causing them unconsciously to underestimate the violence surrounding them. In the 1952 preface Bowen comments on how the events might have affected Lois:

> Why was Lois, at her romantic age, not more harrowed, or stirred, by this national struggle round her? In part, would not this be self-defence? This was a creature still half-awake, the soul not yet open, nor yet the eyes. And world war had shadowed her school-days: *that* was enough— now she wanted order. (1952, 99)

Such a reading would suggest that Lawrence, Marda and Lois (in particular) should be categorised as "politically" innocent. However, there is an explicit and spoken desire among them not to notice the political violence that surrounds them. Marda, for example, asks Hugo Montmorency

"How far do you think this war is going to go? Will there ever be anything we can all do except not notice?" (*LS*, 82), and the ability to "not notice" is one that Laurence believes is vital for survival. Laurence expresses his desire for "something else to happen, some crude intrusion of the actual […] I should like to be here when this house burns" adding, after Hugo's protestations that such a thing will not happen, "Of course it will, though. And we shall all be so careful not to notice." (*LS*, 44). Not noticing, not seeing, is also symbolised by the trees that surround Danielstown; they protect the inhabitants even as they blind them to the events that are taking place outside the demesne, where the trees become "soundless cataracts" (*LS*, 22).

The ability not to notice is also alluded to in the epigraph of the novel: taken from Proust's *Le Temps Retrouvé*, volume twelve of *À la Recherché du Temps Perdu*,[23] the epigraph reads "*Ils ont les chagrins qu'ont les vierges et les paresseaux ...*" ("They will have the worries of virgins and idle people..."). This can be read as a comment on both the inherent innocence of both Lois and the Anglo-Irish as a race (*les vierges*) and as a critique of the Anglo-Irish as an indolent body of people (*les paresseaux*). Thus, the epigraph can serve as Bowen's portrayal of the characters in the novel as either virgins regarding the political situation in Ireland during the Anglo-Irish war (and in terms of sexuality in relation to Lois) or, conversely, a race which remains idle in both thought and action, deliberately shutting their minds to the troubles as does Lady Naylor, who is forever shutting doors in the house, a metaphor for the closure of her mind to the political and violent turmoil which exists just outside the boundaries of her own house but which will, inevitably, encroach on her life in a most dramatic way. Kenney would suggest, however, a reluctance to not know, not to notice, is an habitual reaction of the Anglo-Irish (1975, 34). Although superficially such a statement indicates an unconscious repression of the truth rather than a conscious decision to remain isolated and thus, hopefully, protected from the ensuing violence outside the grounds of Danielstown, Kenney suggests that as a result of "not noticing", "a guilty void at the center of such a life can be maintained – even augmented and elaborated – but all at some psychic cost" (ibid.).

The void can be seen in the lack of direct discussion about politics, for although the violence of the Irish and the English (most particularly the "Black and Tans") is often a topic for discussion, it is rare for politics as an abstract notion to be discussed directly in the novel; when politics are discussed such discussions centre on Laurence. Lois, for example, explains Laurence's purported political stance to Francie, saying that he is not allowed to discuss politics at Danielstown "because the ones he brings over from Oxford are all wrong." Francie expresses her surprise at such a statement, so Lois clarifies this by suggesting that Laurence's politics are "inconvenient" (*LS*, 21). When Laurence and Gerald discuss politics, Gerald is horrified to discover that Laurence might be a socialist:

> [h]e had heard that Oxford was full of Socialism of a wrongness that was the outcome of too much thinking, and in the light of this it did appear to him that Laurence's conversation had been decidedly Sinn Fein. (*LS*, 93)

Gerald's consternation, and his relative political innocence, serves as a contrast to Laurence's more intellectual and cynical political views. Gerald is, after all, a man whose political nature is a reflection of his unquestioning (and boyish) loyalty to his country; Lois' thoughts on hearing of his death highlight this—"[h]e loved me, he believed in the British Empire". (*LS*, 203). However, it is not completely clear, as with his earlier conversation with Hugo, whether Laurence's political stance is merely a flippant response or if his flippancy disguises a greater insight.

Despite Bowen's assertion that Lois "was a creature still half-awake, the soul not yet open, nor yet the eyes" (1952, 99), and in consequence cannot be accused of deliberately "not noticing", Lois is aware of the turmoil that encroaches on her daily life although she is incapable of action. Following the attack on the barracks at Ballydrum she says to Gerald

> Do you know that while that was going on, eight miles off, I was cutting a dress out, a voile that I didn't even need, and playing the gramophone? … How is it that in this country that ought to be full of such violent realness, there seems nothing for me but clothes and what people say? I might just as well be in some kind of cocoon. (*LS*, 49)

Lois, then, is aware of what is happening in Ireland; she appears to be aware, too, of the difficulties faced by some of the British soldiers and their reluctance sometimes to carry out orders knowing that such orders are not necessarily the most suitable in the circumstances:

> You think we don't understand your not being there in time and not doing anything afterwards? We're not all such idiots. We know it's most terribly difficult for you and that you must obey orders. It's bad luck the orders are silly. (Ibid)

Bennett and Royle suggest a further avenue to be explored in relation to any question of political innocence; their reading of *The Last September* is one which identifies abeyances in the novel, particularly recognising in Gerald a lack of identity, being a "non-person", his lack highlighted by Lois's only able to describe Gerald as if he were dead (1995a, 21).

Whilst Lady Naylor may well, as Bennett and Royle indicate, believe the English to be "sub-human" (ibid, 20), the Anglo-Irish community can also be seen to be lacking identity.[24] Living "on the hyphen", they are neither English nor Irish, with Lois perceiving Ireland as an abstract notion (*LS*, 34); they are isolated in their "big houses", unable to connect with the local populace, living out their days filled with tennis parties and luncheons. It could therefore be considered unsurprising that they generally show either no interest in politics or are ambivalent in their responses, not disloyal but having no loyalty because of their hyphenated existence.

Yet it could be argued that Lois and Laurence are very aware of the situation in Ireland during 1920, but that, despite their knowledge and understanding, they are unable to take any real action. If this is so, then they should not, perhaps, be considered as "politically innocent", for a decision not to act following the acquisition of knowledge cannot arguably be considered the action of an innocent person, but does knowledge necessarily preclude innocence? Lois cannot be considered ignorant but she can be perceived as being politically innocent. She is unable to act because she is cocooned in Danielstown, lacking financial or physical independence, suffering from inertia because of her dependency on Danielstown, an argument advanced by Lassner (1990, 38). Although unable to do so, her desire to act suggests a high level of personal integrity, an attribute that few of the Anglo-Irish characters share. If Lois' reasons for not acting (that is, her dependency on Danielstown) demonstrate personal integrity, then perhaps this too indicates a degree of innocence. Laurence's political stance, however, does not suggest a shared innocence with Lois; superficially he is politically aware but he deliberately distances himself emotionally from the problems in Ireland. He recognises the importance of "not knowing" but his conclusion appears to have been reached from his own decision to do nothing; he likes to observe but does not wish to participate. Lassner, however, suggests that Laurence's failure to act results from "Anglo-Irish impotence" (1990, 38). Perhaps, after all, he is an example of the undergraduates so scorned by Hugo Montmorency—an undergraduate who, despite superficial knowledge, remains ignorant of the true nature of the political reality of Ireland in 1920.

Conversely Sir Richard's actions, or rather lack of action, cast doubt on any argument that he too could be considered politically innocent. It is difficult to ascertain whether his political stance results from antipathy, from a desire to maintain his lifestyle, to isolate himself from the actions of other or if it arises from a dislike of violence and waste – is Sir Richard a selfish landowner, keen to preserve his comfortable life, a pacifist or conscientious objector, or, perhaps, as Lassner and Derdiger suggest, a man who is "marginalized, submissive [and in a] powerless relationship to the domestic and political worlds of Danielstown" (2009, 198)? It may well be that his apparent disgust at the way the Irish are treated is a really a deliberate attempt to ensure that no acts of retribution are carried out against his family or Danielstown. If this is the case then, of course, he is not successful for "the death – execution rather" (*LS*, 206) of Danielstown occurs the following February. Certainly Lady Naylor should not be categorised as being politically innocent. Her desire to shut doors is perhaps the most pragmatic reaction to the violence taking place just outside the demesne. Arguably, her attitude to the violence results from a lack of real understanding of the political situation, for whilst Lady Naylor cannot be considered innocent in political terms, she can certainly be seen to be relatively ignorant of the issues germane to the violence. She exists, in Kenney's terms, in a "guilty void", desperately attempting to maintain and protect her way of life, evidenced not only by the literal shutting of doors but also by her unwillingness to talk about such issues, "[f]rom all the talk, you might think almost anything was going to happen, but we never listen. I have made it a rule not to talk, either" (*LS*, 26). Lois and Laurence are aware, to a lesser or greater degree, of the political turmoil and, in Laurence's case, decide that discretion is the better part of valour, but Lady Naylor literally shuts doors, an echo of her aptitude for mentally shutting out anything which she finds disagreeable.

The corruption of innocence

Whilst innocence in political matters is a key element in *The Last September*, the sexual innocence of the main protagonist is a central issue in both this novel and in a great deal of Bowen's fiction: in her fictional world the innocence of the young is often corrupted by the actions of an older man or woman and in her short story "Ann Lee's"[25] (the title story of Bowen's second volume of short stories published in 1926), the violation of innocence is suggested by Letty, a customer in Ann Lee's hat shop. A man enters the shop and is immediately perceived as an intruder who, by his very action of coming into the shop and nearly destroying a hat, violates the two customers, "the two ladies stood at gaze in the classic pose of indignation of discovered nymphs. Then they both turned to Ann

Lee, with a sense that something had been outraged that went deeper than chastity" (*CS*, 106). Letty is aware of the man's rôle of intruder and senses something deeper within the man which she believes is representative of many men for

> [o]ne might almost have believed that she had met him. As a matter of fact, she was recognising him; not as his particular self but as an Incident. He – It – crops up periodically in the path of any young woman who has had a bit of a career, but Ann Lee – really. Letty was vague in her ideas of Vestal Virgins, but dimly she connected them with Ann. Well, you never knew … Meanwhile this was a hat shop, the least fitting place on earth for the recurrence of an Incident. Perhaps it was the very priestliness of Ann which made them feel that there was something here to desecrate (ibid, 107).

Whilst there is a certain ambiguity concerning Lois' innocence of the political situation in Ireland, there can be no doubt that she is an innocent in matters of sexuality. Youth, innocence and inexperience are inextricably linked in Lois who "thought she need not worry about her youth; it wasted itself spontaneously, like sunshine elsewhere or firelight in an empty room" (*LS*, 146). Lois is portrayed in the first section of the novel, "The Arrival of Mr and Mrs. Montmorency", as an adolescent, an innocent child on the cusp of adulthood. Nevertheless, like many of Bowen's female protagonists, and in particular Portia (*The Death of the Heart*), Lois' childhood has not been worry free. She is the child of an unsuitable marriage; her mother, Laura, was "very remote", according to Hugo who had thought at one time that he and Laura might be married (*LS*, 19). Even Laura's death is considered unsuitable, for six months after Francie met her, "without giving anyone notice of her intention, Laura had died." (Ibid). The care of Lois is then given to Sir Richard and Lady Naylor but, like her aunt, Lois too appears remote.

Lois may well be aware that her youth, like her innocence, will soon come to an end; she is, however, unwilling to learn what she will become. Overhearing Francie and Lady Naylor talk about her, Lois becomes afraid, "[s]he had a panic. She didn't want to know what she was, she couldn't bear to: knowledge of this would stop, seal, finish one." (*LS*, 60). She is aware too that she is not like other girls. The narrator suggests this in the opening paragraphs of the novel; although Lois is dressed in a contemporary fashion and is aware that she looks "like other young girls" (*LS*, 7), nevertheless she feels herself to be "clearly […] outside life" (*LS*, 197). Lois is arguably made in the same mould as other Bowen female protagonists and she shares some of her characteristics with others such as

Jane (*A World of Love*), for example, or Portia (*The Heat of the Day*). She is of an age when she is too old for school but too young to be considered an adult. She appears childish when compared to her school friend, Viola,[26] who, on the day after she left school appeared with her hair "woven in bright sleek circles over her ears" (*LS*, 50), and started to pay significant attention to her future marriage plans. Lois appears even more childlike when compared to the apparent sophistication of Marda. However, when Lois is compared to her friend Livvy, Lois appears more adult in her behaviour. She is certainly more restrained and questioning in her relationship with Gerald compared with Livvy's exultations over David Armstrong but, like Livvy, cannot see any future except that of marriage, the only solution perhaps for a girl in Lois' position in Ireland in 1920 who desired independence from her family. Laurence's comment to Francie, "[a]s Lois never does anything or seems to want to, I suppose she must be expecting to marry someone" (*LS*, 54), highlights Lois' acknowledgement of her own lack of options. She tells Marda "I like to be in a pattern" and when Marda tells her that she would like to be a wife and mother, Lois replies "I can't think how to begin to be anything else" (*LS*, 98-99).[27]

On a solitary walk, Lois acknowledges both her fears, and her desire for security:

> Her fear of the shrubberies tugged at its chain, fear behind reason, fear before her birth; fear like the earliest germ of her life that had stirred in Laura. She went forward eagerly, daring a snap of the chain, singing; a hand to the thump of her heart, dramatic with terror. She thought of herself as forcing a pass [...] Silence healed, but kept a scar of horror. The shuttered-in drawing room, the family sealed in lamplight, secure and bright like flowers in a paperweight – were desirable, worth much of this to regain. Fear curled back from the carpet-border ... Now, on the path: grey patches worse than the dark: they slipped up her dress knee-high. The laurels deserted her groping arm. She had come to the holly, where two paths crossed. (LS, 33)

Lois desires the stability that family life will give her and her inability to consider any future other than marriage could be due, in part, to her innocent and childlike perception of the world; it is, however, an innocence that will be corrupted. Such a corruption of both Lois and the Anglo-Irish in the novel is constantly foregrounded by the repeated references to subterfuge, the constant uncertainty, surveillance and isolation, of ante-rooms through which people constantly pass, of "furtive lorries" (*LS*, 31) or a "man in a trenchcoat [who passed Lois] without seeing her" (*LS*, 34). The "furtiveness" of the lorries can be seen as a metaphor for the furtive and immoral nature of some of the characters, particularly evident in Hugo's love affair with Marda. Questions of sexuality and morality are, like the issue of violence, a constant backdrop to *The Last September* and there are frequent references to the sexual morality of the English; David Armstrong for example, according to Livvy, "is accustomed to English girls who are very free", girls who "get kissed before they get engaged" (*LS*, 69) and the anonymous D.I.'s niece comments that "Englishmen never could keep their mouths to themselves" (*LS*, 155). Lois too believes that the "English have quite a different moral standard" (*LS*, 101). However, Hugo's involvement with Marda, combined with his "uxorious" (*LS*, 18) treatment of his wife, leads to a reversal of the stereotypical image of the Englishman as morally bankrupt. Gerald, who can be seen as an archetypal Englishman, is horrified when Lois explains the situation between Hugo and Marda, he "went rigid, something shut like a door on his sensibilities – the thing reeked of adultery. He produced an appalled silence." (*LS*, 171).

The role violence has to play in Lois' loss of innocence can also be seen clearly in the pivotal episode at the ruined mill for, significantly, Lois remains an innocent in sexual terms until the day that she, Marda and Hugo visit the mill where "Lois shied through the gateway with more than affected nervousness. This was her nightmare: brittle, staring ruins." (*LS*, 123). Hoogland's reading of the scene at the mill suggests that Lois' choice is not a simple binary one, a choice between an impossible dream of a continued state of childhood or acceptance of an adult world of sexuality and sensuality; she offers a third option for Lois, an option which is effectively shattered, as is Lois' desire to remain as a child, by the violence, both threatened and actual, of the hiding Irishman. Reading the growing friendship between Lois and Marda as one which would, if allowed to continue, allow Lois to find safety in a lesbian relationship, Hoogland suggests that this third route is no longer a viable option following the threat of violence by the Irishman for "under the threat of his phallic power, Lois and Marda are forced to swear their silence to the Sinn Feiner about the events at the mill" (1994, 82). Hoogland continues

> [t]he fact that it is Marda and not Lois who is injured indicates that the conclusion of the adolescent protagonist's sexual initiation simultaneously marks the older woman's definitive subjection to the Law.[28] Her willingness to silence her transgressive sexuality and to take up her proper gender position is suggested to be no less than an act of self-mutilation, a wound inflicted by the sway of the powerful phallus (Ibid:82-3).

Writing from a "lesbian feminist angle" Hoogland acknowledges that Bowen would not "have defined her work in such terms" (ibid, 21). Nevertheless her reading of *The Last September* suggests that, whilst Bowen might not have written overtly about lesbian relationships in this novel, recognition of the possibility of lesbian sexuality is an important step for a female adolescent. Hoogland's opinion is partially substantiated by the exchange between Marda and Lois as Marda prepares to leave Danielstown for the last time, to return to England and marry Leslie Lawe:

> Lois stood behind the door in the drawing-room, waiting. 'Marda,' she said through the crack. 'Hullo?' said Marda. She came round the door, pushing it a little way to behind her. They kissed.
>   'Marda, I can't –'
>   'Never mind.'
>   'Darling!'
>   'Be good!'
>   'Happy journey!'
>   'Oh yes.' They parted. (*LS*, 139)

Nevertheless, whether the violence which takes place at the derelict mill forces Lois to reject the possibility of a relationship with Marda or, alternatively, provides the catalyst for Lois' recognition that adulthood beckons with its attendant questions of (hetero)sexuality, there is no doubt that the actions of those involved catapult Lois into a state of being into which she is reluctant to enter.

The divide between the childlike innocence of Lois (although becoming aware of the need to move away from her childhood to adulthood), and the sexual knowledge of Hugo and Marda, is highlighted by their walk to the mill; Hugo and Marda walk on ahead in their superior state of knowledge with Lois

> straggling behind [...] she seemed absorbed and remotely dependent, like one of the dogs. If she had fallen in with a loud enough splash and a cry she might have distracted the couple ahead, but she was surefooted and not quite certain enough of herself to fall in on purpose. (*LS*, 120).

For Lois, the entrance to the ruin can be used as an analogy for her entrance into adulthood, not sufficiently certain of herself to "fall in on purpose". Aware that she has to pass through the gateway, Lois is reluctant to do so. Personified by Bowen, the mill, "staring, light-eyed, ghoulishly", (*LS*, 122) startles them; its entrance and Lois' own entrance into adulthood frightens Lois and it is a journey on which she is reluctant to embark for "she wouldn't for worlds go into it but liked going as near as she dared. It was a fear she didn't want to get over, a kind of deliciousness" (*LS*, 123). Whilst the gateway to the mill may also provide a pathway to adulthood for Lois, the journey cannot be without loss and, as *The Last September* is concerned with both the loss of innocence of Lois and that of the Anglo-Irish, the mill too symbolises that loss for all those in Ireland, "[t]hose dead mills – the country was full of them, never quite stripped and whitened to skeletons' decency: like corpses at their most horrible" (ibid). In addition to the violence threatened by the man-made structure, "incredible in its loneliness", its "hinges rustily bled where a door had been wrenched away", a metaphor suggesting the bleeding generally associated with loss of virginity and thus of innocence (ibid). The threat of violence is also symbolised by the river which "darkened and thundered towards the mill-race" and by the recurring presence of the rooks, initially alluded to by Lady Naylor to Francie, and which "disturbed the trees, disturbed the echoes" (ibid).

Even at this late stage, Lois continues to be reluctant to enter the mill, to make that step into adulthood, exhorting Marda *"Don't* go in!" (ibid) but they do enter and the events that follow thrust Lois into an awareness of the potential for human sexuality. The darkness of the mill draws Lois and Marda in; as their eyes become accustomed to the dark, the hiding Irishman becomes visible. His advice, "[i]f you have nothing better to do, you had better keep in the house while y'have it" (*LS*, 125) strikes a chord in Lois. She has nothing to do, "she felt quite ruled out, there was nothing at all for her here. She had better be going – but where? She thought: 'I must marry Gerald' " (ibid). Lois can see no alternative to marriage, and marriage to Gerald seems to be the most obvious solution to her desire to be in a pattern.

The implied threat of violence by the Irishman, his prediction that Danielstown will not survive the ensuing war, is juxtaposed with Hugo's reflections on his relationship with his wife and his newfound love for Marda. His evident horror when he believes Marda has been fatally shot jolts Lois into a recognition of an adult relationship. This is Lois' moment of recognition or *anagnôrisis*, recognition that sexuality is one of the key elements of adulthood; as she exclaims to Marda, " 'I've had a … a revelation,' continuing, 'I had no idea – I was too damned innocent,' she explained with precision—'till we all stood in there and shouted.' " (*LS*, 128). On her approach to the mill and its gateway, Lois is apprehensive about crossing the divide. Once the divide has been crossed Lois is aware, perhaps unconsciously, that the events in the mill have changed her forever, a fact alluded to by Marda: "One won't be girlish again" (ibid), although Lois is not necessarily happy that such a change has been effected: "You know,' she said, 'all this has quite stopped any excitement for me about the mill. It's a loss, really. I don't think I'll ever come down this part of the river again" (*LS*, 129).

Following the incident at the mill, and her internalised reaction to the Irishman's threat of violence, Lois writes to Viola "that she intended to marry Gerald" (*LS*, 148). Lois' motives for making such a decision appear to be based on her perception that marriage to Gerald would provide her with a safe future. Allied to her "revelation", this could suggest that she does not perceive Gerald as sexually threatening, for dancing with Gerald "Lois felt she was home again; safe from deserted rooms, the penetration of silences, rain, homelessness." (*LS*, 150).[29] Dismayed at her aunt's subsequent interference in her plans, realising that the marriage might not take place and threatened by the loss of the promise of sanctuary offered by Gerald, Lois cries out to Gerald "I was so happy, I was so safe." (*LS*, 191). It appears that it is the "safety" of romantic love that Lois is seeking, a romantic love which will subsume Gerald's sexuality and Lois' own fears of her own potential for sexuality. However, following the dance, Lois realises that, even when he is present, she cannot visualise Gerald nor distinguish him from other men for

> [t]hough she watched wherever he went, she could not see him. There was nothing, in fact, to which to attach her look except his smoothness and roundness of head [...] She looked for his mouth – which had kissed her – but found it no different from mouths of other young men who had also been strolling and pausing between the huts in the dark [...] 'What have I done?' she thought (*LS*, 158).

And yet, after she receives a letter from Gerald, Lois reaches the conclusion that she is right to marry Gerald, that if he believes their relationship to be right and "perfect", it cannot be wrong; an "escape of sunshine, penetrating the pale sky in the south-west, altered the room like a revelation" (*LS*, 163) forces her to question her thoughts about marriage to Gerald. Both Hoogland and Lassner argue that Lois perceives Gerald as a sexual being. Lassner suggests that Lois "needs Gerald's passion to energise her individuality, but she must also save herself from identifying with his aggression by insulating herself within her home which rejects her." (1990, 39) and Hoogland reads the possible marriage between Lois and Gerald as offering a "solution to [Lois'] fear of exclusion but also promises the fulfilment of her dawning sexual needs" (1994, 68). Lassner further suggests that Bowen's use of metaphors "signify a fear of being absorbed, by sex or home, into emptiness and loss of self" (1990, 39) and that Lois, whilst beginning to recognise her own sexuality, is fearful that it will absorb her growing independence, but that she is equally fearful of being subsumed into Danielstown. This presents her with a dilemma for, according to Lassner, Lois is aware that "impotence is the key to survival [showing similarities with Laurence's desire to not notice] because sexual energy leads to individual expression which is always anarchic" (ibid). Lois of course remains impotent, and it is Lady Naylor, not she, that breaks up the relationship with Gerald. Whilst it appears to be equally possible to argue that Lois desires marriage to Gerald because he will meet her growing sexual needs or because he will offer her a haven from sexual desires, without doubt it is Lois' experiences at the mill which thrust her into a state of sexual knowledge and which force her to cross the boundary between childhood and adulthood.

The continuing backdrop of violence against which Lois' transition from childhood to adulthood is played out remains a constant throughout the novel. Sir Richard refers to the violence inherent in Ireland (both of nature and of man) immediately upon the arrival of Francie and Hugo Montmorency; answering the question "didn't you clear some trees", Sir Richard responds "[t]he wind had three of the ashes – you came quite safe? No trouble? Nobody at the cross-roads? Nobody stopped you?" (*LS*, .8). The violence at the ruined mill, both implied and actual, provide a pivotal moment for Lois; it is not, however, the final episode of violence in the novel. The continuing violent struggle between the English Army and the Irish provides a stark counterpoint to the relative innocent fun of the dance at the Rolfes' house. The scene is set for an enjoyable evening of dancing, the room having been prepared earlier in the day by Denise Rolfe and Betty Vermont who

> had been more than busy the whole morning. Flustered and happy, they darted about the hut, cutting sandwiches, scattering floor powder, pinning draperies round the walls. They masked the electric lights with pink crinkly paper to produce the desired enchantment. Every now and then, one would collapse on to what remained of the furniture and, catching the other's eyes, burst into delighted laughter. It was all such a rag. (*LS*, 141.)

Dismissive of the patrols that restrict the number of men at the dance, the women are more concerned that there will be too few male partners for the girls, their flimsy grasp on reality highlighted by the adjutant's thoughts about his hostess, "[t]he adjutant took a firmer grip of Mrs. Rolfe, an ethereal girl with a habit of drifting just out of one's reach like a kite" (*LS*, 143). Juxtaposed with the light-hearted preparations for the dance is Daventry's interior monologue, a chilling exploration of the situation in Ireland which details his experiences of the night time raids:

Daventry, a hand on the edge of the cabinet, stood leaning with his back to the wall's art-muslin draperies. He kept shutting his eyes; whenever he stopped dancing he noticed that he had a headache. He had been out in the mountains all night and most of the morning, searching some houses for guns that were known to be there. He had received special orders to ransack the beds, and to search with particular strictness the houses where men were absent and women wept loudest and prayed. Nearly all beds had contained very old women or women with very new babies, but the N.C.O, who was used to the work, insisted that they must go through with it. Daventry still felt sickish, still stifled with thick air and womanhood, dazed from the din. (*LS*, 144).

Violence continues to encroach upon Lois' life through her loss of innocence and eviction from childhood, and her fluctuating relationship with Gerald which culminates in his death, shot through the head after being ambushed by "the enemy" (*LS*, 201). For Lois, Gerald's death becomes the final act which will thrust her out of her own Eden, not only aware now of her own sexuality but also of the inevitability of death. After receiving the news from Daventry, Lois "went into the house and up to the top to meet what was waiting. Life, seen whole for a moment, was one act of apprehension, the apprehension of death" (*LS*, 202). Lois' awareness of the inevitability of adulthood and death casts her out from her own Eden, an Eden to which she will be unable to return. Similarly the death of Danielstown signifies the end of Sir Richard and Lady Naylors' own perhaps Edenic existence. The "execution" of their house, together with that of Castle Trent and Mount Isabel, symbolises not only their eviction but also the eviction of the childlike Anglo-Irish race, and must surely force them into the recognition that they cannot continue "not noticing": "Sir Richard and Lady Naylor, not saying anything, did not look at each other, for in the light from the sky they saw too distinctly" (*LS*, .206). Nevertheless, to the last, Danielstown, personifying both the Naylors in particular and the Anglo-Irish more generally, opens its door "hospitably upon a furnace", still unwilling, or unable, to accept its fate.

Notes

[1] *H* and *LS* will be substituted for *The Hotel* and *The Last September* in future references.
[2] In giving a "backward perspective", Bowen suggests that the narrator is more objective.
[3] During this period Bowen lived, for the most part, in England with her Aunt Laura in Harpenden.

[4] Lois' departure from Ireland following the ending of her relationship with Gerald, and his subsequent death is an echo of Bowen's journey to Italy.

[5] Reprinted in *Collected Stories*, pp.199-210.

[6] In an interview for the BBC production *Bookmark* a friend of Bowen's recounted the occasions when she would insist on her guests dragging cushions out of the house and sitting on the steps after dinner.

[7] Following Francie Montmorency's mistaken identification of Lois' relationship with Laurence, Lois patiently explains to her that she is the niece of Sir Richard and Laurence is the nephew of Lady Naylor (*LS*, 21). Given this careful explanation and Bowen's statement in the preface to the novel that Lois "was niece always, never child, of the house" (1952, 99), it is surprising that two critical works which refer to *The Last September* should state Lois and Laurence's relationship incorrectly. Seamus Deane refers to "the daughter of the house, Lois Naylor" (1986, 205) and Andrew Bennett and Nicholas Royle refer to Laurence as Lois' brother (1995a, 14).

[8] The article is reprinted in *Collected Impressions*. The two books reviewed by Bowen were *Irish Life in the Seventeenth Century: After Cromwell* by Edward Maclysaght and *The Sword of Light* by Desmond Ryan (Bowen 1939, 173).

[9] Distrust

[10] See for example F. S. L. Lyons' study of the period *Culture and Anarchy in Ireland 1890-1939: From the Fall of Parnell to the Death of W. B. Yeats: The Ford Lectures Delivered in the University of Oxford in the Hilary Term of 1978* (Oxford, 1979) and Mike Cronin's work *A History of Ireland* (Houndmills, 2001).

[11] One of Bowen's own relations, Captain John Bowen-Colthurst (the son of her father's cousin) played a significant and dishonourable part in the aftermath of the Easter Rising when he was responsible for the harsh treatment and subsequent execution of Francis Sheehy-Skeffington, a journalist and a university classmate of James Joyce (Kiberd 1992, xi) whose wife was a well-known campaigner for women's rights. The inquiry into Sheehy-Skeffington's death found that he was arrested on 25th April despite having taken no part in the violence of the Rising (Simon et al 1916, 115-152); Bowen-Colthurst was eventually found guilty of murdering Sheehy-Skeffington while insane (Lyons 1963, 373) and sent to Broadmoor (Glendinning 1977, 37). Glendinning suggests that this particular episode did not impinge much on Elizabeth Bowen's life although conceding that this "became another, peripheral Bowen burden" (ibid, 38). Whilst it might not have made an immediate impact on Bowen's life, resonances of the lasting effect of the behaviour of her relation can be seen in *The Last September* and, in particular perhaps, Bowen's portrayal of Sir Richard's own ambiguous political stance. It is interesting to note that in the film of *The Last September* (1999), Gerald Lesworth's name is changed to Gerald Colthurst, thus linking the brutal treatment of the Irish by the English to Bowen's own family.

[12] A rough, unsurfaced minor road.

[13] Such themes are, of course, also apparent in other novels by Bowen and can be found in, for example, *To the North*, *The Heat of the Day* and *Eva Trout, or Changing Scenes*.

[14] Bowen previously used rooks with a different symbolism in her short story "Charity" (1926 and reprinted in *Collected Stories*, pp.190-198) where two young girls, Charity and Rachel, "listened to the rooks going to bed" and where there
> would be a sudden cry, a tree shaken, and the sky would be dark with
> them; then calling to one another again and again, they would drop back
> into the branches. Fewer rooks rose each time, and this gave one a feeling
> of great peacefulness, as though the whole earth were being hushed-up and
> reassured (*CS*, 195).

However, in contrast to *The Last September*, the silent presence of the rooks here provides comfort and reassurance.

[15] Cooney, for example, refers to the Anglo-Irish as "the Raj in the Rain" and quotes Sir Richard Keane who says "[t]his Anglo-Irish thing is just shorthand for the difference between Catholic and Protestant [...] It's shorthand for a set of historical circumstances" (2001, 28, 30). In contrast Jack Lane, in his polemical attack on Elizabeth Bowen, gives the following definition of the term "Anglo-Irish": "They were the English in Ireland, the English of the Cromwellian and Williamite (Orange) conquests, who were established in exclusive control of the country for many generations following the Battle of the Boyne" (1999b, 130).

[16] Patrick Buckland, for example, identifies three broad categories under the genus "Anglo-Irish": small landowners who were active in local politics, larger landowners who were prominent in national politics and those who became involved in British public life (1972, xv-xvii) and Lyons refers to the term "Anglo-Irish" as one which "expresses very precisely the schizophrenia which was their natural condition" (1979, 18).

[17] Lane's acerbic introduction includes a quotation from an earlier book by Lane and Clifford, *The North Cork Anthology* (1993), in which they state their belief that the only difference to Irish life made when Bowen's Court was demolished was "the addition of a good agricultural field to the stock of land." (1999a, 6). Much of their criticism appears to stem from their disapproval of Bowen's activities during the Second World War when she produced reports about Ireland for the British Government, thus in Lane and Clifford's eyes effectively spying on her friends and the people of Eire (an aspect of Bowen's life which will be considered further in Chapter Five when her wartime fiction is discussed).

[18] Identified by Brian Fallon as H. L. Morrow (1999, 176), "The Bellman" portrays her in a very positive and flattering manner, suggesting somewhat obsequiously
> She is, in fact – if she will forgive me – the synthesis of all the Holbein
> family portraits, even to that delicate rose-pink of the cheeks and the
> upper-lip that is not so much a colour, as a tinted shadow or the bloom of
> some rare fruit out of season (The Bellman 1942, 421).

[19] Reprinted in *Collected Stories* pp.124-135.

[20] Reprinted in *Collected Stories*, pp.170-179.

[21] Lady Naylor's dislike of those who are "villa-ry" is a sentiment which Bowen re-visits in *The Death of the Heart* and one which is echoed by Anna Quayne's disdain of Waikiki, the home of her former nurse. It is not, however, a dislike shared by Bowen who speaks of her delight on her arrival in Kent where she found

herself "in a paradise of white balconies, ornate porches, verandahs festooned with Dorothy Perkins roses" a delight which led to her "craze for – [her] infatuation with—villas, unhistorical, gimcrack little bubbles of illusion." (1972, 28, 30).

[22] Regina Barreca deals more fully with this aspect of Bowen's fiction, commenting that "[h]umor is the mainstay of all of Bowen's fictions, italicizing the effects of dislocation and loss rather than expelling them through catharsis or resignation." (1994, 115)

[23] This novel was originally published in French in 1927 and in English in 1931.

[24] See chapter six for a greater exploration of Bowen's use of abeyances within her narratives.

[25] Originally published in *Spectator* (July 1924) and republished in *Collected Stories*, pp.103-111.

[26] The use of the names "Viola" and "Livvy" (the shortened form of Olivia) contain resonances of Shakespeare's *Twelfth Night*. Francie questions the shortening of Livvy's name but the reiteration of the initial letter "L" arguably serves to make a connection between Laurence, Livvy, Lois (and her mother, Laura) which excludes others; although as Laurence explains, Lois is not fond of Livvy, their relationship is the result of "contiguity" (*LS*, p.55). Bowen's use of these names contains a suggestion that *The Last September* might, in part, be considered a romantic comedy.

[27] Winifred Holtby's exploration of women's rights (*Women and a Changing Civilisation*, 1934) charts the many difficulties faced by women should they wish, or need to be employed and the insistence of employers that women should give up their employment on marriage.

[28] Hoogland's notion of Marda subjecting herself "to the Law" is a reference to Marda's engagement to Leslie Lawe.

[29] Lassner, however, suggests that Lois is aware of Gerald's sexuality; to avoid being absorbed by Gerald, Lois' "antidote against such fears is to imagine sexual love as a sanctuary from feelings of emptiness – a holding environment" (1990, 39).

CHAPTER TWO

"PASSION KNOWS NO CRIMES":
FRIENDS AND RELATIONS AND *TO THE NORTH*

[Emmeline] stepped in Paris clear of the every-day, of conduct with its guarantees and necessities, into the region of the immoderate, where we are more than ourselves. Here are no guarantees. Tragedy is the precedent: Tragedy confounding life with its masterful disproportion. Here figures cast unknown shadows; passion knows no crimes, only its own movement; steel and the cord go with the kiss. Innocence walks with violence; violence is innocence, cold as fate; between the mistress's kiss and the blade's is a hairsbreadth only, and no disparity; every door leads to death … The curtain comes down, the book closes – but who is to say that this is not so? (*To the North*, 185) [1]

This melodramatic passage from *To the North* draws the focus away from public and political violence to the violence of the private sphere; as Chapter One focused in part on the nature of political innocence and the chaos caused as a result of this aspect of innocence, so this chapter considers the effect on individuals when the bridge is crossed from innocence to experience, a bridge crossed both literally and metaphorically by Lois in *The Last September*. Bowen contends that it is 'not only our fate but our business to lose innocence' (1946, 264) and this chapter explores the consequences of accepting or rejecting societal rules about standards of behaviour, particularly in relation to notions of sexuality and marriage, and, continuing the employment of Bowen's own analogy, the eviction from an individual's Garden of Eden.

The late 1920s and early 1930s were periods of great change; writing in 1930, F. R. Leavis suggested that "change has been so catastrophic that the generations find it hard to adjust themselves to each other, and parents are helpless to deal with their children [...] 'Civilisation' and 'culture' are coming to be antithetical" (1930, 19 and 22): a time when questions of sexuality were debated more openly in certain sections of society and "a restless age" according to Julian in *To the North*, a sentiment which finds accord with Lady Winters who suggests that "[a]ll ages are restless". She continues however that this period is particularly so, it "is far more than restless: it is decentralized. From week to week, there is no knowing where anyone is" (*TN*, 170). It is within this context of restlessness and major social change that *Friends and Relations* (1931) and *To the North* (1932), and two collections of short stories, *Joining Charles and Other Stories* (1929) and *The Cat Jumps and Other Stories* (1934) were written.

Just one year separates the publication of the two novels and although a cursory summation would suggest that they deal with identical themes (innocence and sexuality), the way in which these are explored is dissimilar. The plots of the two novels can be easily, and superficially, summarised thus: *Friends and Relations* can be read as a novel which follows the trials and tribulations of two young women as they enter into marriage, marriages which have all the fictional problems generally regarded as commonplace in populist romantic fiction; one woman is in love with her brother-in-law, the emotion is reciprocated but, for the sake of the two families, they decide that they can do nothing about their feelings for each other and that life must continue as before without the added emotional entanglement. To add a further *frisson* of excitement to this basic plot, there is the knowledge that the brother-in-law's mother trod the same route many years before but was unwilling to fight temptation and thus became embroiled in an adulterous relationship. In contrast, *To the North* tells the story of one young woman's descent into a personal hell through her sexual behaviour. Unwilling and unable to take the moral high ground, Emmeline's illicit and extra-marital relationship with Markie culminates in their deaths, whilst her sister-in-law and aunt stand on the sidelines in condemnation of the relationship.

From such accounts, and from both novels' lack of closure associated with realist fiction, it could be argued that Bowen wanted to show her readership the consequences of being unable to resist temptation, that such resistance maintains marriage while disregard for societal rules leads to outrage, ostracism and, on occasion, death. However, the narrator of *Friends and Relations* constantly makes oblique references to the artificiality of various situations: on the day of Laurel and Edward's wedding, for example, the "morning-room flowers had been 'arranged' " (*FR*, 7) and, later, "Edward was determined that his wedding, like the execution of Julien Sorel, should go off simply, suitably, without any affectation on his part" (*FR*, 8);[2] the bridegroom's mother "over-acted a little" (*FR*, 10), a comment which suggests that the wedding should be read as a performance. The narrator of *To the North* highlights the unreliability of appearance; Julian for example "looked like one of those nice English actors who look so much more like gentlemen than like actors that beside them an ordinary gentleman would appear theatrical" (*TN*, 21). Such a comment, allied with other issues such as Emmeline's severe short-sightedness[3] and the apparent artificiality of Laurel and Edward's wedding, serve as an indication that a simplistic reading of the two novels will not provide an adequate response to Bowen's increasingly complex narratives. This can be seen in the intricate plotting and characterisation of the novels and her understanding of the complex issues surrounding sexuality and love, innocence and experience. Further, such a reading does not take into account the literary and historical contexts of the two novels.[4]

Literary and Historical Contexts: Locomotion and Location

James Gindin succinctly summarises the direction that fiction was taking in the 1930s, a summary which places *Friends and Relations* and *To the North* within the literary context of the period, he states that many novels of that decade

> are also accounts of travel, gestures against the fears of both insularity and destruction that home represents. Settings are often outside Britain, or, when within Britain, far from the point of origin [...] Geography signifies. The fiction contains a good deal of both conflict and assimilation between the representations of London and the provinces. No single set of values, attitudes or even kinds of representation can apply. (1992, 15)[5]

Reading the two novels from this perspective, it is possible to demonstrate that their subject matter was in tune with the predominant themes of the decade. For example, the opening pages of both novels involve journeys: Cecilia is travelling back from Italy when she meets Markie on the train, Laurel's train journey is, in contrast, metaphorical rather than literal, "for her, these hours before her wedding were like a too long wait on the platform of some familiar station from which, virtually, one has already departed" (*FR*, 7). Travel is foregrounded throughout the two novels; travel on trains, buses, airplanes and by car, travel that invariably leads to re-evaluation or violent change in life, the most extreme of course, being Emmeline and Markie's fatal journey on the Great North Road. *To the North* highlights the obsessive nature of travel, with journeys within England being particularly important (Cecilia's journey with Julian to Pauline's school and, of course, Emmeline and Markie's journey north being specific examples). Travel abroad also plays a central rôle in *To the North*; the embryonic travel industry run by

Emmeline and Peter Lewis provides, for example, the narratorial motive for Emmeline and Markie's journey to Paris and travel plays an equally significant rôle in *Friends and Relations*.[6] However, whilst travel plays an important rôle in the two novels, Coates suggests that this should not be read simply as a Modernist device for whilst Bowen's imagery often "draws on a stock feeling which Modernism inherited from the Romantic movement [...] both the image and the mood behind it are questioned and subverted by Bowen" (1992, 292); in both novels the physical elements of travel can be seen as analogous to the journey from innocence to experience, an aspect of the novels which will be developed further in this chapter.

Location plays an equally important part in both *Friends and Relations* and *To the North*; undoubtedly it plays a significant rôle in all of Bowen's fiction. Indeed, as she asserted in 1945, "Nothing can happen nowhere. The locale of the happening always colours the happening, and often, to a degree, shapes it" (1945b, 253), adding to this argument in 1972 that, for her

> what gives fiction verisimilitude is its topography. No story gains absolute hold on me (which is to say gains the required hold) if its background – the ambience of its happenings – be indefinite, abstract or generalised. Characters operating *in vacuo* are for me bodiless. (1972, 34)

Bowen's use of locale in *Friends and Relations*, with its geographical delineation of town and country (London versus Batts Abbey and, to a lesser extent, the parental home of Laurel and Janet in Cheltenham) suggests another demarcation, one concerned with sexual morality, and one which is exemplified by Lady Elfrida's past. Living in London, her apparently immoral behaviour in the past casts a shadow over subsequent generations. Equally, a London restaurant and hotel provide the backdrop to Janet and Edward's scenes of temptation. It is a city for which the innocent need maps; the youthful, inexperienced and relatively naïve Laurel, for example, is unable to find her way around London without a guide.[7]

In contrast to the London inhabited by Laurel, Edward, Theodora and Lady Elfrida, Batts Abbey, complete with its renovated orchard with Edenic connotations, suggests a place that should be unsullied by the ramifications of the earlier generation's behaviour. It becomes apparent, however, that this rural location cannot remain an innocent idyll, predominantly because it is contaminated by the relationship between Lady Elfrida and Considine Meggat,[8] the owner of Batts Abbey. The consequences of their actions, in Edward's eyes, threaten to corrupt the innocence of his children, as his own childhood was corrupted, and he is unable to countenance any suggestion that Lady Elfrida, Considine and his children should remain together under Janet's roof. Nevertheless, it is in this apparently Edenic setting that Janet makes the decision that she shall not eat, metaphorically, from "the fatal apple tree" (*FR*, 104). Equally it is at Batts Abbey that a serpent, in the guise of Theodora Thirdman, rises from the nest and attempts, subsequently, to ruin the marriage of Laurel and Edward.[9]

As Paris is used by Jean Rhys as the backdrop to the corruption of Marya Zelly, so too can the Modernist motif of the city as a corrupting force be seen in *To the North*,[10] with London and, more specifically, Paris acting as the settings for Emmeline's loss of innocence. Markie, described by the narrator as someone whose features are shaped by "malevolence" with a "mobile, greedy, intelligent mouth and the impassive bright quick-lidded eyes of an agreeable reptile" (*TN*, 7) and who can be read as an evil influence on Emmeline, resides in London and is the instrument of Emmeline's fall from social grace. The reptilian reference can, of course, be considered analogous with the serpent in the Garden of Eden who tempts Eve, and finds its equivalent in the behaviour of Theodora Thirdman. However, the actual point of Emmeline's passive submission to Markie's will takes place in Paris and the descent to the airport at Le Bourget can be seen as a metaphor for Emmeline's descent into her own private hell, a descent in which "blood roared in ears as the plane with engines shut off, with a frightening cessation of sound plunged downward in that arrival that always appears disastrous." (*TN*, 139).

As in *Friends and Relations*, city and countryside are used to suggest the contrast between innocence and corruption, with Paris and London being used as points of comparison with Farraways, Lady Waters' country house. Identified by Lee as "a garden of Eden for Emmeline" (Lee 1981, 75) the house's name, of course, suggests a place far removed from the reality and rigours of city living. It is "a dull-faced, pleasant Victorian house" (*TN*, 43) to which Lady Waters and her second husband, Sir Robert, retreat from life in London. Weekend parties at the house consist of young people such as Gilbert and Gerda Bligh and Tim Farquharson whose relationship difficulties are examined by Lady Waters as she attempts to help them out of their dilemmas by offering long walks and visits to ruins. There is an old-fashioned and innocent air about the house, its occupants, visitors and a strict adherence to societal rules, which is greatly at odds with modes of behaviour in Paris and London and the accepted Victorian social mores of sexuality and marriage are contrasted with the growing debate on sexuality and acceptance of sexual relationships outside marriage. These views might appear to be a simple difference between the older and younger generations, although this somewhat simplistic reading does not take into account Cecilia's belief in marriage nor her apparent condemnation of Markie's behaviour, beliefs which are of course at odds with her inability to "travel without picking someone up" (*TN*, 7). However, as the narrator states "[n]either Cecilia nor Mark had nice characters; all the same, this encounter [on the train from Milan] presents them in an unfair light [… for] she was quite happy only in one relationship: with her young sister-in-law, Emmeline." (*TN*, 10).

Not only does this highlight the contradictions in Cecilia's character, it also raises issues about homoerotic desires particularly when the narrator further states that Lady Waters, for example, "viewed the arrangement with an unshaken mistrust. Women could not live together, sisters-in-law especially" (*TN*, 13). Her misgivings could be construed as unspoken anxieties concerning lesbian relationships, an issue which will be discussed later in this chapter.

Sexuality and Morality

Locating the two novels within the literary context suggested by Gindin also serves to situate them within the historical context of the period, particularly in relation to changing attitudes to marriage and sexuality, including homosexuality, with the work of sexual theorists being discussed more openly in the 1930s. Indeed, Peter Lewis is invited to tea "to discuss Havelock Ellis" (*TN*, 93) and even Gerda Bligh who "was not really a fool [… and] having read a good many novels about marriage, not to speak of some scientific books, […] knew not only why she was unhappy but exactly how unhappy she could still be" (*TN*, 52). Contemporary sexual theories are also highlighted, somewhat ironically, in Bowen's short story "The Cat Jumps" (1934).[11] The Harold Wrights, having recently moved into a house which had been the scene for a very violent murder, invite their close friends for a weekend party to "warm the house" (*CS*, 363). Harold's "library stools, rugs and divans were strewn with Krafft-Ebbing, Freud, Forel, Weiniger and the heterosexual volume of Havelock Ellis. Harold had thought it right to install his reference library; his friends hated to discuss without basis." (*CS*, 366).

As Andrew Thorpe comments in his study of Britain in the 1930s, "one ancient pastime to retain its appeal was sex", further noting that it is evident that more literature about sexuality was available in the thirties, particularly "literature which stressed the importance of sexual pleasure for both partners within marriage". Although, as Thorpe suggests, marriage was seen as the norm, he adds the *caveat* that "pre- and extra-marital sex continued to thrive" although acts of homosexuality remained illegal (1992, 105/6). However, as Maslen notes, "homosexuality and lesbianism tend to be treated circumspectly, implied rather than explored, and, when they are spelt out, often meeting a hostile reception" (2001, 147). Thorpe's acknowledgement that a new sexual discourse was emerging during this period echoes the work of Margaret Lawrence. Considering women writers in 1937, she discusses the changing sexual attitudes of women over the centuries and, in particular, in the first third of the twentieth century and comments that

> '[i]t is upon this [changing] approach to sex that the present generation separates from the past generation. The separation is absolute and divides thinkers and writers and critics. The thinkers of the old order refuse to take seriously the sexual psychology of the thinkers of the new order. They maintain that the sexual function is no modern discovery and that the race has continued reasonably well for centuries without analysing its nervous reactions to sex, and that fiction and drama have in the past done quite well without succumbing to sex [...] The new thinkers maintain that in concentrating interest upon *why* people do as they do in general, or in given sets of circumstances, they have advanced [...] This difference of attitude generally noticeable in a placing of the accent either upon "how" or upon "why" makes a gulf between the generations that goes through the whole of society. It affects politics; it affects religion; it affects individual social conduct; but above all it affects art and philosophy and particularly the blend of these two in writing.
>
> So wide and so deep has been the interest of this generation in the psychology of sex, its analysis and its interpretation, that it no longer needs to be set down as sex in the terms of sex. It is set down in terms of conduct and shock. (1937, 155-156)[12]

To the North, in particular, can be viewed in relation to these opinions, the narrator focusing on motives and emotions, the psychological "why" of events, or future events, rather than the "how", the physical description. But is this element of Bowen's fiction really typical of thirties fiction, or is it, instead, the result of a reluctance on the part of Bowen to go into graphic detail concerning, for example, Emmeline's loss of virginity? While there is no literal description of Emmeline and Markie having sexual intercourse, it is described metaphorically; ostensibly narrating the evening spent wandering in the gardens of Paris, this passage indicates Emmeline's unthinking surrender to Markie's seduction following an afternoon of "suspended crisis" (*TN*, 140),

[h]er attitude even said: 'Must I think at all?' as though, most alive in the heat and shade of the tree, she were reprieved from living. She spread out her fingers along the hot seat: he looked from her hand past her face up into the branches. An intense sense of being forced so close to the other as to be invisible, a fusion of both their senses in burning shadow obscured for the two, as they sat here, the staring quivering city, making remote for Markie a picture he must believe for always imprinted: Emmeline in her white dress watery with green shadow looking down at his hand approaching her hand – for Emmeline, Markie looking her way in an instant of angry extinction as though he would drown. A slackening of tension, the gentleness of the bemused afternoon—in which like someone who has lost his memory he was tentative and dependent and she, like someone remembering everything, overcome – carried them on to night with the smoothness of water, quickening to the fall's brink with a glassy face.

Past midnight, some few voices, or sounds with metallic echoes, dropped into the extraordinary silence behind the hotel. (*TN*, 141)

As Lawrence comments, the writing of the 1930s concerns itself, in part, with "conduct and shock". Consideration of this expression allows a questioning of societal rules about sexuality; Winifred Holtby, writing in 1934, suggests that one of the "conventional ideas about the young modern woman suggest that she is […] uncontrolled in habits, given to drinking, smoking and sexual promiscuity" (1934, 116-117). She writes about the "double standard of morality [which] expected all unmarried women to remain virgin, but cherished no such expectations for a bachelor" (ibid, 131) and discusses the Papal Encyclical upon Christian Marriage (issued December 31st 1930) which "[n]aturally upholds the view that matrimony is an indissoluble sacrament, divorce an unmitigated evil, birth control a sin, and the subservience of wives a divine principle" (ibid, 171). In Emmeline's consideration of her letter to a hotelier in Malaga, the narrator gives us, with a certain archness, one view of the societal expectations of behaviour between men and women,

[a]t the inclusive price she had quoted she must obtain for them everything: occasional chars-à-bancs, wine, the aesthetic amenities, accommodation in accordance with the proprieties – for, as they had intimated with an indescribable archness, their party was to be mixed. (*TN*, 118)

Two of Bowen's short stories are also concerned with the predicament faced by young women. Miss Fox, the sewing lady in "The Needlecase" (1934),[13] is described by one of the children of the house as "one of the wonderfully brave – she's got a child to support that she shouldn't have […] She used to work, years ago for the Fotheringhams, but Aunt Doris only got on to her after she fell" (*CS*, 454). Another short story, ironically titled "The Good Girl" (1934),[14] serves to highlight the double standards which were prevalent during the interwar period; a young girl, Monica, falls in love with an Italian, Captain Monteparnesi. After spending the evening with him, Monica returns very late to the hotel where she is staying with her friend, Dagmar, who is initially horrified at Monica's behaviour. However, after seeing the Captain with his mother and family, "Dagmar, looking down from her loggia, knew that her cousin could not have sinned with a man with so large and black a family, and once more it seemed unlikely to her that Monica would ever sin" (*CS*, 361). In contrast, the Captain's mother rushes her son away to marry his cousin who has just become an heiress, "[i]t was not until months afterwards that she heard how nearly he had been entangled with an English girl of doubtful reputation" (ibid).

One might assume that Bowen equated loss of innocence with the acquisition of sexual knowledge—indeed Blodgett suggests that "Miss Bowen's novels implicitly urge that sexual activity be restricted to the fully committed marriage partner" (1975, 65). There is no doubt that 1930s society would have considered Emmeline's reputation as being in tatters; Lady Waters, for example, expresses her concerns about Emmeline's behaviour in a conversation with Cecilia,

> 'My point is just this: Emmeline is being far worse than simply silly and intellectual: she is doing herself real damage in her own world.'
> 'Which world?' parried Cecilia.
> 'There is only one world,' said Lady Waters. 'That young man's reputation is shocking' (*TN*, 221)

This theory is borne out when one considers the readings of *Friends and Relations* and *To the North* outlined at the beginning of this chapter. Such an interpretation of the novelist's stance would certainly give weight to this argument, particularly when Emmeline's fall from social grace leads ultimately to her death and when Janet's discussion with Edward is considered, "[w]e cannot expect your mother to stay in London without a cook because she once ruined herself – Yes, I did mean ruined herself; isn't that how you've made her see it?" (*FR*, 90). Social ruin for a woman, however, could apparently be avoided if marriage legitimised a sexual relationship: Cecilia and Henry, for example, "became friends, intimates, lovers and soon afterwards married." (*TN*, 12). The pre-marital relationship of Cecilia and Henry contrasts sharply with the engagement of Laurel and Edward who marry following a long engagement; desperate to marry in the summer, the narrator tells us in parenthesis that "to make this possible he and she had devoured each other nervously throughout the endless winter of their engagement" (*FR*, 8). However, the relationship between sexuality and loss of innocence is not, in the author's eyes, as black and white as the initial summary of the two novels might suggest.

Sexuality and Loss of Innocence

Whilst 1930s society, following on from Victorian standards, might well have believed that any sexual activity outside the bounds of marriage immediately classed a woman as "fallen", it is instead the Biblical connotation that equates loss of innocence with the original Fall—that is, the exercise of free will and subsequent eviction from the Garden of Eden—that should be used to examine Emmeline's situation. Her belief that she should be considered "ruined" is evident in the following exchange between Emmeline and Markie when Markie expresses his concern for the future,

> 'I'm alarmed'
> 'If I'm not – and of course I do see in one way I am ruined – I don't see why you should be.'
> 'Oh, all right. As you like. But we *are* riding for a fall.'
> 'I don't care.' Smiling she drew her finger across his angry uncertain lips in a little line that should conclude the argument.
> 'I do,' he said, when the finger had gone. 'You know, you've been idiotic.'
> 'How, a fall?
> 'Oh, I don't know … But it will be the devil.' (*TN*, 184)

A close reading of the novel can infer a complex relationship between innocence and sexual experience, with the narrator ultimately suggesting that perhaps the loss of innocence is a psychological rather than physical state; indeed loss of innocence for Emmeline initially stems from her unconscious deception of Cecilia, not from her journey to Paris.

> When Emmeline realized Cecilia no longer saw [Markie] she was alarmed; it was as though a door shut upon her and Markie, leaving them quite alone for the first time: the nature of their relationship changed for her. When she understood that Cecilia had not realized *she* still saw Markie, taking fully for granted that he was out of the family, Emmeline was dumbfounded. […] This was her first break with innocence. Something weakened in her defences that were not till now defences, so unconscious had they been and so impassable. (*TN*, 49-50)

The narrator specifically refers to Emmeline's acknowledgement that she and Markie have a relationship, one which excludes Cecilia, and it is this acknowledgement which is "the first break with innocence"; for Emmeline this realisation forces her to start her journey along the path to knowledge, a path which could, ultimately, result in her total loss of innocence. Yet it could be argued that her naivety and lack of sexual knowledge helps to prolong any state of innocence. Like Laurel, who confesses to Janet that "[s]he liked London better even than she had expected, and carried (though Edward must never suspect this) a map of it in her handbag, also a guide to the buses" (*FR*, 22), Emmeline is also, at times, lost. However, whilst Laurel's lack of knowledge and unfamiliarity with London is founded on both a literal basis and a psychological naivety, Emmeline's confusion relates solely to her state of mind (she is, of course, far more knowledgeable about the geography of London than Laurel). Arriving at Markie's flat for the first time and having encountered his sister before climbing the stairs to his flat, Emmeline "looked bewildered – like a gentle foreigner at Victoria, not knowing where to offer her ticket, to whom, if at all, her passport, uncertain even whether she had arrived" (*TN*, 70).

The journey from innocence to experience does not appear to be one of simple linearity as the passivity with which Emmeline succumbs to Markie in Paris further complicates the binary opposition of innocence and its loss. Leaving Kent, frequently referred to as the Garden of England and thus perhaps, for her, synonymous with the Garden of Eden, Emmeline is tempted by Markie; in Paris she loses both her virginity and, as 1930s society would probably suggest, her innocence. Her loss of virginity, the narrator suggests, is a loss for which Emmeline is not ready; Markie, waiting for Emmeline to meet him in the evening was "unused to going about with a woman on these terms, had yet to learn that a woman who seems to be ready early is never ready" (*TN*, 146). Whilst ostensibly this passage relates to Emmeline fetching her gloves, it can be read as a statement that Emmeline was not ready to lose her virginity, particularly if this is taken in conjunction with the description of Emmeline's actions earlier in the day,

> [t]he passionless entirety of her surrender, the volition of her entire wish to be his had sent her a good way past him: involuntarily, the manner of her abandonment had avenged her innocence. As though she were conscious of her unwilling departure, of a disparity isolating for him in their two expressions of passion, he had read in her look today a kind of entreating gentleness. Following him with eyes that saw at once nothing and too much, she had seemed unwilling to be a moment apart from him, her

finger-tips in the palm of his hand, in which every swerve and jar of the taxi became recorded' (*TN*, 142-143)

Despite Emmeline's physical loss of virginity, she retains the vestiges of innocence; such a retention could be allied to Emmeline's perception, on the flight to Paris, that she and Markie were inextricably linked together,

> [s]he was embarked, they were embarked together, no stop was possible; she could now turn back only by some unforeseen and violent deflection – by which her exact idea of personal honour became imperilled – from their set course. She could not see at what point the issue became apparent, from what point she was committed: committed, however, she felt. (*TN*, 138)

Markie's previous comment "[b]ut it will be the devil" is an interesting one: throughout the novel Emmeline is referred to as "angelic" (not least by her aunt's Vicar who refers to her as a "thin girl with the social passivity of an angel" (*TN*, 64)); in contrast Markie is considered to be devilish, "satanic" according to Lee (1999, 69). Such a statement by Markie however suggests that Markie too can be considered as retaining an element of innocence. Is he aware of the moral dilemma in which he is placing Emmeline or does he have no concept of morality? Consideration of Markie's close contemporary in Bowen's writing, John ("The Last Night in the Old House", 1934[15]), helps to shed a little more light on Markie's character. Having effectively lost all his family's money, a loss which leads to the auction of the family home and all its contents, John is described thus: "[h]ard-hit, John felt really innocent. Not once had he been deliberate: if mess bills ran up, horses he backed turned out rotten, cards he held worthless and women he loved exacting, was John to blame?" (*CS*, 373)[16]

Indeed Blodgett sees Markie as a "notable victim ... [who] is a complex devil delineated with a modern sense of perversion in human nature" (1975, 60). Markie's relationship with Daisy would support Blodgett's reading; perversely Daisy provides Markie with a "source [...] of endless satirical pleasure" for "he liked women lowish" and the more she became "the clergyman's daughter"[17] instead of a woman who has an "acute sense of having departed from virtue" (*TN*, 179) in reaction to Markie's attitude towards her, the more he enjoyed her company. In contrast to Blodgett's opinion, Coates is not prepared to consider Markie a victim at all likening, for example, Markie's dissolute appearance at Oudenarde Road early one morning to Milton's Satan's entry into Eden (1998, 93); certainly he sees Markie in the rôle of a corruptor, describing the train journey on which Cecilia and Markie meet for the first time as a meeting between "a Jamesian young American girl about to fall prey to European corruption" (ibid, 71).

Homosexuality

Gindin recognises three recurring themes in 1930s fiction, the importance of geographical location, a psychological exploration of sexuality and, thirdly, "an increasing interest in homosexuality" (1992, 15). In the 1930s there were, as there are today, many differing and divergent attitudes to sexuality, homosexuality and lesbianism and it is within this context that it is interesting to consider Bowen's position in relation to this particular issue, both textually and biographically.[18] It is apparent that Bowen experienced difficulties with her own sexuality; in a letter to Alan Cameron dated 1923 she wrote,

> You are very precious to me – I feel sometimes I am stupid. My love for you seems very childish – I mean sexless and imaginative. You see I have loved you for a long time as a friend, and that feeling still goes deepest and doesn't seem to have changed very much. (1999b, 194)

Arguably, this would probably be considered an appropriate emotion in a young woman of the 1920s who was not yet married (she married Cameron in August later that year) but various commentators suggest that Bowen's marriage to Cameron was a relatively sexless relationship. Ellmann, for example, states that Bowen's marriage to Cameron was never consummated (2003, 30) and comments that

> [l]ike Edith Wharton, who discovered passion after many years of sexless marriage, Bowen reached her mid-thirties before she embarked on her first love affair, with a young Oxford don named Humphrey House, who was dumbfounded to discover she was still a virgin. (Ibid, 32)

Glendinning alludes to this in her discussion of Bowen's sexuality stating "The man himself believed – as he told his wife – that he had taken Elizabeth's virginity" (1977, 88); Hoogland suggests that Bowen's affair with House left her "with a radically changed sense of self [which allowed] her to discover the strength of her hitherto restrained passions." (1994, 12). Wyatt-Brown adds to the debate over the consummation of the Camerons' marriage by suggesting that Cameron was homosexual, commenting that "[h]e conducted his affairs – whatever they were—… discreetly" (1993, 171). There appears to be no doubt that Bowen enjoyed a number of affairs, particularly during the 1930s and 1940s, with various names being linked to hers including Sean O'Faolain and Charles Ritchie. Virginia Woolf, however, in a letter to Vita Sackville-West dated 18th October 1932, suggests that Bowen might not be as heterosexual as others, or as Bowen herself, might think. Having received a copy of *To the North* from Bowen, Woolf writes

> [a]nyhow my Elizabeth [Bowen] comes to see me, alone, tomorrow. I rather think, as I told you, that her emotions sway in a certain way. (that's an elegiac) I'm reading her novel to find out. Whats so interesting is when one uncovers an emotion that the person themselves, I should say herself, doesn't suspect. And it's a sort of duty don't you think – revealing peoples true selves to them selves? I dont like these sleeping princesses. (1979, 111)[19]

Hoogland also mentions this facet of Bowen's sexuality, commenting that following her affair with Humphrey House, Bowen continued to have "a series of short-lived affairs, mostly with men but occasionally also with women." (1994, 12).

Although acts of homosexuality were illegal in the 1930s, nevertheless a great deal had been written about this specific area of sexuality, writing which was being discussed more openly during this period and much of the groundwork had already been carried out by sexual theorists such as Edward Carpenter, Havelock Ellis[20] and Krafft-Ebbing.[21] Whilst Crossland might well believe that "Elizabeth Bowen in the 1930s made a few indirect references to lesbian relationships" (1981, 222) other critics challenge this reading of Bowen's fiction; Coughlan, for example, says of Theodora Thirdman, "[a]part from, or as well as, her lesbian characterisation, Theodora is one of a type in Bowen" (1997, 118).[22] She continues that Theodora is not "constructed with pity, or even with charity" (ibid) but, nevertheless Theodora's question "Mother, are we so absolutely *superfluous?*" (*FR*, 28), whilst directly referring to her family's lifestyle can also be read as a plea for understanding for she knows that, even at this early age, she is at odds with society. Such a reading would find accord with Coughlan who suggests that characters such as Theodora, the "odd man out" according to Janet (*TN*, 94), who finds herself an outsider,

> glower from peripheral niches in the plots, while the protagonists gliding up the central aisle of the story generally have beauty, social poise, parents, the warmth of human regard or some combination of three of those four which makes them adequate for life. (1997, 118)

Theodora's continued questioning of her mother also draws on the analogy of a train journey, alluded to by Laurel on her wedding day, "But don't we want to *matter* in this place? Aren't we ever going to begin? Mother, you're like someone sitting for always on a suitcase in a railway station. Such a comfortable suitcase, such a magnificent station! *Eeooch!*" (*FR*, 28). The Thirdmans are of course equally at odds with society, not by dint of their sexuality but rather their "long exile" (*FR*, 27) and, like Pauline, Julian's niece, they enjoy travelling round London by bus; as Mrs Thirdman tells Theodora they "are so happy going about on buses looking at all the types" (*FR*, 28).

Theodora may well "glower" from a "peripheral" niche in *Friends and Relations*, but her actions play a significant rôle in the lives of Laurel, Edward, Janet and Rodney. Sent by her parents to Mellyfield, a school whose headmistress was, according to Mr and Mrs Thirdman, a woman of "striking originality, who set great score by individual development" (*FR*, 29), Theodora initially remains an outsider at a school where the girls "developed very early a feeling for character [...] They read psychology to each other on Sunday afternoons" (*FR*, 43-44). Mellyfield is a school concerned with its pupil's characters; like the school attended by the eponymous protagonist in Bowen's short story "Maria", a school which was "one of those comfortable schools where everything is attended to [... where Maria] was having her character 'done' for her' " (*CS*, 408),[23] Mellyfield's "diluted Freudianism" (Coates 1992, 296) enables Theodora to find her own rôle to play in school life, particularly when "[s]he distinguished herself as a young man in one of the Saturday night plays – these improvised, un-rehearsed, in the manner of *commedie dell'arte.*" (*FR*, 44). Naturally, a propensity to taking on male rôles in school plays does not automatically suggest any lesbian tendencies on the part of Theodora but, nevertheless, when read in connection with her attraction to Janet on the day of Laurel's wedding, her living arrangements with Marise suggest a homosexual rather than heterosexual relationship.

Theodora's manipulative letter to Laurel, telling her that both Considine and Lady Elfrida were present at Batts Abbey, sets in train a series of events which serve to make Theodora very unhappy. In her actions she exhibits those attributes ascribed by Coughlan to the lesbian characters in Bowen's fiction:

> When in her fictions she created explicit representations of adult lesbian characters, she tended, as I have said, to place them in the margins, and with a high degree of irony, distance, and even moral approbation – not, to be sure, specifically of their presumed sexual acts, but of a range of characteristics with which she chose to endow them, characteristics

sometimes including over-emotionality, sometimes manipulativeness. (1997, 111)

Theodora's "over-emotionality" comes to the fore when she mistakenly believes that Janet has run away with Edward, based on Lewis Gibson's false assumption. Theodora's conversation with Lewis prompts him to accuse her of being hysterical, to which Theodora responds, "I can't stand this; I love her! I tell you, idiot, I love her beyond propriety-" (*FR*, 146), but as Lewis reflects,

> She really was unhappy. And what a good thing, thought Lewis, viewing the entire collapse of any charm she ever had, that she was not unhappy more often. 'I suppose,' he thought, 'that they do really suffer.' She was so entirely to pieces that Lewis [...] had no difficulty in edging her from the flat. (Ibid.)

Theodora's surname (Thirdman) is also suggestive of her sexuality, the name having resonances of Edward Carpenter's belief that homosexuals were effectively a third gender. Although Carpenter was referring to male homosexuals, this argument can be applied in this instance to Bowen's choice of names, for Bowen never chose a name lightly for her characters[24] and, in Theodora's case, "Thirdman" can also be read as an interloper. Ellmann draws parallels between this novel, gothic fiction of the nineteenth century and Henry James' short story "The Third Person" (2003, 73) and also traces the use of the third person in the narrative to Freud's work *Jokes and their Relation to the Unconscious*.[25] Whilst not completely fulfilling Freud's description of the third person (most noticeably Freud's third person is male), Theodora's intervention in the relationship between Janet and Edward does have lasting consequences. However, it is not Theodora's intervention that causes Janet to reject Edward, but rather Janet's own sense of duty towards Rodney and her daughter and her refusal to lose the safety of Batts Abbey, with all its Edenic connotations.

Margaret Lawrence suggests that "Lesbianism is admittedly flourishing in either its implication or its actuality in an astonishingly large number of women." (1937, 262) She continues

> [w]hether the largeness of the number is to be accounted for by the world shock sustained by the war and post-war generation of women, and the sickening of the civilized mind against the animality of war, and consequently against all other phases of animality, is a subject for thought. (Ibid, 263)

Whatever the root causes of this increase might be (if indeed there was an increase), Bowen's introduction of homosexual characters within her novels obviously merits discussion and, whilst Theodora might well be the main embodiment of that element of thirties' fiction, Bowen continues to employ this theme in *To the North*, albeit in a less overt manner in the guise of the unfortunate Miss Tripp, Emmeline and Peter's stenographer. Like Theodora, Miss Tripp does not appear to be comfortable in her life. She believes herself to be invisible to Emmeline, a state of affairs that she finds increasingly impossible to live with. She dresses in a vain attempt to attract Emmeline's attention, she is banished from the room when Emmeline's friends call and, in an analogy for her own lack of position in this society, has nowhere to hang her hat. Miss Tripp is distraught because Emmeline fails to recognise her emotional attachment, but worse, does not seem to recognise her as a person. Although having rehearsed the words "I shouldn't stay here a moment if it were not for you" (*TN*, 122), Miss Tripp is unable to express her emotions clearly and, eventually, Emmeline sends her home without really understanding why Miss Tripp should be so upset. As she later tells Peter "she didn't seem very well, she was rather upset about something: I gave her a week or two's rest" (*TN*, 126).

There are a number of ways in which this comedic episode can be read. When taken into consideration with Bowen's characterisation of Theodora, it could suggest that Bowen believed that her reading public would not welcome a sympathetic treatment of homosexuality. Alternatively, if Woolf is right, it could suggest that Bowen was not aware of her own attraction to women or that she was uncomfortable with the idea of lesbianism and her own sexuality: however, Bowen's work is always self-conscious, both here and elsewhere.

Of more interest, perhaps, is the relationship between Cecilia and Emmeline. Lady Waters does not approve of two women living together and yet it is not a passionate or sexual relationship; nor, I would argue, should their relationship be read from a solely lesbian perspective. However, it is possible that Virginia Woolf would have read this fictional relationship as evidence of Bowen's "emotions sway[ing] in a certain way" (1979, 111). Emmeline and Cecilia's relationship fulfils a significant rôle in the lives of the two young women. As Lassner suggests, their relationship is one which has more significance than the mere convenience of sisters-in-law sharing a house (1990, 64). We are told, for example, despite Cecilia's unwillingness to commit herself in another relationship with a man, and being "[m]istrustful, tentative, uncertain whether to marry again, she was quite happy only in one relationship: with her young sister-in-law, Emmeline" (*TN*, 10). It is a situation which has a bearing on both

Cecilia's relationship with Julian and Emmeline's with Markie in which both passion (or rather its lack) and jealousy play a large part.

Passion

Margaret Lawrence's opinions, although often strident and perhaps unusual in the 1930s, provide an insight into how certain sections of society viewed women, men and matters of sexuality and with Markie in mind, Lawrence's views about men can be seen to be particularly apt,

> [m]en, with rare individual exceptions, care fundamentally very little about women and, except in their momentary mating urges, are interested only in their own particular game. They like business; they like war; sometimes they like politics; and sometimes they like golf. They do not really like love affairs. They never quite see why women cannot take sex as sex and let it be; yet somehow they never quite trust the woman who does […] if he by any chance is involved with a romantic it is too bad for her. She wants so much more from him than he can give, and if she can adjust at all after her first disillusionment, the process is likely to take some length of time, during which anything may happen (1937, 207-208).

Lawrence thus makes a distinction between love affairs and relationships that are based solely on a sexual attraction; in her opinion passion for men equates with war, politics, golf and sex, for women passion is closely linked with love and romance. With this in mind it is particularly interesting to note that throughout these two novels there is a continual suppression of passion of which Emmeline's "passionless" surrender is just one example, nor is passion a constant. We are told, for example, that

> [p]assion, with Markie, went in curves of caprice: under the fairly imposing surface of his masculinity there whirled currents of instability, of exactingness, of an incapacity to be satisfied, of whose ravages on serenity he was not aware: missing repose vaguely he made it impossible. (*TN*, 145)

However, whilst sexual passion might well be constrained at times, emotional passion is given a full rein, and it can be seen to be present in varying guises in both novels. There is the passion which is denied in the premarital relationship between Laurel and Edward and the later exhaustion of sexual passion in their marriage; when Edward, Laurel, Janet and Rodney meet for lunch before Janet and Rodney's wedding, Rodney's emotions are all too present for "Rodney's look narrowed; love became momentously present and the young Tilneys, obliterated, wanted to walk away. Recollecting their own passion they rallied and were benevolent" (*FR*, 35). It is perhaps strange that, so early in their marriage, Laurel and Edward should have to recollect their passion, a passion that seemed to be fully alive only the previous day when discussing the possibility of the lunch party

> [t]hey lay side by side on their two low beds as on tombs and were each aware in the other, falling asleep, of the same carven air of finality. Now, shading their eyes, they turned discover each other again in the light of the new day.
> 'Perhaps not today.' Determining in her heart to be first with Janet alone, she put out a hand; their fingers groped for each other over the chasm between the beds. A small thrill animated the tombs. (*FR*, 21)

Whilst passion might well have existed in Laurel and Edward's early marriage, it is not an emotion which, from Edward's point of view, continues, to play a part in their life; reflecting back on his marriage, it appears to him to have an almost childlike quality, both providing comfort for the child within the other,

> If [Laurel] was not serene she was gay and professed to find in Edward the spring of her comfort. Her solicitude reached him almost before he suffered, fostering sensibility. 'And life after all,' thought Edward […], is an affair of charm, not an affair of passion.' (*FR*, 99)

Equally, there appears to be an awareness on Laurel's part that all is not well with their marriage. As Theodora becomes the third person in the putative relationship between Laurel and Edward, so Laurel, at a very early stage in her marriage to Edward, perhaps subconsciously acknowledges that Janet might be the third person in her marriage and may well be the one who might cause trouble in the future. This can be seen from her desire to see Janet first when she comes to London. Of course, her need to be the first to meet Janet, excluding Edward from the meeting, could arise simply from the close relationship that exists between the sisters. Laurel's misapprehensions are not misplaced; having received Theodora's manipulative letter, Janet and Laurel meet up in London, Laurel is distraught and after an initial period of consoling Janet "in her passionate fatality" (*FR*, 128), Laurel eventually unleashes her emotions.

> '[…] What a long time you've waited, Janet. You've waited, haven't you? And how well Elfrida knew. She's always been seeing something over my shoulder; she's been my most frightful enemy. No wonder Edward was restless. Funny, I seemed to have everything, didn't I? And

I've got no friends really but people like Mother and Willa and Mrs Bowles. I've never been anything but a daughter.'
    'I wish you'd be angry – '
    'Have I seemed very ridiculous all these years? I thought I was doing so well. What a wedding day, what rain, what a frightful mistake! But no one could tell me.' (*FR*, 128-129)

Laurel, however, also apportions blame for the apparent failure of the marriage on Lady Elfrida's affair with Considine. She continues to Janet

'[…] I love him so much; I do love him. But this idea of Elfrida, what she had, what she was, has been fearful; it's ruined us all. We've been certain of missing something, we've all watched the others. Like that game, a ring going round and round on a circle of string under everyone's hands – you never know where it is, who may have it. It's been terrible, Janet, it has, it has really. It's ruined us all.' (*FR*, 129)

Yet, although Theodora Thirdman might well be the physical embodiment of the third person in the relationships between Janet and Laurel, and Laurel and Edward, there is, to borrow a phrase from Maud Ellmann, a "shadowy third" (2003, 69), a psychological manifestation whose presence is keenly felt by Janet, "[t]hese weeks, a grotesque, not quite impossible figure, had come to interpose between herself and Laurel. A woman, an unborn shameful sister, travestying their two natures, enemy to them both." (*FR*, 122)

In contrast to the highly charged scenes with both Laurel and Edward, Janet is initially portrayed as being unemotional and cold, and yet the narrator suggests that, rather than lacking in emotion, she disguises her feelings by looking "blankly up with her very dark eyes" at her mother and "[i]f in her twenty years she had formed opinions, she never expressed them. No one knew what she thought. She had now, of course, her happiness, but it had been difficult – Cheltenham did not know" (*FR*, 15). When Edward writes to the Studdarts expressing his horror that Janet should be considering marriage to the nephew of "Lady Elfrida's co-respondent" (*FR*, 16) and whilst those all around her are concerning themselves with her future happiness or unhappiness, "[m]ercifully, the Girl Guides kept [Janet] busy during this difficult period: a rally was being organized" (*FR*, 17). Yet this apparently passionless demeanour is at odds with her thoughts; at the lunch organised by Laurel "Janet, deliberately not looking [at Edward], thought with her cold dispassionate passion, I could hold you, yes, and make you run about, in the palm of my hand" (*FR*, 36).
    Whilst there would appear to be no doubt that Janet does have a passionate side to her nature, her effective suppression of her passion for

Edward allows her, one could suggest, to retain her own notion of innocence. She becomes aware, following Edward's dramatic journey to Batts Abbey to "rescue" his children from any possible corruption arising out of the relationship between Lady Elfrida and Considine, that any action she takes to alter her own life, to allow herself to advance her relationship with Edward, will effectively ruin not only her life, but the lives of others too. If she does attempt to make any substantive changes in her life, or as she herself verbalises internally, "[i]f you felled the tree, or made even a vital incision [...] down they all came from the branches and scattered, still green at the core like July apples, having no more part in each other at all: strangers" (*FR*, 104), that life will become intolerable. Coates suggests that an affair with Edward is never really possible for Janet; in his view,

> *Friends and Relations* makes it abundantly clear that Janet's predicament is that she has fallen in love with a man who cannot respond to the kind of feeling she has to offer. It is not a question of compromise or conventionality strangling love or of a passion being 'relinquished'. Such passion is never a possibility (1992, 298).

An alternative reading is one which recognises the passion that Janet and Edward share cannot be acted upon because of Janet's realisation that many lives will be altered if she and Edward pursue their own feelings for each other; it is through her own passion for Edward that she married into the Studdart family. Lady Elfrida is aware of Edward's love for Janet ("Nonsense, Janet, of course he loves you" (*FR*, 105)) and becomes aware of Janet's need to be connected; this becomes very clear in an exchange between Lady Elfrida and Janet:

> 'So you've married them both.'
> 'It seemed *something* for me – I wanted to be related. I suppose that seems odd to you – I can see now it was odd,' said Janet, with her calm precision.
> 'So you took Rodney – ' Her friend re-examined the situation from this angle. 'Of course,' she added, 'it is extraordinary to me that a woman as little cold as you are should keep so quiet.'
> 'It was a question of what I wanted – couldn't you have kept quiet once?'
> 'We're not speaking of passion,' returned Elfrida impatiently. '*This* was – determination. Perhaps that's the only passion you have ...' (*FR*, 106).

For Janet, however, it is not just the passionate need for a connection with Edward which leads her to marry Rodney, but also the knowledge that such a marriage would connect her to Lady Elfrida; the connection between them all is of utmost importance to Janet, a desire which is in stark contrast to Markie's unwillingness to be connected to anyone. His living arrangements are a metaphor for his desire to remain unconnected; he rarely talks to his sister, in whose house his flat is located, and he communicates with the cook by whistling down a tube.

In contrast to Janet's hidden passionate nature and the sexual passion of Markie for Emmeline, Cecilia's relationship with Julian appears to have no basis in any such emotion; rather it appears to be of a more platonic friendship. Cecilia acknowledges this lack of emotion when she and Julian are organizing their trip to see Pauline at her boarding school,

> Julian suggested that they should take the whole day out and lunch in the country. But Cecilia said no: Buckinghamshire was too small, not many times the length of his car; they would soon overshoot the school and run out of the county; they must not overshoot the school. The fact was, to lunch at a country inn one must be in love (she thought). The musty red entrance, hat-racks, long solid menu, short wine-list were bare of charm for her nowadays. She could not attempt this with Julian ...' (*TN*, 74)

It is a lack she acknowledges again when she is staying at Farraways without Julian, "[s]he was missing him these days, not that she saw him less but his absences seemed longer: the possibility of their ever falling in love remained, however, remote" (*TN*, 156). Cecilia's ability to love, to experience passion, was extinguished on the death of her husband (and Emmeline's brother), Henry. Cecilia's love for Henry is destroyed by his death, a death which casts her out of her own Eden, her marriage. In a passage which resonates with echoes of the burning of Danielstown in *The Last September* and Bowen's own fears for Bowen's Court during the Troubles in Ireland in the early part of the nineteen twenties, the narrator suggests that it is not possible to regain that existence, "[w]hen a house has been destroyed by fire – left with walls bleached and ghastly and windows gaping with the cold sky – the master has not, perhaps, the heart or the money to rebuild" (*FR*, 99). Cecilia does not have the "heart [...] to rebuild", and although "[w]ith the quick fancy, the nerves and senses Cecilia could almost love [...] she could not regain some entirety of the spirit" (*FR*, 100). Despite Lady Elfrida's distrust of women living together, and Emmeline's own perceptions of their relationship, Cecilia is not able to love Emmeline completely. Standing at Emmeline's bedroom door, Cecilia contemplates the possibility of Emmeline leaving Oudenarde Road and,

> not going in [to Emmeline's bedroom], leant against the doorway trying to read the name of a book by the bed, and thought: 'She is not my lover; she's not my child.'
> Though the idea of parting from Emmeline could seem intolerable there was not much more, it occurred to Cecilia, than the idea of company in her company. Saying: 'I live with Emmeline,' she might paint for ignorant eyes, and even dazzle herself for a moment with a tempting picture of intimacy. But she lent herself to a fiction in which she did not believe; for she lived with nobody. (*FR*, 133)

Jealousy

Whilst Cecilia might well feel as though "she lived with nobody", this is a feeling which is not shared with Emmeline and, with this in mind, another aspect of passion and sexuality which should be considered, one which has a considerable bearing on any reading of the two novels, is jealousy. It is an issue which arises specifically in the latter stages of *To the North* when Markie reads a chapter from Stendhal's *De l'Amour* entitled "De La Jalousie" ("Concerning Jealousy").[26] Stendhal's chapter examines the nature of jealousy, particularly the jealousy experienced when a man in love believes he has a rival for his affections. He starts with the basic premise that

> [w]hen you are in love, no matter what you see or remember, whether you are packed in a gallery listening to political speeches or riding at full gallop under enemy fire to relieve a garrison, you are always adding new perfections to your idea of your mistress, or finding new and apparently ideal ways of making her love you more (1822b, 111).

However, Markie continues to read; this notion of perfection, according to Stendhal, can lead one to believe that the target of one's affections is in love with someone else. Such a thought turns to jealousy, an emotion which is often illogical. Markie's declamation that this is "Rot" surprises Emmeline, "who though already too familiar with *De l'Amour* from which Cecilia frequently read aloud, had politely stopped stirring her tea to listen". His explanation that "One's got no time for all that" (*TN*, 203-4) leaves many unanswered questions. Markie's life, for example, appears to be predicated on his desire to be completely in control of his own life, evidenced in part by his choice of career and his living arrangements. He does not want overwrought emotions to play a part in his carefully controlled environment and yet the narrator would have the reader believe that Markie's choice of reading material was completely random. As Bowen comments in "Notes on Writing a Novel", "[c]haracters should, on the whole, be under rather than over articulate. What they *intend* to say should be more evident, more striking (because of its greater importance to the plot) than what they arrive at *saying*." (1945b, 256) and Markie's reading provides a timely reminder, therefore, that his words should not be taken simply at face value. In as much as the author (according to Bowen) is a manipulator of plot, so Markie is a manipulator of emotions. Having already effectively seduced Emmeline and, possibly, completely ruined her reputation, nonetheless, like John in "The Last Night in the Old House", in his own eyes he feels that he has done no wrong, after all he has constantly reminded Emmeline that he will not marry her but his apparent openness about their situation does not accord with the part that deception has to play in his own life.

Whilst the inclusion of this lengthy reading by Markie raises questions about Markie himself, it also allows discussion of the nature of jealousy within the two novels, an emotion which plays a significant rôle in the lives of the main protagonists. By the very virtue of his reading that particular passage from Stendhal, the narrator highlights Markie's own jealous nature, begging the question of whom is Markie jealous? The telegram from Cecilia perhaps provides one answer as it provokes a very strong reaction in Markie:

> To say that Markie had minded would not be adequate. Any talk of return to Cecilia he blithely discredited overnight, and had taken as done with. This morning Emmeline said she *was* going back; nervousness made her assertive; she could not have put things worse. Upon this, the dead stop of his tenderness, flicked off sharply as electricity, his incomprehension and ice-cold anger had given that hot bright Sunday – downs bald in sunshine, heat quivering in through the cottage doors – the lucidity of a nightmare […] A profound and slighting contempt for her point of view, that must have underlain at all times his tenderness, was apparent in all that he said and did, most of all in silence. This complete disconnection between them, so disorientating to Emmeline, meant, he made evident, little enough to Markie. (*TN*, 209-210).

Thus it can be seen that an element of Markie's jealousy is the relationship between Emmeline and Cecilia and although it might seem irrational given his unwillingness to marry Emmeline, nevertheless he is exceedingly unhappy at the thought of Emmeline abandoning him and returning to London to Cecilia. Markie's jealousy of this relationship is echoed by Emmeline's own strong feelings of jealousy when she contemplates the possible marriage between Cecilia and Julian, "[t]imber by timber, Oudenarde Road fell to bits, as small houses are broken up daily to widen the roar of London. She saw the door open on emptiness: blanched walls as though after a fire. Houses shared with women are built on sand." (*FR*, 207-8) This echoes the despair felt by Cecilia following Henry's death and her inability to feel love for another man.

As Cecilia's capacity for love and her feeling of safety and security had been removed when Henry died, so is Emmeline's own perception of safety altered once she realises that Cecilia will marry Julian and she is thrust into the insecurity that her relationship with Markie brings. Not only does Emmeline have to contend with her feelings of jealousy in relation to Cecilia's impending marriage, she also has to deal with the jealousy she experiences when Markie talks about his friends, particularly Daisy, feelings of jealousy that Markie does nothing to ameliorate. However, these tangled emotions force Emmeline to consider her own life, a consideration which leads to *anagnôrisis* and, ultimately for Emmeline, to death.

Anagnôrisis, Edenic Eviction and Endings

Just as *anagnôrisis* plays an important role in Lois' transition from innocence to experience in *The Last September*, so it plays an equally important part in the lives of the main protagonists in both *Friends and Relations* and *To the North*, but whilst for Emmeline recognition leads to her death, its effect on Janet and Laurel, as will be seen, whilst not physically fatal, has a potentially far-reaching effect on their future happiness. Coates suggests that

> [t]he weight of interest in *Friends and Relations* rests not on the revelation of a secret to the reader but in examining the problem of maintaining order in the personal life and the poignancy of carrying out duties undertaken within relationships. It is concerned with the quality of love viewed as an institution rather than as a form of self-fulfilment. (1992, 294)

The main thrust of the plot, as Coates' rightly suggests, is how Janet, in particular, resists her desire to be with Edward in an attempt to protect herself, and her family, within the framework of marriage, to remain, in effect, in the Eden promised by Batts Abbey; after all, knowledge of Janet's love for Edward does not manifest itself as a blinding revelation, rather there are many signs which indicate the true nature of Janet's love for Edward. Theodora, for example, is aware of this on Laurel and Edward's wedding day, "Theodora, intently listening [to a conversation between Mrs Daubeny and Lady Elfrida], inferred that Janet loved Edward, that his mother preferred Janet; that for Janet this was a day of chagrin, possibly or despair" (*FR*, 13); even Laurel's servants acknowledge that Edward is married to the wrong sister, Sylvia, the cook, thinks that "[a] wife like [Janet] would have been the makings of Mr Tilney, to get him out of his fanciful ways" (*FR*, 26). Equally, when Edward returns from home on the day that Janet and Laurel meet for the first time since Laurel's wedding the reader is given a further indication of the possibility that Janet and Edward are in love, "Mr Tilney stood blindly, as though the hall were the coal-hole. Putting out a hand to the dining-room door he said: 'My darling?' And Miss Studdart said in her decided low voice: 'Hullo … Edward.' " (ibid)

However, whilst recognising the viability of Coates' theory, this book is also concerned with the effect that revelations have on the individual characters in Bowen's fiction and, with this in mind, it is interesting to note the different ways in which Bowen treats *anagnôrisis* in *Friends and Relations* and *To the North*. Recognition for Janet comes slowly, with individual episodes finally culminating in an understanding of her own life, whereas for Laurel and Emmeline, as implied by the quotation used at the very beginning of this chapter, the moment of *anagnôrisis* is far more melodramatic. The effects on the protagonists' lives cast them all out of their own particular Eden, albeit in very different ways.

Janet's recognition and acknowledgement of her feelings for Edward, and her subsequent realisation that their love for each other cannot be acted upon, stems from Edward's visit to Batts Abbey to "rescue" his children from the corrupting presence of his mother and Considine. Janet is appalled by Edward's decision to remove Anna and Simon, it is as though she needs their presence in her life because of their connection to Edward; when Edward questions Janet's motives, she exclaims "[b]ecause they're *your* children!" (*FR*, 91) and then,

> [h]e committed her fully to this, underlining the remark by a complete silence. She had to turn round: he replaced a book. Nothing further had to be understood; they let the remark remain between them, a sheer awkwardness. 'Edward—' she began; this was the first break in her manner; despair came through, so personal, so positive that it was like the carrying-in of a light in which the whole subject wavered a moment, to become smaller and plainer. 'This does no good,' said Janet. (ibid)

As the narrator similarly suggests of Emmeline when she realises that Cecilia no longer sees Markie, "[t]his was her first break with innocence" (*TN*, 50), so this is Janet's first major realisation of the depth of her feelings for Edward. Her contemplation of Edward, linking them with Elfrida and Considine in relation to the tree of Jesse[27] and the Tree of the Knowledge of Good and Evil (more commonly known as the apple tree in the Garden of Eden) forces her to realise that she needs to make a choice between her marriage with Rodney and the possibility of a life with Edward. She is well aware, however, that if she chooses the latter, then the result will be chaos. For Janet, her innocence, and her Eden (despite her desire for Edward) remain rooted in Batts Abbey and in her marriage to Rodney. It is an innocence of which Edward is only too well aware. When they meet up in London he becomes aware of what he perceives as her nobility and integrity, an aspect of her personality which "he had not loved" (*TN*, 119). Edward is alarmed to discover that she has changed, the "goodness" which he felt epitomised Janet has disappeared,

> [a]nd if that virtue of wholeness had been simply a quality in her behaviour, if her present noble innocence in affection denied her nobility, light went out of the scene instantly; it became indifferent to him, in his groping, where he rested or if this hand he touched in the dark were indeed her own. Her very innocence, her unguardedness, the approach there was to extravagance in her slow, dark looking, the directness she brought from her practical life to express passion, seemed in their present triumphant misuse to shadow decay, so that the whole bitterness of an unfruitful autumn was present in this belated flowering. (*FR*, 119-120)

Janet's love for Edward, and her acknowledgement of this love, has caused her to lose innocence, and whilst her decision to remain with Rodney at Batts Abbey provides her with the physical element of her Eden, psychologically by deciding to cross the divide between innocence and experience she has effectively cast herself out of her own Garden of Eden and, to revert to Bowen's thesis, "once we have lost that [innocence] it is futile to attempt to picnic in Eden" (1946, 265).

A similar fate awaits Laurel in her recognition of the relationship between Janet and Edward. The ultimate moment of *anagnôrisis* for Laurel comes on the receipt of Theodora's letter, which brings to the forefront of Laurel's mind all the worries that have remained in her subconscious from the beginning of her marriage. Her interview with Janet, following Janet's meeting with Edward, serves to highlight the tenuous state of her marriage. They meet in the drawing room which was once full of wedding presents but

[i]n ten years, many of the wedding presents had been broken or put away. The room was sadder, civiller, less inconsequent, a room that ten years ago, with some tears and quarrels but all in a glow, had been contrived together and chatted about. Its order was now fixed; you must not move the furniture or a patch of ghostly new carpet appeared, that had not faded. (*FR*, 127)

With the revelations in Theodora's letter and the recognition that it brings to her when she and Janet meet, Laurel can no longer pretend that her marriage provides her Eden. She is thrust into a world of experience, a world in which her childish acceptance of life allowed her to remain unquestioning in an unsuitable marriage. *Anagnôrisis* comes with a jolt to Laurel, "[a] shiver, as at some terrifying awakening, passed for a sob. Wide open, Laurel's unseen eyes, unseeing, were dark and steady with incredulity" (*FR*, 128).

Bowen's comment that "it is not only our fate but our business to lose innocence" (1946, 265) suggests that for a person to continue to develop it is necessary to cross the boundary from innocence to experience, although this may not always arise from a conscious choice as if it is "our business" then it is also essential that innocence should be lost. However, Laurel and Janet's loss of innocence results in an eviction from their own particular Edens without the possibility of any compensating happiness from their acquisition of experience. Janet returns to Batts Abbey, to continue to be a dutiful wife and mother, and Laurel continues to "mother" both her children and Edward in a marriage that "had been carried along on the smooth stream; they had only to keep still, not rocking their boat" (*FR*, 153). Most tellingly, rather than emerging as individuals in their own right following their loss of innocence and their subsequent transition to a life of knowledge and experience, the novel ends as it begins, with Janet and Laurel reverting to their original status as daughters of Corunna Lodge.

In contrast to this rather anticlimactic ending to *Friends and Relations* and, as indicated by the opening quotation of this chapter, Emmeline's eviction from her Eden, and the ending of the novel, are far more melodramatic. Melodrama, in fact, is never far from the surface in *To the North*; whereas there are frequent signs of Janet's love for Edward from the day of his wedding to Laurel, so there are numerous indications that the relationship between Markie and Emmeline will lead to disaster. These include the initial tone of violence when Cecilia and Markie first meet and Emmeline and Markie's flight to Paris: "[s]he was embarked, they were embarked together, no stop was possible; she could now turn back only by some unforeseen and violent deflection" (*TN*, 138), a Paris which is "approached by its macabre north" (*TN*, 140).

Anagnôrisis for Emmeline starts with an awareness that all is not as it should be in her life; sitting in Markie's flat one evening following their return from Paris, Emmeline is *"distraite"* (*TN*, 180),

> the room kept for her the ghost of its early strangeness […] But this touch of strangeness upon her nerves was becoming familiar: an isolation from life she felt here bound her up more closely than life itself […] intense experience interposed like a veil between herself and these objects' (ibid)

The loneliness Emmeline feels when she realises that Cecilia is going to marry Julian is exacerbated both by Markie's jealousy of the relationship she has with Cecilia and the realisation that she will never know the happiness that Cecilia is experiencing because of the very nature of the situation between herself and Markie, a relationship which is not recognised by society; it is perhaps the knowledge that Cecilia is to marry which forces Emmeline to recognise the inadequacies of her own relationship. When Markie doesn't understand why Emmeline cannot tell Cecilia about their weekend together in the cottage, Emmeline tries to explain,

> 'If I don't go back I must tell her … But I couldn't; I can't, Markie: it would be too cruel. You don't know how she feels. She's … not like us, she wouldn't ever see why … Just now when she's so safe and happy – it would be cruel! You see, she'd think I was ruined. She'd blame herself; she'd never be able to understand – Why did that telegram have to come? Interruptions like this, don't you see, are a tax on our sort of love. People in love like Cecilia and Julian, people married, have passports everywhere. They don't get telegrams, nobody sends for them: everyone understands. But you and I – wherever we go there is something to keep us separate. Someone is out to break us. We're not nearer each other for being tied up in lies!' (*TN*, 211)

She desires stability in her life, a security which is not offered by Markie; it is perhaps a realisation of her need to be like Cecilia, and knowledge that such a need is not going to be fulfilled which, in part, drives her to suicide. It is Emmeline's deception of Cecilia, when Cecilia does not know that Emmeline is seeing Markie, that is Emmeline's "first break with innocence" (*TN*, 50) and its continuation causes her great anguish. It is this which casts Emmeline out of her own Eden, for Emmeline a psychological rather than a physical place, one in which she feels secure, where deception does not play a part, one in which she longed suddenly to be fixed, to enjoy an apparent stillness, to watch even an hour complete round one object its little changes of light, to see out the little and greater cycles of day and season in one place, beloved, familiar, to watch shadows move round one garden, to know the same trees in spring and autumn and in their winter forms (*TN*, 144).

Lawrence suggests a hypothesis which could arguably account for Emmeline's reaction to her situation,

[t]he girl who, by some peculiar set of circumstance, grows up to be romantic is an image-worshipper [...] She is never aware that her illusions are illusions; that her beliefs are beliefs; or that legends are only legendary. [...] For the first impact of reality upon her imagery is usually shattering to her nervous system. (Lawrence, 1937, pp204-205)

There is no doubt that this is the effect that Markie has on Emmeline; he shatters her "nervous system", throwing her into a decline. The narrator of *To the* North suggests that "passion knows no crimes, only its own movement" (*TN*, 185) and yet both novels show that passion for the wrong person has a long lasting and detrimental effect on a person's life. Passion, for Emmeline, leads to the ultimate act of violence; her only avenue of escape is death, both for herself and the man that she once passionately loved. As the narrator tells the reader "[i]nnocence walks with violence; violence is innocence, cold as fate; between the mistress's kiss and the blade's is a hairsbreadth only, and no disparity; every door leads to death [...] The curtain comes down, the book closes" (*TN*, 185).

Notes

[1] When subsequent mention is made in parenthesis to these novels, *Friends and Relations* will be referred to as *FR*, *To the North* as *TN*.

[2] See Stendhal's *Le Rouge et Noir* although, of course, Stendhal is narrating an execution rather than a wedding.

[3] The ability to see occurs with symbolic significance in other novels by Bowen. For example, specific reference is made in *The Heat of the Day* to Harrison's eyes, the "lag or inequality in his vision gave her [Louie] the feeling of being looked at twice – being viewed then checked over in the same moment." (*The Heat of the Day*, 12).

[4] Bennett and Royle make this point in relation to their own reading of *To the North*. Initially providing a brief summary of the plot, they go on to observe that it is misleading since it "presupposes a reading of the novel as a literary and fictional tragic narrative, predicated on the basis of the most classical literary critical concepts, namely the constitutive rôle of plot, of a linear narrative progression or unfolding, and the determining force of character" (1995a, 24). Their reading of

the novel, however, is one which examines the "tragic power [… which] is inseparable from an acknowledgement of its displacements of concepts of person and individuality and from a dissolution of the linearity and teleological structure of narrative" (ibid). Anna Wyatt-Brown makes a similar, albeit briefer, observation: "Bowen's fiction resists superficial reading" (1993, 164).

[5] See also Paul Fussell's account of the importance of travel highlighted by the fiction of the inter-war period (*Abroad: British Literary Travelling Between the Wars*: London, 1980). Fussell's exploration has been expanded by David Farley's book *Modernist Travel Writing: Intellectuals Abroad* (Columbia and London, 2010).

[6] Even the Channel Tunnel is discussed in *To the North*, some 60 years before it was actually built in 1994 (*TN*, 129).

[7] Gindin suggests a further recurrent theme in the fiction of the 1930s, that of "an increasing interest in homosexuality" (1992, 15), an element of *Friends and Relations* and *To the North* which will be explored later in this chapter.

[8] Bowen's choice of names warrants further discussion. Continuing the analogy of childhood figuring the Garden of Eden, a motif found in varying forms throughout Bowen's novels, Meggat, for example, is only two vowels away from maggot, an insect commonly found in rotten apples. Theodora Thirdman's surname is also very suggestive, raising questions of sexuality which will be dealt with later in this chapter.

[9] Coveney, amongst others, points to the contrast between the arcadian rural life in Blake's *Songs of Innocence* and the urbanity of *Songs of Experience* (1967, 60).

[10] This aspect of Modernism is discussed by, for example, Hynes (1976, 25); T S Eliot's *The Waste Land* is one of the best-known pieces of twentieth century literature to employ this motif. Bowen also employs the device of compartmentalizing urban and rural motifs in her earlier short story "Aunt Tatty" (1929) where the apparently sophisticated London way of life of Eleanor is juxtaposed with the rural, almost Edenic existence of her family (*CS*, 263-275).

[11] Reprinted in *Collected Stories* pp.362-370.

[12] Her book was initially published in New York as *the School of Feminity: a Book for and about Women as They Are Interpreted through Feminine Writers of Yesterday and Today* under the alias F. A. Stokes in 1936. According to D. M. R. Bentley (the editor of *Bliss Carmen's Letters to Margaret Lawrence 1927 – 1929*) Lawrence was a Canadian feminist who remained single until 1943. She corresponded with Bliss, a Canadian poet, from 1927 until his death in 1929 (Bentley, 1995).

[13] Reprinted in *Collected Stories* pp.453-460.

[14] Reprinted in *Collected Stories* pp.355-361.

[15] Reprinted in *Collected Stories* pp.371-374.

[16] Markie could also be compared with Eddie in *The Death of the Heart*.

[17] Daisy's change of demeanour to that of a "clergyman's daughter" is perhaps not surprising for she is, according to Markie, an archdeacon's niece (*TN*, 205).

[18] Bennett and Royle rightly suggest that caution be employed when considering biographical and autobiographical material in relation to fictional texts commenting

"it is well to be aware that the relationship between life and work is at least highly complex and highly mediated, and that a key to the authorial life is by no means necessarily a key to the literary text" (1995b, 26). Nevertheless an appreciation of the life of the author is in this case, I would argue, germane to the discussion.

[19] There is a later comment in a letter to Ethel Smyth dated 17th June 1934 which also refers to Bowen. It is an oblique reference but it does suggest that perhaps others were beginning to question Bowen's sexuality. Woolf asks of Smyth

> "Why is Mrs Cameron [Elizabeth Bowen] so touchy? I cant myself feel that even if the aspersions you make were of my dearest I should resent them. An odd trait in human nature: throw it down the WC. if you can spare the water – and think no more of it." (Ibid, 310).

In both this quotation and the one above the spellings, punctuation and parenthetical inclusions are as published.

[20] See, for example, *Socialism and the New Life: The Personal and Sexual Politics of Edward Carpenter and Havelock Ellis*, Rowbotham and Weeks' exploration of the life and theories of these two sexual theorists (London, 1977).

[21] See Sheila Jeffreys' exploration of these issues, *The Spinster and her Enemies: Feminism and Sexuality 1880 – 1930* (1985) for a further discussion of the theories of these pre-eminent sexologists.

[22] It is interesting to note that, despite the fact that Theodora Thirdman is one of Bowen's more overt lesbian characters, Hoogland does not comment in depth on *Friends and Relations*, preferring to concentrate on *The Last September*, *The Heat of the Day* and *Eva Trout, or Changing Scenes*.

[23] Reprinted in *Collected Stories* pp.408-417.

[24] Bowen's choice of names will be discussed further in later chapters.

[25] Freud suggests that the "presence of a third party precludes seduction (for the first person cannot assault the second under the observation of an onlooker), yet ensures the perpetuation of sexual excitement through its transformation into verbal play. Hence the third person acts as both an obstacle and an incentive to desire" (Ellmann, 2003, 71).

[26] Two editions of this work are referred to in this chapter, the Penguin edition (1986) translated by Gilbert and Suzanne Sale and a 1965 French edition published by G F Flammarion. Unless otherwise stated, all quotations are taken from the Penguin edition. *De l'Amour* is Stendhal's analysis of love, written at a time when he was passionately in love with Mathilde Viscontini Dembowski (Stewart and Knight, 1975, pp.12-22); he attempts to define four varying forms of love, "Passionate Love", "Mannered Love", "Physical Love" and "Vanity Love" (Stendhal, 1822b, 43).

[27] Coates explains the imagery referred to by Janet's contemplation of the tree of Jesse—it:

> draws on a […] medieval mythic mode for understanding history and the relationship between individual choice and action to its wider social context. The Tree of Jesse first appeared in iconography in the twelfth century […] Based on Isaiah, II, 1-2, it is a genealogical linking of David's father with Christ and the Virgin Mary, a means by which the most private

and domestic of Old Testament stories, that of Naomi, Ruth and Boaz, is
joined to the ultimate cosmic drama. (1992, 297)

CHAPTER THREE

"THE CRACK ACROSS THE CRUST OF LIFE":
THE HOUSE IN PARIS

Written in the middle of the last decade before the onset of the Second World War, *The House in Paris* (published in 1935)[1], is one of Bowen's most complex novels; its tripartite structure lends itself not only to discussions of childhood innocence (a key element in the novel) but also to the rôles of the narrator and *anagnôrisis* in conveying that innocence. Writing about women's fiction of the 1930s, Clune, Day and Maguire suggest that "what happens in many of these novels is a sense of fracture within the home" (1997, 60), it is "the crack across the crust of life" (*HP*, 127). The "crack" however often represents the movement from innocence to experience, a "crack" that can have both positive and negative repercussions. Baxendale and Pawling extend Clune et al's argument to one which encompasses contemporary European history. They highlight the climate of "crisis and transformation" during the interwar period (1996, 3) and discuss the position of critics who

> have picked up on the importance of travel and travel writing in the Thirties [… who] interpret the journey as a *metaphysical* movement through a 'landscape without maps', a quest for values which rewrites the universal archetype of the Fall. Europe in the Thirties is seen as a land without God, whose more 'aware' inhabitants, the intelligentsia, are embarked on a voyage 'out of Utopian notions of innocence into a Christian awareness of sin'[2] (ibid, 14).

The 1930s was a turbulent decade both in Great Britain and Europe; during the years leading up to the onset of the Second World War much debate took place about the apparent inevitability of war and the necessary steps to avoid such a catastrophe, a debate which included the Oxford Union Debate of 1933, the Peace Ballot and Canon Dick Shepherd's Peace Pledge Union, a pledge that was signed by many, including Vera Brittain (Deane 1998, 69).[3] Just one year before the publication of *The House in*

Paris, in an article entitled "Can the Women of the World Stop War?" Brittain stated that

> [t]he world today is threatened by the gravest danger that has confronted it since 1914. During the last twelve months there have been international crises in every part of this earth [...] Unless humanity makes a mightier effort to save itself than it has yet achieved, the civilisation that we know may well go the way of Greece and Rome, and mankind be plunged into a new Dark Age. (1934, 69-70).

Rebecca West highlighted the major threats of Nationalism and Fascism in her essay, "The Necessity and Grandeur of the International Ideal", published in 1935. West comments that "[t]he concentration of Europe on nationalism has led to a situation which must be terminated, because it has already produced an unprecedented crop of horrors, and threatens to produce worse" (1935, 80). She refers to Fascism as "a headlong flight into fantasy from the necessity for political thought" (ibid, 82) and continues that supporters of Fascism

> wish to return to the psychological conditions of an ideal childhood, in which they will be given every provision and protection by an all-powerful father if only they are good and obedient children. This attempt to organise the State on nursery lines gives many people a degree of emotional satisfaction far greater than they would receive from participation in political activities, and puts them into an exalted state, comparable to that of young persons in love, when the merest trifles seem of tremendous and delicious significance. A punctual train is an object which in a democratic country arouses nearly no emotional reaction in its beholders save in circumstances too particular to be taken into account; but in a Fascist country it is the cause of glowing pride and joy. (Ibid)[4]

Fascism took hold in many parts of Europe and was supported in England by Sir Oswald Mosely's British Union of Fascists and National Socialists whose uniform of black shirts reflected the similar uniforms and growing influence of German Nazism; the exploitation of anti-Semitism led to the "Battle of Cable Street" when a large group of Fascists attempted to march through the predominantly Jewish East End of London (Thorpe 1992, 30,66). The position of the Jewish population had been seen, in some quarters, as problematic for many years. Large numbers of Ashkenazi Jews from Eastern Europe had emigrated to Britain towards the end of the nineteenth century and the East End of London saw an increase in racial tension; David Bradshaw notes that by June 1934 anti-Semitism "had become a key component of Mosely's demagogy" (1999, 179).[5]

Storm Jameson noted the effect of this turbulence on both political and personal life during this decade and, writing in 1937, she commented that the "process of change, of decay, of growth, is taking place everywhere all the time" (1937, 312). Dealing "with the complexities of anti-Semitisim at the time of the European-wide political crisis between the world wars" (Tylee 2009, 123),[6] *The House in Paris* is concerned, in part, with this process of cultural and political change.

Patricia Craig offers the following reading of the novel: "it's centred on a gigantic piece of bad behaviour: getting pregnant by your friend's fiancé rather than your own" (1986, 68), but the novel encompasses many more issues than Craig's statement would suggest. Jean Radford states that "*The House in Paris* is not just a Modernist parable about time; it is also a novel *of its* time, a historical novel which reflects upon England and Europe between the wars and the political history of Paris since 1789" (1999, 39) and she argues that "[a]ll three features— the weakness of liberalism, migration and anti-Semitism— are textualised in *The House in Paris*" (ibid, 41).

The history of both Ireland and France are also reflected in the novel: Karen's uncle by marriage, Uncle Bill, has photographs of his former house, Montebello, burnt down during the Irish troubles of the early twenties, hanging on the wall in his new house, Mount Iris; they are photographs which recall the violence of earlier times in Ireland and anticipate the violence to come, they are "[g]hastly black staring photographs" (*HP*, 75). In contrast, nineteenth-century French history, in particular the siege of the Paris Commune of 1870-71, is represented in a more metaphorical fashion, its bloody past alluded to in the description of Henrietta's first impressions of Paris. Travelling in a taxi with Naomi across Paris from the Gare du Nord,

> [i]n a sort of slow flash, Henrietta had her first open view of Paris – watery sky, wet light, light water, frigid, dark, inky buildings, spans of bridges, trees. [...] Windows with strong grilles looked ready for an immediate attack (Henrietta had heard how much blood had been shed in Paris); doors had grim iron patterns across their glass; dust-grey shutters were almost bolted fast (*HP*, 21/2)[7].

Not least amongst the three features identified by Hobsbawm is that of anti-Semitism: it is one which is predominantly associated with Max Ebhart and his son, Leopold. Throughout the novel Max is written as "the other" and descriptions of the man and boy indicate their visible alterity. Henrietta, looking at Leopold, for example, "saw a dark-eyed, very slight little boy who looked either French or Jewish" (*HP*, 28) whilst Max, according to Karen's letter to her fiancé, Ray Forrestier, "is not a person to trust" (*HP*, 89). As Coates suggests, "The first readers of *The House in Paris* would be aware of anti-Semitism in the Third Republic, far more open and virulent than the equally unpleasant but more genteel English middle-class insinuations of Mrs Michaelis" (1998, 123).[8] The issue of anti-Semitism is most explicit in *The House in Paris* when Karen's mother, Mrs Michaelis, talks to Karen about Max. With an ironic touch which is so often evident when Bowen "allows" her characters to articulate opinions with which she might not agree or wish to be associated with in public (a device utilised with great success in *The Last September* when Lady Naylor and her friends discuss the habits of the English), Mrs Michaelis voices her anti-Semitic feelings,

> 'Though he has such good manners, I don't think he is as confident as he seems. He looks sensitive, and might easily be touchy [...] The question of background: curious, isn't it? For instance: here today at tea he was charming; not suspicious or "sticky", not tiresomely at ease. But then, he was alone with us: if we had had him here with so many other people no nicer than he is, and not nearly so clever, he might have been different, on the defensive at once. Yes, it is curious: social things matter so little, yet somehow one cannot be with people who do not "mix" when they have to ... And there is always that touch – Jewish perhaps – of womanishness about him [...]'
> [...] So Mrs Michaelis dismissed Max; he melted into thin air while still on his way to the bus. Should he ever come up again – which was unlikely, for no one they knew in Paris had heard of him – she would have him at her fingers' ends, to discuss once more with understanding and tact. (*HP*, 117-118)[9]

Her comments, particularly her use of the term "womanishness", can be seen to echo Otto Weininger's theories in *Sex and Character* published in Vienna in 1903, a work which had a great influence on Modernist Europe. Weininger, who is described by one critic as an "extreme" misogynist and "rampant" anti-Semite (Cheyette and Marcus 1998, 3), ascribed the characteristics of women in the 19th century to the Jewish population, thus representing the Jewish male as "essentially effeminate" (ibid).[10] However, as Lee suggests, Mrs Michaelis's "middle class anti-Semitism, typical of its time, is only partly satirised: Max's Jewishness *is* meant to make him seem suspect. Socially and racially, Max is an undesirable lover" (1999, 92).[11]

Whilst Max's portrayal highlights the growing issue of anti-Semitism in Europe, it is not just European politics which provide the context for *The House in Paris*: arguably, elements of autobiography can also be found in the novel. Bowen is aware of this facet in her fiction; in the "Preface" to *Stories by Elizabeth Bowen*[12] (reprinted in *The Mulberry Tree*) she states,

> [t]o return to the matter of the personal, I repeat that one cannot wholly eliminate oneself for a second [...] any fiction (and surely poetry too?) is bound to be transposed autobiography. (True, it may be that this is at so many removes as to defeat ordinary recognition.) I can, and indeed if I would not I still must, relate any and every story I have written to something that happened to me in my own life. (1959, 129)

Bowen's "Preface" therefore gives a certain validity to the quest to identify the autobiographical context of both this novel, and indeed all her fiction, in relation to both character and place; it can be seen that *The House in Paris* contains "transposed autobiography" with its oblique references to Bowen's personal life, in particular to a love affair which took place when she was in her early thirties. In 1933, Bowen fell "immoderately in love" with Humphrey House, their affair continuing even after he married his wife, Madeleine, at the end of the year (Craig, 1986, pp.66-67). Whilst there are no obvious similarities between House and Max Ebhart, (House was English; Ebhart is Jewish), Glendinning notes that "*The House in Paris* draws on her love affair" (1997, 94). She continues "[but] Max is not a physical portrait of Elizabeth's lover. Elizabeth did seem to model Naomi on the wife, or on her own version of her" (ibid, 95)[13]. This assumption is borne out by a letter dated 31st August 1935 to A. E. Coppard; writing to thank him for his letter regarding *The House in Paris* (and for sending her a copy of *Polly Oliver*[14]) Bowen states, "Max is a portrait of someone I knew quite passingly and superficially once, so of course I do see him [...] Naomi Fisher I see the whole time, even her clothes" (1999b, 199) and, in a later letter to William Plomer dated 5th June 1938, she writes of Madeleine House "she looks pop-eyed with anxiety the whole time, poor little creature: I always feel at once sorry for and depressed by her" (1999b, 205), a description which is most apposite when one considers Naomi Fisher.

The Garden of Eden

In addition to any autobiographical elements contributed by her affair with Humphrey House, Bowen also utilises geographical contexts in her novels, drawing on specific locations which had, for Bowen, a particularly personal resonance. Place, as Bowen once asserted, was very important to her; in "Pictures and Conversations" she poses the question "[a]m I not manifestly a writer for whom places loom large?" (1972, 34). She continues, "[... but] the Bowen terrain cannot be demarcated on any existing map; it is unspecific. Ireland and England, between them, contain my stories, with occasional outgoings into France or Italy" (Ibid, 34/5).

Of prime relevance to this book is the more metaphysical notion of exile from Eden. A sense of Eden is found in *The House in Paris* in both literal and metaphorical locations; in all cases, however, Eden is presented as a place threatened by outside influences. Geographically, Eden can be found in Ireland, Bowen's childhood home and the island to which Karen flees whilst she is considering the possibility of marriage to Ray Forrestier.[15] Karen's first impression of County Cork as she approaches the dock is made up of a girl on a bicycle, the sound of a "holy bell", "a snuggle of gothic villas", "stucco houses" with "Palladian columns, gazeboes, glass-houses, terraces [...] misted with spring green", a view which "looked like a hill in Italy faded" and yet the scene is one "in which you think of the past". It is evident that this town also shares the negative aspects of Eden; whilst it does "not look like a country subject to racking change", it is a town whose geography hints at its dark past and uncertain future, a town whose "[e]very hill running down, each turn of the river, seemed to trap the ship more and cut off the open sea", a place which "consumes its own sound: the haze remained quite silent" (*HP*, 71-72). The apparently idyllic nature of the Irish town provides a stark contrast to the "hellish" appearance of the eponymous house in Paris with its dark hall, its walls covered in "a red flock wallpaper" which has "stripes so artfully shadowed as to appear bars", a hall with no windows and therefore no natural light (*HP*, 23-24). However, just as the landscape surrounding the town of Cobh suggests a false promise of Eden, it is equally desirable to read Madame Fisher's house in a less superficial fashion, for Henrietta

> felt that the house was acting, nothing seemed to be natural; objects did not wait to be seen but came crowding in on her, each with what amounted to its aggressive cry. Bumped all over the senses by these impressions, Henrietta thought: If *this* is being abroad ... (*HP*, 24)[16]

Yet although the house may appear to be "acting", the sensation of aggression found in the house can arguably be read as being a psychological reminder of the aggressive act of Max's suicide.

Karen recognises the deceptive nature of the Edenic promise of Ireland; writing to Ray just before she leaves her aunt and uncle's house, she comments "something in Ireland bends one back on oneself" (*HP*, 89), indicating an awareness of the island's ability (and that of its inhabitants) to superficially ignore the "racking change" which has taken place over recent decades.[17] Commenting on the duality of Ireland as a place of Eden, Lee states "[a]s usual, Ireland stands for a lost innocence. But the country's deceptively peaceful look […] is an image for all quietness at risk" (1999, 89). Similarly at risk is the apparently Edenic world occupied by the Michaelis family. For Karen, it represents safety; it is a world in which she will continue if she marries Ray, but it is also an imprisoning world. Echoing the sentiments of Laurence in *The Last September*, Karen exclaims to Aunt Violet

> […] With Ray I shall be so safe. I wish the Revolution would come soon; I should like to start fresh while I am still young, with everything that I had to depend on gone. I sometimes think it is people like us, Aunt Violet, people of consequence, who are unfortunate: we have nothing ahead. I feel it's time something happened. (*HP*, 86)

Karen's desire for something to happen culminates in her trip to Hythe. Her night with Max is, according to James Hall, Karen's "one night revolution that will demonstrate her feeling against Aunt Violet, her mother, and Naomi" (1968, 30). From a biographical point of view, Bowen's use of Hythe as the geographical location for Karen's loss of virginity and acquisition of sexual knowledge might appear to be at odds with her own feelings for the town. It was the town to which she retired following the publication of *The Little Girls* and a town which she described in a letter to Charles Ritchie as "a nice little town" (Bowen quoted in Glendinning 1977, 222). Bowen continues to explain her affection for it: "I suppose I like Hythe out of back-to-the-wombishness, having been there as a child in the most amusing years of one's childhood—8 to 13. But I can't see what's wrong with the womb if one's happy there, or comparatively happy there." (Ibid)

However Hythe, for Karen, represents a pivotal moment in her life, a moment of *anagnôrisis*, and the events which take place there, as will be seen below, force her to re-evaluate her life and her future, thrusting her out of the comfort of the metaphorical womb into a world of experience.

Whilst Hythe might represent the break with the past, Chester Terrace, the Michaelis London home, can be seen to represent the continuity of the Michaelis' way of life. Lassner highlights the role that the house plays in this world of safety and certainty, suggesting that Bowen uses houses to "embody a wish for continuity" (1990, 75). She continues that these houses provide the "arena where parents and children struggle for individuation and attachment [which] must itself remain stable for its combatants to survive" (ibid). For Karen to marry Ray will be a continuation of both her childhood and her parents' way of life, but it would also be a suppression of her own identity, and she acknowledges that this is not necessarily the right path to follow, that she needs to escape from this world of certainties into a world of uncertainty and possibilities. Not wishing to emulate her brother who "had come safely through the war to marry a very nice woman with property in the north; he managed his wife's property, hunted two days a week, sometimes published clever satirical verse and experimented in artificial manures" (*HP*, 71), Karen remains unconvinced as to whether she should remain in "this inherited world" (ibid). Tylee suggests that in the novel "Bowen has satirically displayed the cowardice, selfishness, and coldness of English middle-class culture" continuing that "the novel can suggest no alternative because it itself is symptomatic of that very culture" (2009, 130): in order to escape from the future too precisely mapped out for her by her station in life, Karen needs to move from a world of childhood innocence to a world in which experience is the only acceptable currency.

Authorial manipulation

This novel is one of Bowen's more complex novels, the narrative of *The House in Paris* evolving from the relatively simplistic, linear style of her earlier novels. Bowen's treatment of time and perspective, together with her use of interior monologues throughout the novel, all serve to manipulate the reader's understanding of the novel and experience of moments of *anagnôrisis*. *The House in Paris* does not follow a teleological progression (that is, a sequence of beginning—middle—end) often associated with nineteenth century and popular fiction. In a teleological novel, according to Bennett and Royle, the "readers' desires are directed towards the end" (Bennett and Royle, 1995b, 56), thus the ending confers structure, order and significance—it is "characteristically the place of revelation and understanding" (ibid, 57). Using Genette's classification of time within a novel, it can be seen that *The House in Paris* follows the pattern A1, B2, C1 where A1 and C1 indicate the present and B2 indicates the past. The reader is alerted to the fact that B2 (the middle section of the novel) is set in the past, not only by the title of the section, "The Past", but also by the narrative signpost "This is what he would have been told"; "anachronies" (Genette 1972, 35) which highlight Bowen's departure from her treatment of time in her earlier novels which follow a linear progression with only occasional forays into the past, constantly manipulating the reader.

Not only does the narration in *The House in Paris* provide a temporal shift from present to past, and back to present, but within this manipulation of time, Bowen presents the narrative from two different points of view: that of Leopold in the beginning and final sections of the novel, and that of Karen in the middle section, providing differences which could lead the reader to question the reliability of either narrator. Despite these differences, Karen and Leopold remain the central characters. Karen retains her centrality even when not physically present, as Leopold explores his own identity in her absence. Leopold occupies an equally pivotal position throughout the novel, even before his conception in the middle section, which is, after all, a story apparently told for Leopold's benefit, an effect reinforced by the various direct addresses to Leopold by the narrator. In the middle section the reader seems to be not only the audience of the narrator, Leopold also attends to the narration, although, of course, there is no evidence that Leopold has overheard the narration. He becomes, however, to borrow a phrase of Gerald Prince, a "narrattee-character" (1973, 214).[18]

It can be argued that the narrative structure employed by Bowen in *The House in Paris* with its temporal shifts and the implied reader/narrattee, together with the shifting point of view serve to reinforce the manipulation of the moments of *anagnôrisis* both for the reader, and for Karen and Leopold as the epistemological journey of the reader often parallels that of the characters. As in detective fiction which invariably starts with a murder, followed, by means of analepsis, by a discussion of motives and opportunity, so Bowen presents the reader first with the predicament faced by Leopold, then an exposition of his parentage and the circumstances of his conception, followed, in the true fashion of populist detective fiction, by something of a *denouement*; though, of course, like *Friends and Relations* and *To the North*, the ending of *The House in Paris* poses more questions than it answers.

Bowen's manipulation of time within the novel alerts the reader to the history of Leopold; it also provides the reader with a sense of understanding of the predicament of both Karen and Leopold. *Anagnôrisis* for the reader comes in stages: first the early recognition that Karen is somehow central to Leopold's life (she is referred to only as his mother, rather than by name, in the first section of the novel) and then the later recognition that the circumstances surrounding Leopold's conception, coupled with Max's later suicide, are events which force Karen into a false existence, one in which she would like to remain, dependent on others.

Innocence, Recognition and Identity

Literary moments of recognition, or *anagnôrisis*, are fundamental in the transition from innocence to experience, from childhood to adulthood. While Bowen did not formally acknowledge her use of *anagnôrisis* as a narrative ploy in her fiction, nevertheless, she was concerned with the recognition which arises from the impact of the actions of one character on another, particularly the psychological effect of "the conflicting desires between two people" (1942, 13). In *The House in Paris* Karen acknowledges the importance of psychological growth, rather than a growth which is determined purely by outside factors. On her return journey from Ireland to England in the company of "Yellow Hat", Karen reflects that she does not really know what the future holds for her. Looking at the engagement ring on Karen's finger, "Yellow Hat" seems surprised that Karen does not seem "settled": " 'Surely to dear goodness,' said Yellow Hat, nodding glumly at Karen's ring, 'you wouldn't look beyond *that*? You know what's coming, all right' " (*HP*, 93) but Karen is not certain:

> She returned to eye humbly and with no inner smile Yellow Hat's heavy frills and honest, heated face. 'I meant, apart from shipwrecks and outside things,' she said, 'surely what happens to one is what one makes happen oneself?'
> Lighting a cigarette with momentous boldness, Yellow Hat let this pass. (*HP*, 94).

Karen's transition from adolescence to adulthood results from a number of instances of recognition; it initially arises from the knowledge of Aunt Violet's impending death and is compounded by a letter from Ray, by Naomi's engagement to Max and Karen's acknowledgement of her love for Max. Coates suggests that the "change in Karen's consciousness begins with her visit to Aunt Violet and "Uncle Bill" in Cork. Here she encounters historical tragedy and impending death and, through both, begins to realise the fact of impermanence" (1998, 117). Coates identifies a defining moment in Karen's life: it is the fact of Aunt Violet's death which, according to Mrs Michaelis, is "[…] not the worst that will happen. They both saw the crack across the crust of life" (*HP*, 127-128) and for Karen, her aunt's death is a moment of *anagnôrisis* which "seemed to crack [her] home" (*HP*, 136). Blodgett too notes the effect of Aunt Violet's death on Karen's life and comments that

[t]he symbolic solitary journey during which an initiate learns the nature of death begins Karen's cycle of change. [… Bowen] subjects Karen to the same emotional experience of mortality [experienced by Sydney in *The Hotel*] that makes the waste of one's days seem unendurable." (1975, 91).

Her aunt's death is a "crack" which will allow Karen to consider the exploration of other avenues of life in addition to the accepted route of marriage to Ray, a minor "crack" which opens her mind to the possibility of loving Max, an option which becomes apparent when she has lunch with Max and Naomi. Although Karen knew Max when she stayed with Naomi and her mother in Paris, the narrator tells us

[Karen] was ashamed, looking at Max across the table, of the unfair way her fancy, then her revenge on her fancy, had misused him.
    For Max was very nice. As her host at lunch today she met him for the first time.
    […] Karen, looking at Max, against a stuffy draped curtain, thought: This is like an epilogue to a book. You hardly read on, the end is so near: you know. (*HP*, 108-109)

It is not, perhaps, the *coup de foudre* experienced by Jane Danby at the end of *A World of Love*, nevertheless Karen's moment of recognition that her life is about to change can be considered, to borrow Lucas's words, as "the realization of the truth, the opening of the eyes, the sudden lightening flash in the darkness". It is an epiphany in Karen's life, one which is to have serious consequences, consequences which will be explored further in this chapter.

The loss of innocence is predicated on many issues; at a basic level, innocence is lost when one person has been corrupted by another, but this suggests a negative connotation for such a loss. Innocence is also lost when a person gains experience, usually of a sexual nature, or when a person becomes aware of his or her own identity and self-knowledge is gained. In these circumstances, loss of innocence can be perceived as a necessary and vital aspect of human nature if one is to exist and function happily in society, so that one does not remain an "incurable stranger to the world" (*The Death of the Heart*, 106). However, childhood cannot necessarily be equated with innocence nor does a person's age always indicate their stage in the journey from innocence to experience.[19] Sister Rose Margaret Dostal highlights this in her unpublished thesis of 1964; discussing the position of children within the dichotomy of innocence and experience she states,

[c]hildren become both active and passive, both agents and patients in their relationship to the innocence-knowledge theme. They are at once innocents and the destroyers of innocence in others; they suffer the destruction of their own innocence, but in their suffering, they cause agony to their aggressors. (1964, 29)

Equally, and quite as obviously, the innocence of children is not synonymous with being kind. After facing probing questions from Leopold regarding her feelings about her dead mother, questions that suggest a small boy removing legs from a spider, Henrietta experiences new emotions, feeling

quite a new kind of pain. She saw only too well that this inquisition had no bearing on Henrietta at all, that Leopold was not even interested in hurting, and was only tweaking her petals off with the intention of exploring himself. His dispassionateness was more dire, to Henrietta, than cruelty. With no banal reassuring grown-ups present, with grown-up intervention taken away, there is no limit to the terror strange children feel of each other, a terror life obscures but never ceases to justify. There is no end to the violations committed by children on children, quietly talking alone. (*HP*, 31)

The small children who inhabit the Bowen landscape are rarely creatures of unremitting kindness; they include Maud, for example, younger daughter of the Danbys in *A World of Love*, who is "specially feared by children with whom she attended school" (*WL*, 109), and the young Theodora (*Friends and Relations*).

The cruelty of children is particularly evident in Bowen's short story "The Inherited Clock"[20] where Paul, a young boy of nine, on finding out that he will not inherit the clock he so desires, forces the finger of Clara, a six year old girl, into the mechanism of the clock. This act of torture is the culminating moment in a relationship in which "The children worked on each other like two indestructible pieces of sand-paper" (*CS*, 625). When Clara inherits the clock, all her fears come to the fore, fears which threaten to overwhelm her when Paul visits her and asks for the clock. He forces Clara to remember the terrifying occasion and gradually the memories return:

'I'll tell you something, Clara. Have you ever SEEN a minute? Have you actually had one wriggling inside your hand? Did you know if you keep your finger inside a clock for a minute, you can pick out that very minute and take it home for your own?' So it is Paul who stealthily lifts the dome off. It is Paul who selects the finger of Clara's that is to be guided, shrinking, then forced wincing into the works, to be wedged in them, bruised in them, bitten into and eaten up by the cogs. 'No, you have got to keep it there, or you will lose the minute. I am doing the counting – the counting up to sixty.' … But there is to be no sixty. The ticking stops. (Ibid, 639)

However, Leopold does not share Paul's delight in physical cruelty and Henrietta is right to acknowledge that Leopold is dispassionate rather than cruel. Nevertheless such a state of mind can be seen to inflict cruelty (whether consciously or not), not caring can often be just as cruel as a specific act of malice, and Henrietta must be correct in her assumption that Leopold is trying to discover who he is, rather than specifically trying to hurt her, so that he can begin his own journey from childhood to adulthood, a journey which necessitates the acquisition and acknowledgement of identity and self-knowledge. The narrator uses the analogy of the emotions felt when entering a house for the first time in order to discuss this journey:

It is a wary business, walking about a strange house you know you are to know well. Only cats and dogs with their more expressive bodies enact the tension we share with them at such times. The you inside you gathers up defensively; something is stealing upon you every moment; you will never be quite the same again. These new unsmiling lights, reflections and objects are to become your memories, riveted to you closer than friends or lovers, going with you, even, into the grave: worse, they may become dear and fasten like so many leeches on your heart. By having come, you already begin to store up the pains of going away. From what you see, there is to be no escape. Untrodden rocky canyons or virgin forests cannot be more entrapping than the inside of a house, which shows you what life is. To come in is as alarming as to be born conscious would be, knowing you are to feel; to look round is like being, still conscious, dead: you see a world without yourself (*HP*, 77).

Whilst ostensibly a discussion of the experiences felt on arrival at a new location, this passage can also be read as an examination of the emotional upheaval which takes place during the transition from innocence to experience, from childhood to adulthood. In order to grow, to cross the divide between innocence and experience, the narrator suggests that knowledge is important, self-knowledge is vital and that all experiences add to one's identity. It is, perhaps, the acknowledgement and recognition that "you will never be quite the same again" that becomes a pivotal moment, a moment of hidden *anagnôrisis*, in the journey of discovery of identity and self-awareness.

A. S. Byatt, in her introduction to the 1976 Penguin edition of *The House in Paris*, suggests that it "is a novel about sex, time and the discovery of identity" (1976, 9); the issue of identity is one which pervades *The House in Paris*, an issue which both starts and finishes the novel, which begins with Miss Fisher collecting Henrietta from the Gare du Nord. A system of cockades has been arranged for identification purposes, and both Miss Fisher and Henrietta have "pinned to their coats, the cerise cockades which had led them to claim one another, just now, on the platform" (*HP*, 17). The presence of the cockade is not, however, sufficient means of identification for the unnamed lady under whose care Henrietta has travelled to Paris, and she insists on further proof of identity from Miss Fisher which is produced in the form of a letter from Mrs Arbuthnot, Henrietta's grandmother. After spending a day in the Fisher household, Henrietta is taken to the Gare de Lyons by Ray Forrestier and Leopold. Once again, identity is established by means of the cockades but this time, having no more need for it, Henrietta gives her cockade to Leopold. Questioning the wisdom of this course of action, Henrietta replies to Miss Watson, the lady who is to accompany her on the last leg of her journey, saying "[t]he person I'm meeting next is my own grandmother, and if she doesn't know me without it I might as well be dead." (*HP*, 236)

However, identification by cockades does not equate with recognition or (in its most literal form) self-knowledge and Henrietta, in questioning her own identity, echoes the sentiments expressed by Lois in *The Last September*, for

> [t]oday was to do much to disintegrate Henrietta's character, which built up by herself, for herself, out of admonitions and axioms (under the growing stress of: If I am Henrietta, then what is *Henrietta?*) was a mosaic of all possible kinds of prejudice. She was anxious to be someone, and no one having ever voiced a prejudice in her hearing without impressing her, had come to associate prejudice with identity. You could not be a someone without disliking things... (*HP*, 25-26)

In this regard, it can be seen that Henrietta could well become a successor to Mrs Michaelis, whose prejudices, which include her anti-Semitic views, help to shape her personality.

Dostal suggests that Leopold "has lived in an intellectual incubator" (1964, 65) and for Leopold, self-knowledge is inextricably linked with knowledge of his mother, and his mother's acknowledgement of (or failure to acknowledge) who Leopold is, but Karen's abortive visit (echoing her

abandonment of Leopold as a baby) allows Leopold to nurture his own
dreams of what he is, of who he is:

> by her not coming the slate was wiped clean of every impossibility; he was
> not (at least that day) to have to find her unable to speak in his own, which
> were the true, terms. He did not have to hear out with grave discriminating
> intelligence that grown-up falsified view of what had been once that she,
> coming in actually, might have given him. She, in the flesh, could have
> offered him only that in reply to the questions he had kept waiting so long
> for her: 'Why am I? What made me be?'
>   He expected from her a past as plain as the present, simply a present
> elsewhere. (*HP*, 67)

Leopold's desire to know the answers to such questions is also
connected with Karen's decision to allow Leopold to be adopted and to
keep his birth a secret from the world; when Henrietta asks him why his
name is different to that of his mother, Leopold replies "Because no one
knows I'm born" (*HP*, 59). Although he obviously wishes this was not the
case, Leopold appears to revel in the position in which he is placed. He is,
according to Blodgett, "a heroic child [who] symbolize[s] the creative or
reborn self: not only does he himself mature; he has a beneficent effect on
others" (1975, 21) and there is no doubt that Leopold's very existence has
an effect on those around him, nor that Leopold is eager to discover his
place in society, in a world in which he can be sure of his own identity.

Leopold and Henrietta are not the only people in *The House in Paris*
who are searching for identity; it is a quest shared also by both Karen and
Max. Karen is obviously aware of her physical identity; as an artist (albeit
an occupation which she has discarded),[21] she can enumerate her facial
qualities and describe them in terms of an artist, "[b]ut her pencil had
always lacked something, not quickness or energy, simply power,
perhaps" (*HP*, 73), a lack which Coates perceives as "the first hint of
something defective in her world" (1998, 116). Whereas Leopold believes
that his identity, his knowledge of who *he* is, will be apparent once he has
met and knows his mother, Karen believes her identity to be reflected in
the eyes of other people; her identity does not, therefore, arise from self-
knowledge, rather it is one which is constructed by others. This form of
identity "makes any lover or friend a narcissus pool; you do not want
anyone else once you have learnt what you are; there is no more to learn."
(Ibid.)

Whilst it can be assumed, perhaps optimistically, that Leopold and
Henrietta will be allowed by society to pursue their quest for self-
knowledge and identity, it is a pursuit that, to a lesser or greater extent,

others have tried to deny Karen, Naomi and Max. Karen's mother, by her
desire to retain Karen within her own social world, an attempt particularly
highlighted by her lack of willingness to discuss Karen's duplicitous
arrangements when she goes to Hythe to see Max, can be seen to be
denying her daughter the transition from childhood to adulthood, from
innocence to experience. Karen's thoughts during the lunch with Naomi
and Max further suggest the influence a mother can have in restricting her
daughter's ability to evolve from a childhood existence to one in which
she emerges as an adult, as necessary an evolution as that of a chrysalis
into a butterfly:

> She thought, young girls like the excess of any quality. Without knowing,
> they want to suffer, to suffer they must exaggerate; they like to have loud
> chords struck on them. Loving art better than life they need men to be
> actors; only an actor moves them, with his telling smile, undomestic, out of
> touch with the everyday that they dread. They love to enjoy love as a
> system of doubts and shocks. They are right: not seeking husbands yet,
> they have no reason to see love socially. This natural fleshly protest against
> good taste is broken down soon enough; their natural love of the cad is
> outwitted by their mothers. Vulgarity, inborn like original sin, unfolds with
> the woman nature, unfolds ahead of it quickly and has a flamboyant
> flowering in the young girl. Wise mothers do not nip it out immediately;
> that makes for trouble later, they watch it out. (*HP*, 108)[22]

When considering this particular passage, O'Faolain poses the
following question, "[t]he large question, indeed, about the Bowanesque
heroine is whether she is ever truly adult. Carnally and sentimentally her
women are incontinently involved in the toils of their own adolescence.
They go on dreaming too long." (1956, 166). His reading would suggest
that it is the girls who somehow delay their entry into a world of
adulthood, however I would argue that a mother can influence and, should
she so desire, delay this transition. Karen's thoughts suggest that her
mother's actions should be read as a protective mechanism, both of her
daughter but also of her own way of life, in the one "class in England
[that] changes least of all" (*HP*, 70). However, Karen sees the actions of
Mrs Michaelis as detrimental to her own development, an awareness
which stems from the afternoon spent in the garden of Naomi's aunt;
speaking to Max, she says:

> [...] Since you were in London in April, then went away, I have been
> either possessed or else myself for the first time. I found I was in prison –
> no, locked into a museum full of things I once liked, with nothing to do
> now but look at them and wonder why I had. *They* keep me away from

everything that has power; they would be frightened of art if I painted really well. When it thundered last month I used to wish I could be struck by lightening. (*HP*, 161)

In contrast to Mrs Michaelis's motivation lie the actions of Madame Fisher, Naomi's mother. Lassner and Derdiger see Madame Fisher and Mrs Michaelis as "gothicized characters", suggesting that, whilst Mrs Michaelis's anti-Semitism is overt, Madame Fisher can be read as equally anti-Semetic:

> The novel's depiction of Max as a rootless, wandering Jew serves as a critique of Mrs. Michaelis's anti-Semitism whose rhetoric relies on processing Max as primitive in its most sinister and gothicized sense [...] While there are no signs of antisemistism in Mme. Fisher's utterances, between her gothicized character and home and her monstrously oppressive control, one can detect resonances with fascism and with colonial dominance, both of which relate to Max's fate as a Jew and as a symbol for colonized people. (2009, 207)

Madame Fisher too has stultified her daughter's progression from childhood to adulthood leaving Naomi in a "no man's land", for Naomi "had outgrown years ago any girlish naturalness, without having learnt how even to imitate any other" (*HP*, 98). However, it can be seen that Madame Fisher is not acting altruistically, nor is she attempting to protect her daughter from the harsh realities of life; in fact her selfish manipulation of the lives of both Naomi and Max Ebhart have disastrous consequences. Max's identity is completely constrained by the influence of Madame Fisher, a truth which Naomi discloses to Karen following Max's death: "I saw then that Max did not belong to himself. He could do nothing that she had not expected; my mother was at the root of him [...] I saw then that evil dominated our house." (*HP*, 182). It is an influence which Madame Fisher tries to exert over Leopold as she has done to his father; Coates suggests that

> Mme Fisher offers a worldly wise, demystifying, yet in a subtle way destructive and false, analysis of the characters of Uncle Dee and Aunt Marion and, far more importantly, of Ray and Karen. The old woman's apparent power to clarify Leopold's life for him in shrewd, elegant and economical phrases captivates the boy. (1998, 113).

Dostal argues that Leopold's initial lack of self-knowledge occurs because he is "[d]ispossessed and disinherited [... his] life is a vacuum with no past, no atmosphere pressured with those germs of knowledge which the child can breathe naturally" (1964, 65)—arguably he could also be read as a metonymic character, representing the dispossessed European Jew[23].but his subsequent quest for identity also echoes the search for identity undertaken by both Karen and Max. Karen's refusal to acknowledge the existence of Leopold, her repeated betrayal of him from conception and adoption to her last-minute decision not to go to Madame Fisher's house, thrusts the boy into a premature exploration of his own identity. Lacking a mother and father to whom he can turn to for guidance, Leopold believes that Madame Fisher can supply the answers to the questions that have plagued him all his life, to provide a release for all his pent up emotions and to help him understand who he is; in a mute appeal to Madame Fisher who appears to be asleep, he says:

> [d]o not seal me up again, listen, listen! At Spezia when I am angry I go full of smoke inside, but when you make me angry I see everything. If *this* is what men come to women for, what is love then? Madame Fisher, listen – I could not help being helpless. Nothing makes me belong to them. Open your eyes again; make me see what I saw. You said I was not the young man with the sword, but – (*HP*, 208-209).

Bennett and Royle read Madame Fisher's room as a "tomb of knowledge" (1995a, 53). They continue

> Leopold is also born inside the tomb of this knowledge, a tomb that he will have to crack in order to live […] The inner tomb of Leopold's consciousness both contains and is contained by the tomb of Mme Fisher's room, a tomb which its occupant is herself instrumental in making. (Ibid)

To escape from this tomb Leopold requires knowledge and whereas Leopold believes that Madame Fisher will provide the answers he seeks and thus provide the means of escape from childhood,[24] Max, perhaps with a maturity which can be attributed to his age, is aware of the undue influence Madame Fisher has had on him, and it is an influence from which he is desperate to escape:

> 'Till this year, I have not tried to separate what she made me from what I am. From the first, she acted on me like acid on a plate.'
> 'Corrosive?'
> 'Yes. No. What her wit ate out is certainly gone. But more happened than that, as she saw me, I became. Her sex is all in her head, but she is not a woman for nothing. In my youth, she made me shoot up like a plant in enclosed air. She was completely agreeable. Our ages were complementary. I

had never had the excitement of intimacy. Our brains became like senses, touching and drawing back.' (*HP*, 138-139)

It is, however, Max's desire for separation from Madame Fisher which ultimately leads to his suicide. Having acknowledged his love for Karen, Max realises that he too must cross the divide and become a self-determining adult. To do this he has to renounce the patronage of Madame Fisher, but this is an act which he is never able to carry out. When Madame Fisher confronts Max, he realises that he is incapable of stepping out from her shadow[25] and, in a moment of *anagnôrisis*, realises that he will never be free of her influence, will never be able to be independent. In response, Max cuts his wrists. Max would have known that to cut his wrists would be a quick death; with a distant echo of Shylock's sentiments from *The Merchant of Venice*, Max asks, "When I cut myself even slightly, I bleed like a pig, profusely. Does that make me nobler?" (*HP*, 139) It would appear that, for Max, death is a nobler state than one in which he would be eternally suppressed by the will of another. Thus, there are several elements needed to enable a person to move from childhood to adulthood. Of these, self-knowledge is of paramount importance and yet, paradoxically, it is Max's awareness of his subjugation to Madame Fisher, his realisation that he can never be a self-determining adult, that leads him to the conclusion that he cannot be independent, that his life will never be his own and, rather than be dominated by Madame Fisher, he decides that his life can only truly be his own if he takes the irrevocable step of cutting his wrists in the darkened hallway of her house.

Sexuality

Of equal importance in the journey from innocence to experience is the acquisition of sexual knowledge and, whilst it might have been hoped that Leopold would be "allowed" to make the transition from childhood to adulthood by Ray and Karen, the Grant Moodys' attempt to deny him knowledge of sexuality reflects their desire for Leopold to remain a child. Not only is he dressed childishly, but his adoptive parents have decided that he should not yet know about sex or religion. Denying Leopold an environment in which he might grow and develop the Grant Moodys have carefully selected "the chosen childish children" (*HP*, 34) with whom he can safely play, their definition of safety obviously being an environment where sexuality does not rear its ugly and complicated head but, "all the time he impressed [the children], he despised them for being impressed; he wanted to crack the world by saying some final and frightful thing" (ibid.)

In a letter from Marian Grant Moody, his adoptive mother, to Miss Fisher, she writes "We feel that, apart from the circumstance of his birth, Leopold's heredity (instability on the father's side, lack of control on the mother's) may make conduct difficult for him, and are attempting to both guard and guide him accordingly." She continues:

> "We do not consider him ripe for direct sex-instruction yet, though my husband is working towards this through botany and mythology. When the revelation regarding himself must come, what better prototypes could he find than the Greek and other heroes, we feel. (*HP*, 41)

It is a letter which fills Leopold with "revulsion" (*HP*, 42). Theirs is, however, a false premise, for Leopold has already been influenced by the sexuality of others, albeit without being aware of the precise details of his birth for "[y]ears before sex had power to touch his feeling it had forced itself into a view as an awkward tangle of motives. There was no one he could ask frankly: 'Just how odd *is* all this?' " (*HP*, 34). It is a question that could have, and should have, been answered by his mother, but her non-appearance at Madame Fisher's house allows Leopold a further moment of introspection. Leopold's interior monologue about what might have happened had his mother appeared at the house, a monologue that is also a source of authorial comment, highlights the divide between childhood and adulthood, a divide which is, in this instance, predicated on sexual knowledge:

> Having both looked at the world they know that, as you compose any landscape out of hills, houses, trees, the same few passionate motives go to whatever happens. Experience at any age has the same ingredients; the complexity of the rainbow is deceiving but its first colours are few. He has travelled less, so his imagination is wider; she has less before her but a more varied memory: referring backwards and forwards between imagination and memory she relives scenes, he sees them alive. The mystery about sex comes from confusion and terror: to a mind on which these have not yet settled there is nothing you cannot tell. Grown-up people form a secret society, they must have something to hold by; they dare not say to a child: 'There is nothing you do not know here.' (*HP*, 68)

However, despite all the attempts by the Grant Moodys to keep Leopold in a state of safe ignorance, they have not been able to suppress his passionate nature, an aspect of his personality which is apparent even to Henrietta, particularly the passion with which he conjures up an image of his mother. Henrietta cannot believe that Leopold will lead a dull life in England with his mother, "Leopold's mother swept brilliantly through one's fancy; he commandeered, to make her, every desire, not only his own. He was a person whose passion makes its object exist. She will be in his own image, she will not hesitate or mind what they say." (*HP*, 62) This examination of Leopold's passion and Henrietta's belief that she will be "forgotten, luckless, cold" suggests that Henrietta, too, would like to be passionate about something, even if she is not too sure what form this might take. Blodgett argues that Henrietta matures psychologically during her day at the Fisher's house and suggests that she experiences "a growth in her differentiation into female being, or sexual maturity conceived of in far more than, but certainly not excluding, physical terms" (1975, 103). Certainly Henrietta is aware of her femininity but she has not yet crossed the divide into adulthood; she remains a child. Charles, her monkey, is of course, evidence of her childlike state but nonetheless Henrietta is delighted when Ray asks her if she has her handbag and gloves—"[s]he was too much uplifted to tell him she had no handbag yet." (*HP*, 235)

Despite Henrietta's momentary desire for a passionate relationship, or perhaps just a familial warmth, and in contrast to Leopold's yearning for understanding, she appears to be generally content with her position as a child for, undoubtedly, Henrietta remains happily in her childhood Eden, an Eden complete with uneaten apples (*HP*, 35)[26]; contemplating the marriage of Captain and Madame Fisher,

> Henrietta, being not ripe for grown-up reflections, did not wonder how he had treated his wife, or speculate as to the lastingness of his passion for the ironical French governess, never pretty, not from the first young. He had married Mme Fisher. Love is the unchallenged motive for some kinds of behaviour: Mrs Arbuthnot said: 'You will understand some day,' and Henrietta was still willing to wait. (*HP*, 50)

However, in terms of sexuality, Henrietta and Leopold remain innocents for, despite being aware that there are facets of adulthood that are, as yet, beyond their understanding, they do not have sufficient knowledge of their own sexuality to begin to cross the divide. This does not, of course, apply to the other main protagonists in the novel, Karen, Max, Naomi, Madame Fisher and Ray who are all, to a lesser or greater extent, aware of their sexuality although this knowledge is acquired at different times and in different ways in their lives. The acquisition is most apparent when one considers Karen, though questions of sexuality underpin much of the novel and shape the lives of all the protagonists, including Madame Fisher.

Madame Fisher exerts an enormous influence on both Max and Naomi and arguably in both instances her influence is based on sexual jealousy, albeit a sexual jealousy which has psychological rather than physical roots. Karen sees Madame Fisher in the rôle of a malevolent *Madame* in a brothel: "[s]he is a woman who sells girls; she is a witch" (*HP*, 155) suggesting that Madame Fisher uses sexuality as a destructive force. Karen is aware of Madame Fisher's shadowy presence even in the hotel room at Hythe, an awareness that is voiced during an interior monologue when Karen contemplates the position in which she finds herself: "She is here; she is that barred light. She can never have wanted Max to be quiet; when he's quiet he's not hers. He was hers tonight when we saw the lighthouse, hers when we came in" (Ibid). However, Madame Fisher's sexuality is not overt, rather, as Max comments to Karen, "[h]er sex is all in her head, but she is not a woman for nothing." (*HP*, 138) Karen is aware that Madame Fisher's feelings for Max are not those simply of a patron but when she tells Max that she believes that Madame Fisher is in love with him, Max, whilst not denying the accusation, reacts violently stating "I cannot think of her in that way" (*HP*, 139). Yet it is Madame Fisher's sexual jealousy, together with her desire for control, that ultimately leads to Max's suicide.

In contrast, Karen's acquisition of sexual knowledge takes place at the hotel in Hythe where she has gone with Max, although the process begins when she meets Max in Boulogne and the physical aspect of their love begins to surface. Walking along the ramparts of Boulogne

> [a]n incoming tide of apartness began to creep between Max and Karen, till, moving like someone under the influence of a pursuing dream, he drew the cigarette from between her fingers and threw it over on to the boulevard. Moving up the parapet, he kissed her, and with his fingers began to explore her hand. Their movements, cautious because of the drop below, were underlined by long pauses. They were hypnotised by each other, the height, the leaves ... (*HP*, 145)

It is a love that is to be consummated in Hythe, an act which provides the pivotal moment in the novel, not only in terms of Karen's acquisition of sexual knowledge but also through the way in which the author and narrator convey the emotional upheaval felt by Karen. The narrative constantly shifts from past to present tense, the narrative voice from omniscience to interior monologue, to a direct address to Leopold. It has already been suggested that this is a tale told for the benefit of Leopold; as he contemplates the conversation he would have had with Karen had she arrived at Madame Fisher's house, the narrator says, as a prelude to the central section of the novel, "This is, in effect, what she would have to say." (*HP*, 68). This notion is reinforced when Karen herself asks, "What have I done?" (*HP*, 151). Indicating that Karen has taken precautions to avoid the possibility of pregnancy, the narrator continues, "[h]aving done as she knew she must she did not think there would be a child: all the same, the idea of you, Leopold, began to be present with her." (*HP*, 151-152). The changes from past to present tense within this section add to the notion that this is a story being told for Leopold alone. The description of Folkestone in the present tense contributes to the verisimilitude of the tale and the use of tense in this instance is in contrast with the previous description of Cobh harbour and Paris, both of which are described in the past tense. These narrative techniques, added to the episode's centrality within the novel, all help to highlight the importance of this particular event in Karen and Max's life, as well as for the future life of Leopold.

Max is conscious that this is a momentous occasion in Karen's life and interrogates Karen about her readiness to accept the consequences of their behaviour. Karen appears to be aware of her actions but, nonetheless, waking at three o'clock in the morning, begins to question herself:

> [t]he weight of being herself fell on her like a clock striking. She saw the clothes she would put on to go home in hanging over a chair. While it is still Before, Afterwards has no power, but afterwards it is the kingdom, the power and the glory. You do not ask yourself, what am I doing? You know. What you do ask yourself, what have I done? you will never know.
>   Had this not been escape? She was washed back ashore again. (*HP*, 152)

By gaining sexual knowledge, Karen has gained knowledge of her own identity, "the weight of being herself". It is a moment of *anagnôrisis* for Karen yet it is a knowledge which she does not wish to accept. Karen's interior monologue is an introspective study of the consequences of her actions that night with Max. The very act of sexual intercourse with Max has opened and, paradoxically, closed many avenues for her. Despite having been "further out than you dare go", Karen now feels that she is "let back, safe, too safe; no one will ever know. Naomi and my mother, who would die if they knew, will never know" (ibid). However, Karen's belief that Naomi and her mother will not know about her sexual relationship with Max leaves Karen in a metaphorical dead-end from which there is no escape; not noticing, not knowing, means that Karen will not be able to escape from the world so loved by Mrs Michaelis. Ostensibly describing the streets of Boulogne, the narrator emphasises this fact, that denial leads to imprisonment in a system from which Karen desires to be free, for "the silence in *culs-de-sacs* is the silence of not hearing the sea." (*HP*, 137). Yet, despite her belief that she will not become pregnant, there is an unconscious desire for a child to be borne as the result of her love for Max. However, such a child would inevitably lead to her mother being aware of her duplicitous arrangement with Max; this is a knowledge that first manifests itself as deliberately "not noticing" for, despite Karen's awareness that Mrs Michaelis knows that she did not spend a weekend with her friend, "[n]othing was to be said." (*HP*, 172). That Leopold does exist is a fact which, ultimately, leads to her mother's early death.

Despite Karen's acknowledgement that life has changed forever, she truly believes that if no one else ever knows that she has crossed the divide from innocence to experience, she can marry Ray and remain a child for, as Aunt Violet recognised, Ray represents safety and continuity: "*She* saw Ray was my mother" (*HP*, 154), but if Karen has become pregnant as a result of her night with Max, the wedding will not take place. Of course, this is not the case and Ray does marry her despite the knowledge that she has had Max's child. Nevertheless in the bleak hours of the early morning, Karen fears the future. If she is not carrying a child then, using war as a metaphor for her life, Karen believes that "whoever wins, the streets are laid again and the trams start running again" (*HP*, 152). However,

> [b]eing caught is the word for having a child, sometimes. Then Ray would not marry me; mother would not buy me the sofa I wanted to shoot. The street would stay torn up, the trams could not begin again … How silent it is! Surely it must be time for a clock to strike? You would never think there was the street out there. Yes you would; it takes a street to be silent, a stone silence going nowhere. Besides, we walked back down a street last night … I wonder whether so much rain tires that tree? When do they put the lamps out? This is the time of night when they say you feel most afraid. Only, I have nothing to be afraid of: no one will know. (*HP*, pp.154-5)

Max and Karen's night together is the ultimate "crack across the crust of life". It is a "crack" which has serious repercussions on the lives of all the main protagonists in the novel. For Max, the realisation that he cannot marry Naomi, allied to his inability to escape the patronage of Madame Fisher and his acknowledgement that he will not be able to become a self-determining adult, leads to his decision to commit suicide. However, in contrast Karen appears to have survived the "crack", indeed the "happiness of the Forrestiers' marriage surpassed the hopes of those friends who had received the engagement with so much pleasure" (*HP*, 218), but, of course, her past is always present in her life. Leopold's birth and subsequent adoption weigh heavily on her, a weight which is added to by the death of the child fathered by Ray. Throughout their marriage Karen and Ray are constantly aware of Leopold's presence, he becomes another shadowy third. In an extraordinary change in narrative style, an unspoken dialogue occurs between Ray and Karen which appears to exist only in Ray's consciousness; Ray states his belief that until Karen acknowledges the presence of Leopold their marriage is in danger:

> SHE: All I want is for us to be alone.
> HE: We are not alone: there is Leopold.
> SHE: Leave my child alone.
> HE: I can't, because he *is* your child.
> […]
> HE: But we are never alone, while you're dreading him. It is you who remember. If he were here with us, he'd be simply a child, either in or out of the room. While he is a dread of yours, he is everywhere. (*HP*, pp.216-217)

According to Dostal, Bowen's children "acquire that knowledge which is awareness, sometimes prematurely; they cause a revelation in others, sometimes without receiving any illumination themselves" (1964, 29). The very idea of Leopold and his later quest for his own identity provides the catalyst, the "illumination", for Karen and Ray. Bennett and Royle suggest that "throughout the novel, Leopold is specifically conceived as an embodiment of knowledge" (1995a, 52), knowledge of Leopold is suppressed by Karen and, to a lesser extent, Ray but, nonetheless, Leopold is continually present in their marriage; there are constant reminders of his existence, "[t]hat third chair left pushed in at a table set for a couple … The third bed in their room at the simple inn" (*HP*, 219-220). The "crack", the act of love which results in Leopold, acts as a barrier to Karen's much hoped for but overlong existence as a child, dependent on both her husband and the society in which they live.

Her denial of Leopold's existence which initially takes place on the night of his conception, and her later decision to leave England to give birth secretly and then to hand the child to Naomi for onward transmission, places Karen in a false Eden, an Eden which is no longer innocent or idyllic, an Eden constantly interrupted by the fact of Leopold. Although Karen has lost her sexual innocence, she remains in the prison of her false Eden, a prison in which she will remain until she is completely willing to acknowledge the presence of Leopold and "the weight of being herself" (*HP*, 152). This is, however, an acknowledgement that she seems unwilling or unable to make as evidenced by her refusal to meet Leopold in Madame Fisher's house. Karen's denial of Leopold and her refusal to accept and embrace the knowledge of her own identity have disastrous consequences for Karen, becoming trapped in the very society from which she wished to escape, fearful of becoming, at last, an adult.

Despite, or perhaps in spite of, Karen's refusal to acknowledge the fact of Leopold, his day under the roof of Madame Fisher provides him with moments of *anagnôrisis* which help him to understand who he is, to begin to achieve self-knowledge, and to start the journey which will ultimately lead to his crossing the divide between innocence and experience, childhood and adulthood. It is, perhaps, Karen's negation of Leopold which allows him to explore his own identity through his interrogation of Henrietta, his reading of the letter from Marion Grant-Moody, the "virtual" reading of the missing letter from his absent mother to Naomi and his discussions with Madame Fisher.

In contrast to Karen's fears, the meeting between Ray and Leopold culminates in a moment of *anagnôrisis* for both Leopold and Ray. Whilst Leopold's breathing symbolizes that he is coming alive for the first time, that he has been reborn, Ray too experiences a moment of illumination, both literally and metaphorically, as he contemplates Leopold on the steps of the Gare du Nord:

> Ray had not seen Karen's child in bright light before; now he saw light strike the dilated pupils of Leopold's eyes. Egotism and panic, knowing mistrust of what was to be, died in Ray as he waited beside Leopold for their taxi to come: the child commanded tonight, I have acted on his scale. (*HP*, 239)

The novel ends with Leopold looking down from the steps of the station asking, "[i]s it illuminated" (ibid.) It is to be hoped that when Karen and Leopold eventually meet, Karen's life will be illuminated by the physical presence of Leopold enabling her, with the acknowledgement of his existence and the acceptance of the knowledge of her own identity, to cross the divide from adolescence to adulthood, from innocence to experience, and become, belatedly, an individual in her own right; that acceptance of the various cracks "across the crust of life" will enable Karen finally to come of age.

Notes

[1] When subsequent mention is made in parenthesis *The House in Paris* will be referred to as *HP*.
[2] Quoted from Cunningham (1995, 467).
[3] The Peace Pledge Union began with a letter from Canon Shepherd to *The Guardian* on 16th October 1934 in which he asked men to send him a postcard

undertaking to "renounce war and never to support another". According to the PPU website, by 1937 over 100,000 men and women had signed the Pledge. Its signatories included, as mentioned above, Vera Brittain together with Aldous Huxley, George Lansbury (a former leader of the Labour Party) and Siegfried Sassoon. (www.ppu.org.uk/ppu/ppu_hisx.html). The Peace Pledge Union was not, of course, the only pacifist movement or peace initiative in Britain during the 1930s. Martin Caedel's work on this aspect of British politics, *Pacifism in Britain 1914-1945: the Defining of a Faith*, is a comprehensive study of such initiatives.
[4] West is, of course, referring to Italy's much trumpeted reliability of its railway system.
[5] Bradshaw's study of the rise in anti-Semitism particularly focuses on Virginia Woolf's novel *The Years*.
[6] Tylee notes that *The House in Paris* was published by Gollancz in the same year that he refused to publish Betty Miller's *Farewell Leicester Square* and suggests that Miller's attempts to "politicize the woman's novel", in contrast to "Bowen's more circumspect novel", led to its rejection by the publisher (2009, 124). Tylee further suggests that "Bowen's own novel on the Jewish issue in 1930s Europe […] suffers […] from (liberal, middle-class) racial assumptions which it implicitly (if unintentionally) confirms" (ibid, 126).
[7] Lee comments on Bowen's repeated use of a taxi journey and compares Henrietta's taxi ride in Paris with the taxi ride in Bowen's short story "The Demon Lover" and the overriding sense of danger found in the opening pages of *To the North* (1999, 87).
[8] The issue of anti-Semitism is not, of course, portrayed in Bowen's fiction alone. Amongst the many novels which either alluded to, or were solely concerned with, this issue is Katherine Burdekin's *Swastika Night*. Published in 1937 under the pseudonym Murray Constantine, Burdekin portrays a dystopian world set in a feudal society which recognises Hitler as God, a world in which women are viewed as animals whose sole purpose is to reproduce and who are considered only marginally superior to Christians. All pre-Hitlerian history has been destroyed and the Jewish population has been completely eradicated. It is a world in which the ordinary men are perceived by both themselves and those further up the hierarchy as children, and people are kept in check by their Knight, a portrayal that accords with Rebecca West's view of Nazi aims at this time. Conversely, Betty Millar's novel *Farewell Leicester Square* (1941) explores the position of the Jew as an outsider in British society.
[9] Mrs Michaelis' dismissal of Max is very similar to Lady Naylor's reaction to Gerald and his Surrey relations (see Chapter One).
[10] See Jean Radford's essay 'The Woman and the Jew: Sex and Modernity' (1998, 91-3).
[11] Tylee castigates Bowen for her portrayal of Max: he "is the token Jew Bowen has created. If Karen's mother can be accused of genteel anti-Semitism for suggesting that Max conforms to the Jewish stereotype of financial astuteness, what should we say of the author who created Max and his selfish, mercenary behaviour?" (2009, 131).

[12] Published in 1959 by Vintage Books, the collection contained a selection of Bowen's short stories, chosen by the author, and included "Coming Home", "The Storm", "The Tommy Crans", "Her Table Spread", "The Disinherited", "The Easter Egg Party", "No. 16", "Reduced", "Look at All Those Roses", "A Love Story", "Summer Night", "Songs My Father Sang Me", "The Inherited Clock", "Sunday Afternoon", "The Demon Lover", "Ivy Gripped the Steps", "The Happy Autumn Fields" and "Mysterious Kor". (Sellery and Harris, 1981, pp.80-81)

[13] Whilst Glendinning does not name Humphrey House, other commentators, including Lee and Heath, do not share this reluctance.

[14] *Polly Oliver*, a collection of short stories by A E Coppard, was first published by Jonathon Cape in 1935.

[15] R. F. Foster mistakenly suggests that Karen was "secretly pregnant" during her visit to her aunt in Ireland (1993, 107).

[16] Bowen's frequently uses the notion of artificiality in her novels; see, for example, the artificial nature of the wedding day of Edward and Laurel in *Friends and Relations*.

[17] This phrase is echoed in Bowen's essay "The Bend Back" (1951), an essay which will be discussed further in relation to *The Little Girls*.

[18] Prince states that the role of the "narrattee-character" "is that of relay between the narrator and the reader(s) or rather between the author and the reader(s). Should certain values have to be defended or certain ambiguities clarified, this can easily be done by means of asides addressed to the narratee" (Prince 1973, 229).

[19] See, for example, Henry James' *The Turn of the Screw*.

[20] This short story was originally published in the *Cornhill* in November 1944, reprinted in *The Demon Lover and Other Stories* (1945), in *Stories by Elizabeth Bowen* (1959) (Sellery and Harris, 1981, pp58 and 81) and *Collected Stories* (pp.623-640). The setting of this short story is further evidence of Bowen's use of autobiographical details as the settings for her fiction. Writing about her childhood on the Kent coast, she states that she and her mother were looked after by a "grapevine of powerful Anglo-Irish relatives", one of whom was Lilla Chichester "a childless dowager who commanded Sandgate from an ilex-dark eminence". Bowen continues in parenthesis, "Enfield, her Victorian-Italianate home appears in one of my stories, "The Inherited Clock"." (1975, 13), as does her Christian name in *A World of Love*.

[21] An abandonment which is reminiscent of Bowen's own decision not to continue with her education after two terms at the Central School of Arts and Crafts in London when she was 20 (Craig 1986, 51).

[22] This emphasis on the theatrical quality of the lives of young girls is reminiscent of the air of theatricality which is evident in *Friends and Relations* and the apparent artifice of the Parisian house. O'Faolain also comments that Bowen's female adolescents "have a weakness for the cad" (1956, 166). This weakness could, of course, result from an aspiration to share the cad's greater knowledge.

[23] See Maslen (2009, 202-203) for a further discussion of Leopold's Jewish identity.

[24] Bennett and Royle's use of the tomb as a metaphor for Leopold's state of mind

might suggest an echo of the tomb in which Jesus' body was placed after he was crucified and from which he was resurrected on Easter Sunday. It is, perhaps, a tomb from which Leopold will be resurrected once he has gained self-knowledge.

[25] Ellmann suggests that Madame Fisher resembles "other shadowy thirds in Bowen's fiction, such as Elfrida in *Friends and Relations*" (2003, 119).

[26] The uneaten apples can perhaps be associated with the apple on the tree of good and evil not yet eaten by Eve.

CHAPTER FOUR

"INCURABLE STRANGERS TO THE WORLD":
THE DEATH OF THE HEART

The title of Bowen's fifth novel, *The Death of the Heart* (1938), suggests a romantic novel, one in which the heroine "loses her heart" to some unsuitable man, and, of course, this is the basic premise of the plot. However, the novel is more complex than this superficial reading would suggest; as Stephen Wall comments, *"The Death of the Heart* is Elizabeth Bowen's most secure presentation of the lonely desolation of innocent immaturity wounded by the shifty compromise of the worldly" (1970, 256). The plot of the novel revolves around a young girl, Portia Quayne. Orphaned at the age of 16, she goes to live with her half-brother, Thomas Quayne, and his wife, Anna, in their house in Windsor Terrace, London. Portia is catapulted from a life of living in small hotels in unfashionable parts of Europe into a sophisticated and superficial world which she does not understand. Bewildered by the society in which she finds herself, she struggles to understand the people who surround her, not least Anna and her friend, Eddie. Portia has particular trouble in understanding the language of those with whom she lives and is unable to decipher the meaning of her life, "[i]n her home life (her new home life) with its puzzles, she saw dissimulation always on guard; she asked herself humbly for what reason people said what they did not mean, and did not say what they meant." (*DH*, 59).

Equally, Portia is unable to understand, or fully participate in, life at "Waikiki", the home of Anna's old governess, Mrs Heccomb, where she fails to understand the conventions and rules of Seale-on-Sea society. During her stay with her brother and sister-in-law Portia falls in love with Eddie, "the near cad" according to Sean O'Faolain (1956, 163). Her love is betrayed when she sees Eddie holding hands with another girl in a cinema and it could be suggested that this betrayal leads to the death of her heart.

However, even this reading, whilst giving an overview of the novel, belies the intricate plot; it is a reading which elides the complexities both of Bowen's language and the structure of the novel. The reader is initially alerted to the possibility of multiple subtexts when St. Quentin asks Anna "But why was she called Portia?" to which Anna replies simply "I don't think we ever asked" (*HP*, 21). In his discussion of this novel, O'Faolain suggests in parenthesis that "Symbolists may decide why the child was called Portia. She does seem to sit in judgement on Thomas and Anna" (1956, 162). There is an allusion to *The Merchant of Venice* in Max's character in *The House in Paris*[1] and it would appear that Bowen, in this novel, is again employing an intertextual reference to that play. William Heath, however, suggests that Bowen's choice of name might simply have been influenced by Henry James: "[t]he narrator's language for describing Portia at first suggests James ("Portia", it should be remembered, was his generic term for the "young person intelligent and presumptuous" in his preface to *The Portrait of a Lady*.)" (1961, 83).[2] James was, of course, writing about Shakespeare's Portia; in his preface he continues that

> Portia matters to Antonio, and to Shylock, and to the Prince of Morocco ...
> but for these gentry there are other lively concerns; for Antonio, notably,
> there are Shylock and Bassanio and his lost ventures and the extremity of
> his predicament. This extremity indeed, by the same token, matters to
> Portia – though its doing so becomes of interest all by the fact that Portia
> matters to *us*. (1907, 50)

Whilst superficially the novel appears to be bound up in Portia's story, suggesting that therefore the reader's concerns should be focused on her predicament and the effect that her loss of innocence has on her, a reading of *The Death of the Heart* which gives credence to James' discussion of Portia in *The Merchant of Venice* could suggest that Bowen is attempting to show the effect that the innocence of an individual can have on society, that Portia's loss of innocence should matter to "us", for, as Bowen comments in her draft synopsis of the novel, "it is *not* uniquely the heart of Portia that we contemplate".[3]

Indeed, Gindin comments that one of the major themes in fiction of the 1930s "is that of betrayal. In social, political, religious, personal or sexual terms, referring to both individuals and societies, the pain of betrayal, of disastrously broken promise or expectation, reverberates through all literature. (1992, 16)[4] Betrayal is a predominant theme in *The Death of the Heart*, a theme which manifests itself in many ways throughout the novel. Bowen's exploration of Portia's adolescence continues her discussion of innocence to be found in her previous novels but, within this particular novel, this is extended by questioning the nature of betrayal, both the betrayal of innocence and the betrayal by the innocents.

Contexts

Gindin's work helps to place *The Death of the Heart* within its literary context and provides a starting point for a discussion on Bowen's style; he states that the fiction of the 1930s is "dependent on metaphor that combines or does not distinguish between private and public experience. Often, individual and sexual experience is intrinsically related to the social and historical, the language of each realm becoming a way of understanding the other." (1992, 85)

It is a literary style often associated with modernism and one which can also be found in the fiction of Elizabeth Bowen, amongst others. Nicola Humble suggests that Bowen's fiction can be considered as "middlebrow fiction": she contends that "middlebrow fictions" "range from intellectual abstruse novels such as those of Ivy Compton-Burnett and Elizabeth Bowen to light *jeux d'esprit* by P. G. Wodehouse and E. F. Benson" (2001, 13) and continues that the novels of Compton-Burnett and Bowen, despite their narrative and syntactical complexities "acquired middlebrow status because their intense interest in class and domestic interiors spoke to the increasing middle-class fascination with status" (ibid).[5] Humble also highlights the reassessment of Bowen as a modernist writer:

> In one sense middlebrow fiction is the 'other' of the modernist or avant-garde novel, the bugbear continually reviled by highbrow critics and literary experimenters as corrupting public taste and devaluing the status of the novel. Yet the feminine middlebrow also provides the brimming bowl into which recent revisers of the modernist canon have dipped for new plums: Rose Macauley, Antonia White, and Elizabeth Bowen are among the once squarely middlebrow writers who have recently been co-opted into a new feminized modernist history. (ibid, 24-25)

Whilst the novel can be placed within a literary context of this kind, it can also be placed within a historical context. Published two years after *The House in Paris*, Bowen's fifth novel was written during a period which was increasingly overshadowed by the seemingly inevitable threat of war in Europe. Indeed, Miss Paullie, Portia's teacher, tells Portia and her fellow students that they "must do all that [they] could to prevent a future war" (*DH*, 118). Such a contextualisation suggests that the turmoil of Portia's life could be read as an allusion to the turmoil facing Britain in the late 1930s, a turmoil described by Gindin as "a premonition of defeat and disaster" (1992, 21). Martin Kitchen suggests that "1937 [the year before *The Death of the Heart* was published] was a year of uncertainty and foreboding." (1988, 290). This was the year Neville Chamberlain became Prime Minister and his search for appeasement, his apparently naïve belief that "Hitler and Mussolini were at heart […] practical men with whom it was possible to negotiate in good faith" showing a man with "a strong sense of mission resulting in a rigidity, an inability to adjust to unpleasant facts and a narrowness of vision which in the end proved disastrous" (ibid). Whilst the turmoil facing the British public can, in a limited way, be read into Portia's own turbulent life, Major Brutt, thought of as outdated by Thomas Quayne, embodies many of the characteristics of Chamberlain, particularly his "inability to adjust to unpleasant facts". Deliberating over Major Brutt's position in society, Thomas suggests that "[m]akes of men date, like makes of cars; Major Brutt was a 1914-18 model: there was now no market for that make. In fact, only his steadfast persistence in living made it a pity he could not be scrapped." (*DH*, 90)

Bowen's references to the popular culture of the 1930s also place the novel firmly within the context of the latter part of the decade; the two visits to the cinema, first by Anna, Thomas and Portia,[6] and the subsequent visit during Portia's visit to "Waikiki" both reflect the increasing middle-class patronage of cinemas in the 1930s. There was an Odeon in every major town, cinemas with "streamlined curves, clean fins and floodlights […] the quintessence of modernism" (Richards 1997, 193). It was an element of popular culture which Bowen thoroughly enjoyed. According to Keith Williams, Bowen took "hedonistic pleasure in the whole cinema going rite" (1996, 79). Writing in 1937 Bowen said that, whilst she preferred the architecture of the "pre-War façades, with caryatids[7] and garlands" (1937, 212), the cinema remained

> like a chocolate box lid, the entrance is still voluptuously promising: sensation of some sort seems to be guaranteed. How happily I tread the pneumatic carpet, traverse anterooms with their exciting muted vibration, and walk down the spotlit aisle with its eager tilt to the screen. I climb over those knees to the sticky velvet seat, and fumble my cigarettes out. (Ibid)[8]

Bowen's fascination with the cinema provides a biographical context for the novel, as does the location of both the Quaynes' house in London and "Waikiki"; her own house in Clarence Terrace can be seen as the model for 2 Chester Terrace, and "Waikiki" has more than a passing resemblance to some of the villas that Bowen lived in with her mother as a child. However, whilst houses were of great importance to Bowen, it is perhaps the betrayal of her love by one man which provides the principal element of biographical contextualisation in this novel. Both Glendinning and Lee record the attraction that Bowen felt for Geronwy Rees, a man for whom Bowen "formed an attachment which was to be, in the event, short-lived" (Glendinning 1997, 114). He visited Bowen at Bowen's Court for a house party which included Rosamond Lehmann and during his visit, despite his attraction for Bowen, Rees turned his attention to Lehmann, for "the *coup de foudre* had struck both him and Rosamond – they fell in love there and then" (ibid). Bowen must have felt betrayed by his actions, a betrayal which manifests itself in the character of Eddie in *The Death of the Heart.* Rees obviously recognised aspects of his personality in Eddie and was, at first, amused by the characterisation. However, his amusement did not last and, feeling betrayed by Bowen, he considered suing her for libel (Lee 1999, 116). Whilst Rees may well have been the model for Eddie, Charles Ritchie's diary entry for 18th October 1941 highlights his belief that Thomas was based on Alan Cameron: "[the novel] is an exact description of her house and of her husband. [...] What is alarming is the husband is an unsparing portrait of A" (2009, 25).

Literary contextualisation can also be obtained from Bowen's unpublished manuscript of *Anna* in which Anna and St Quentin appear for the first time. The manuscript, which Sellery and Harris suggest was written in about 1932 (1981, 232), focuses on two characters, Anna Murgatroyd and St Quentin, who appear to be the literary prototypes for the characters in *The Death of the Heart.* There are, of course, many differences between the eponymous protagonist of the unfinished manuscript and Anna Quayne, not least in the family circumstances of the two Annas. The early Anna lives in London with her parents having fled Ireland following the Troubles in which their house was burnt to the ground. She shows a propensity for living a vicarious life through the lives of her friends, spending her days either in the shops of London or at her friends' homes: "[a] good deal of her life was spent in her friends' houses; she went about hopefully, not knowing whom or what she was likely to pick up where. She was on dropping-in terms with a good many people and when not specifically invited often came in and sat".[9]

In contrast, Anna Quayne, a sophisticated married woman, has been brought up in an English country house, motherless but having been given a free reign by her father. It is possible, however, to read fragments of the earlier Anna in the character of Anna Quayne with Anna Murgatroyd's friendship with St Quentin surviving the intervening years. The earlier St Quentin bears only a passing resemblance to the later version but both are interested in the techniques of writing. While the later St Quentin is a novelist, the earlier version, although claiming to know a lot about novels, bases this claim on the number of novels he has read, stating to Anna, "I know a lot about novels [...] I read one almost every day". Nevertheless, this does not stop him offering Anna Murgatroyd detailed advice about her own career as a novelist. Despite Anna's statement that her putative novel "[…] is not autobiographical; it has not really much plot […] It's my collected impressions",[10] St Quentin tells her "do not be too subtle" and continues "[i]f you must be clever, be clever in such a way as nobody can suspect, in fact be point blank obvious. On days when you don't feel clever be just comfortably muzzy; that will be what they call atmospheric prose."[11] Such advice is, of course, contrary to the opinions of the older St Quentin.

Narrative

Narrative in *The Death of the Heart* returns to the (mainly) linear, or teleological, form of Bowen's earlier novels. However, like Bowen's other novels, the ending of *The Death of the Heart*, which might be expected to confer meaning, fails to answer many of the questions posed by the novel and the reader is left to wonder about the future of Portia, Major Brutt, the Quaynes and, indeed, the future of the society in which the Quaynes move. Within the narrative there are moments of completing analepsis which do provide a limited amount of information for the reader, for example Anna's narrative to St. Quentin explaining, from her point of view, the circumstances surrounding Portia's conception, early childhood and arrival at the Quaynes' household in London. However, Anna's version of the marriage of Thomas' father and mother, gleaned, one supposes, from Thomas' somewhat limited understanding of his parents' marital breakdown, is sometimes at odds with another episode of analepsis in the novel, that of Matchett's deliberations on that same marriage, the differing points of view serving to highlight two different approaches to morality. Analepses within the novel provide biographical detail which aids understanding of a character's behaviour, as does the narrative means by which the analepses are presented. For example, the objective manner in which Eddie's formative years are narrated provides an understanding solely of Eddie's character; conversely Anna's subjective deliberations on Mr. Quayne's marriage and Portia's childhood serve not only to provide information about Mr. Quayne and Portia but also illuminate facets of Anna's own personality.[12]

In addition to moments of analepsis, there are many instances in *The Death of the Heart* where there are direct addresses to the reader, addresses through which the authorial voice is frequently heard, particularly in relation to issues such as innocence and betrayal. Lanser makes a distinction between the use of external and internal narratees (the public and private voices of the narration) and these direct addresses in the novel could be considered, in Lanser's terms, to be "extrarepresentational", that is discourse which is "not strictly required for telling a tale" (1992, 17). Lanser suggests that although there may be no overt authorial voice, the maxims of the author can be read into the comments of the character (ibid, 115). This can be seen in *The Death of the Heart*, particularly in relation to St. Quentin's comments about style in writing, opinions which appear to be strikingly similar to those of Bowen. Chessman states that *The Death of the Heart* explores the "question of authorship more directly than almost any other Bowen novel", continuing that it "is no accident that one of the central characters, St Quentin, is a novelist" (1983, 78). His speech to Anna about Portia's diary serves both to address the process of writing and the idea of style. Equally it highlights the relationship between the author and the implied reader. Portia's diary has, of course, three different readers; although initially written by Portia to express her emotions in a private space, the diary then becomes a text which is written specifically to be read by Eddie. Added to this is the surreptitious reading of the diary by Anna and, of course, the ultimate reading by the reader of the novel; each reader will engage with the diary in different ways.

Anna is deeply upset by Portia's diary, finding her entries "completely distorted and distorting" (*DH*, 10). However, as St. Quentin suggests,

> [y]ou've got to allow for style, though. Nothing arrives on paper as it started, and so much arrives that never started at all. To write is always to rave a little – even if one did once know what one meant, which at her age seems unlikely. [...] St Quentin, looking frustrated, started feeling about for his handkerchief. He blew his nose and went on, with iron determination: 'Style is the thing that's always a bit phony, and at the same time you cannot write without style. Look how much goes into addressing an envelope – for, after all, it's a matter of set-out. And a diary, after all, is written to please oneself – therefore it's bound to be enormously written up. The obligation to write it is all in one's own eye, and look how one is when it's almost always written – upstairs, late, overwrought alone ... All the same, Anna, it must have interested you.' (*DH*, 10-11)

How many of St. Quentin's opinions can be attributed to Bowen is impossible to say. However, Bowen was concerned with both style and the value of writing good quality prose: in a letter to William Plomer dated 27th June 1936[13] she tells Plomer how much she appreciated his comment on her handwriting, "you said once it was *stylish*" (1999b, 200) and in a subsequent letter dated August 17th 1936[14] in which she writes about a collection of short stories she is editing, her comments to Plomer suggests that she views her own writing rather highly in comparison to some other authors:

> Yes indeed I am doing those abominable short stories (the collection, I mean). […] 4/5ths of what I try out shows a level of absolute mediocrity; arty, they are, and mawkishly tenderhearted. […] I long more and more to make a collection of *Great Middlebrow Prose*. Would this be actionable? Would you collaborate? I suppose it would ruin one. (ibid, 202)[15]

By questioning whether or not such a comment would "be actionable", Bowen highlights one of the issues surrounding middlebrow writing for, as Humble comments:

> The term was used throughout the period [1920s to 1950s] (and has been ever since) as a form of disapprobation, suggesting a smug 'easy' read, lacking significant intellectual challenges. For many who applied the term, one suspects that the central tenet that allowed a novel to be dismissed as middlebrow was the issue of whom it was read by: once a novel became widely popular, it became suspect, and bestseller status, or adoption as a Book-of-the-Month choice by a major book club was sufficient to demote it beneath serious attention." (2001, 12-13)

Issues surrounding the act of writing permeate *The Death of the Heart*. There are, of course, Portia's diary entries which so disturb Anna, but there are also questions of the implied readership of the diary, together with the value of letters. With both Eddie and Thomas working in an advertising business, it becomes apparent that the written word cannot always be considered truthful; Eddie's distrust of the written word and worries concerning his representation in Portia's diary serve to highlight the multiple meanings inherent in *The Death of the Heart*.[16] Letters and diary entries provide varying points of view within the novel and their shifting perspectives allow Bowen to portray innocence and betrayal in differing ways.

Anna highlights the importance of letters by noting how seriously Portia takes any correspondence; talking to St. Quentin she says "[Portia] seems to like hoarding paper; she gets almost no letters, but she'd been keeping all sorts of things Thomas and I throw away – begging letters, for instance, or quack talks about health" (*DH*, 9). There can be no doubt that Portia places a high value on any correspondence she receives but she places particular value on a letter received from Eddie, a letter which she carries around with her at school, first in her handbag and latterly secreted "inside her woollen directoire knickers [where] it stayed just inside the elastic band, under one knee." (*DH*, 55). In this instance, not only does

Portia's determination to hold onto the letter from Eddie arguably shows her childishness, the episode also raises issues of class. On discovering that Portia is surreptitiously reading a letter, Miss Paullie turns on her:

> Surely that is not a letter? This is not the place or time to read your letters, is it? I think you must notice that the other girls don't do that. And, wherever one is, one never does read a letter under the table: have you never been told? What else is that you have on your knee? Your bag? Why did you not leave your bag in the cloakroom? Nobody will take it here, you know. Now, put your letter away in your bag again, and leave them both in the cloakroom. To carry your bag about with you indoors is a hotel habit, you know. (*DH*, 55)[17]

Loss of Innocence and the Search for Identity

Incorporated into Bowen's discussion of innocence in *The Death of the Heart* are two separate but intertwined issues; the search for identity and the rôle of innocence in society. From the very title of the novel and given Portia's central position within it, it would appear to be inevitable that Portia should be betrayed and, by such a betrayal, start to lose her innocence, a loss which could lead to the "death of the heart", although, as will be seen, Portia is not the only character in the novel who can be considered innocent.

Allied to the question of innocence and its loss, which is addressed in so much of Bowen's fiction, is the search for identity; according to Keith May this search is "part of a tradition in Western literature from Sophocles onwards, and certainly many a novel since the beginnings of the novel form has turned on a question of identity" (1977, 64). Heather Ingman suggests that when a child becomes an adult s/he necessarily loses any remaining vestiges of innocence. However, it is possible for adults[18] to retain their innocence and many adult characters in Bowen's fiction have been identified as retaining their innocence; in *the Death of the Heart* these include Major Brutt, Mr. Quayne and, to a certain extent, Eddie.

Ingman employs Freudian and Lacanian psychoanalytical theory to explain the transition from innocence to experience in the novel; in particular, she predicates her work on Lacanian theory, specifically the journey from the pre-Oedipal stage through the mirror and imaginary stages to the symbolic stages. She suggests that in order for Portia to develop into a fully functioning adult in society she first has to leave the pre-Oedipal relationship that she has had with her mother, Irene. Irene is a person who would never had dared "to cross the threshold" of Miss Paullie's school (*DH*, 56) but Portia must, according to Ingman, cross this threshold, leaving "behind the symbiotic relationship with the mother and join the world of the father, the world of language and civilisation", and suggests that, for Portia, Anna is the "patriarchal" mother (1998, 79). Whilst Anna does appear to have the dominant rôle in the Quayne household, Anna's position as the patriarch is, of course, debatable.

Lacanian theory highlights the phases that a child goes through before he or she acquires language and starts the process of socialisation. Obviously the time frame usually associated by this theory cannot be applied literally to Portia; nevertheless an examination of Portia's life does allow a reading of Lacanian theory to be applied to Portia in a less literal fashion if one considers that until Portia arrives in London to live with Thomas and Anna she remains in the mirror stage, with no real understanding of her own identity. Using this premise it can be argued that, following Irene's death, Portia enters Lacan's symbolic phase, utilising language in order to identify herself and her position in the social order. Her entrance into the symbolic and linguistic order is represented by her diary in which she records her thoughts and fears. By taking up her pen Portia is, according to Ingman, attempting to understand the patriarchal society in which adults and, in particular, Thomas and Anna live. Her diary is the tool by which she represses "her desire for her pre-Oedipal mother [Irene …] in order to understand the patriarchal 'mother', Anna." (1998, 79).

Ingman's argument can be substantiated, to a certain extent, by the authorial voice in *The Death of the Heart* which also seems to suggest that innocence can only be found in those who have not yet entered the symbolic order where "[i]nnocence so constantly finds itself in a false position that inwardly innocent people learn to be disingenuous. Finding no language in which to speak in their own terms they resign themselves to being translated imperfectly" (*DH*, 106). Bowen would appear to suggest that the innocent have no language, they exist alone in an imaginary, solipsistic world, misunderstood and unable to fully understand others.[19] Without this understanding, this key, which Ingman suggests will lead to self-knowledge, the innocent are unable to participate fully in society. The recurring image of the key throughout the novel adds weight to the argument that Portia, in particular, is searching for understanding. However, undermining this is Anna's comment to St. Quentin in relation to the *escritoire* in Portia's room, "But she seems to have lost the keys" (*DH*, 9). Portia's literal loss of this particular key, which suggests a desire to remain a child, is reiterated during her conversation with St. Quentin about the diary, but St. Quentin's comment, "You ought to want some key to why people do what they do", highlights his own concerns for Portia, his belief that people need understanding to participate fully in society is echoed by Matchett who tells a taxi driver, "You've got to know your own mind" (*DH*, 314).

However, before Portia can begin to know her own mind and utilise the key to a world of experience it is necessary for her to leave her imaginary world which is particularly represented by her arrangement of bears in her bedroom, an arrangement that Anna has difficulty in understanding, seeing only the dust that the bears collect, rather than any intrinsic or emotional value that they might have to Portia. It is perhaps interesting to note that Anna believes Portia's diary and bear arrangement are equally important and, if Ingman's reading of *The Death of the Heart* is valid, the two objects are of equal status; one (the bears) representing the imaginary and a state of innocence and the other (the diary) representing Portia's attempt to enter the symbolic and social order, an attempt which will, inevitably, lead to the loss of innocence. Equally, an alternative reading of the novel could suggest that both the bears and the diary represent a valid view but one which would embarrass a more conventional person such as Anna.

As Portia seems unwilling to keep safe the key which will allow her understanding and acceptance in the social world, the narrator is also aware that the innocent might be frightened and unwilling to take this step, to move away from a solipsistic existence and to acknowledge and accept a place in society, that there "are moments when it becomes frightening to realise that you are not, in fact, alone in the world" (*DH*, 170). However, the narrator seems to reach the conclusion that solitude might be preferred if the sterility of Windsor Terrace is the only real alternative, an alternative in which each "person [...] lived impaled upon a private obsession" (*DH*, 171). There are, of course, other alternatives to the constricted lifestyle of the Quayne household; one of these is represented by the "uneditedness of life [...] at Waikiki" (ibid). One of the main differences between life in Windsor Terrace and life at "Waikiki" is predicated on passion. As Thomas is well aware, Windsor Terrace and, in particular, his marriage, lacks passion despite his own feelings for Anna. His passion for his wife is not reciprocated as Thomas discovers following their marriage,

> [w]hen they had agreed to marry, Thomas was happy enough, and Anna was perfectly willing. Then they married: Thomas discovered himself the prey of a passion for her inside marriage, that nothing in their language could be allowed to express, that nothing could satisfy (*DH*, 39).

He is fully aware that his passion for Anna is not returned, equally that passion has the potential to be all-consuming, particularly when it is not mutual. An exchange between Anna and Thomas highlights his position;

Thomas expresses his dismay that he is never alone with Anna, after kissing her "angrily", "[h]e left her and looked round for his glass again. Meanwhile, he said to himself in a quoting voice: 'We are minor in everything but our passions' " (*DH*, 37).

In contrast life at "Waikiki" is "pushing and frank" (*DH*, 171). However, "[n]othing set itself up here by the naïvest propriety – that made Daphne shout not swear, that kept Dickie so stern and modest" (ibid). It is a life lived in a "primitive state", "the fount of spontaneous living" (ibid), life, in fact, lived with exuberance and passion. However, as Portia can find no place for herself in Anna's society, she also has difficulty in understanding, and assimilating, the alternative life as experienced at "Waikiki".

The Age of Innocence?[20]

Whilst we might expect to consider the child, as opposed to the adult, as an innocent this, obviously, is not the case. In Bowen's earlier novels she portrays the adolescent as the innocent, an adolescent such as Lois who is on the verge of adulthood and of experience, while her later novels, *Friends and Relations* and *To the North* explore the innocence of adults. Bowen most effectively considers the innocence of children in *The House in Paris* but returns to the innocence of the adolescent in *The Death of the Heart.* In his reading of the novel, Cole poses some interesting questions in relation to the adolescent and innocence, stating

> The myths about children cling to adolescents […] Was Portia capable of her moments of cruelty and spite? Do these moments preclude innocence? Does adolescent innocence, when it is at its height, as with Portia, surpass even the childlike kind we more or less take for granted as present, if with qualifications, even in our unsentimental moments? (1974, 120).

Despite her age (she is sixteen) Portia is portrayed as a child with childish interests. She is, for example, particularly fond of her arrangement of a teddy bears' picnic in her bedroom and her childishness, represented metaphorically by her distaste for the necessity of carrying a handbag, is noted by St. Quentin who says to Anna (in Portia's presence), "I'm afraid we can't do much about your character now it must have set – I know mine has. Portia's so lucky, hers is still being formed." (*DH*, 28).

However, it becomes immediately apparent that Portia's childishness, and innocence, is a fragile entity, for "Portia fixed St Quentin with her blank dark eyes. An alarming vague little smile, already not quite childish, altered her face, then died. She went on saying nothing— " (ibid). Portia would appear to be aware of her changing status from child to adult; although having the appearance of a child with "thin hips", "thin arms" and a "body [which] was all concave and jerkily fluid lines", "she looked cautious, aware of the world in which she had to live. She was sixteen, losing her childish majesty. The pointed attention of St Quentin and Anna reached her like a quick tide, or an attack." (*HP*, 29)

Her childlike nature is also based on the false premise that she has experienced a typical childhood of the period,

> for little girls in England spring means the Easter holidays: bicycle rides in blazers, ginger nuts in the pockets, blue violets in bleached grass, paperchases, secrets, and mixed hockey. But Portia, thanks first to Irene, now to Anna, still knew nothing of this. She had come straight to London … (*HP*, 125).

It is evident that due to her circumstances Portia has not experienced such a life, she has never really had the opportunity to be truly childlike. Her entry into the adult world is, not therefore, a desire to cling to a way of life in which she feels comfort, rather it is a delay based on lack of knowledge, being the daughter of a woman who, despite the circumstances of Portia's conception (that is her adulterous relationship with Mr. Quayne), remained naïve until her death.

Age, of course, is not necessarily the defining factor in the transition from innocence to experience. Eddie, Major Brutt and Thomas' father, for example, all retain vestiges of innocence; in the case of Major Brutt and Mr. Quayne this is through their own naivety, although arguably it is Mrs. Quayne who has kept Mr. Quayne in such a state. Apparently the dominant partner in their marriage, Mrs. Quayne treated her husband as a child; according to Anna, "she was a woman who thought all men are great boys at heart, and she took every care to keep him one" (*DH*, 18). Irene, a "plucky" widow (ibid), whom Mr. Quayne met on one of his frequent trips to London, trips suggested by Mrs. Quayne, appealed to him. She was a woman who needed to be looked after in contrast to Mrs. Quayne who, according to Anna, treated Mr. Quayne like a small boy. Having deliberately kept Mr. Quayne in a state akin to childhood, Mrs. Quayne threw him out of their home and out of an apparently Edenic existence, albeit a false Eden predicated on the subservience of Mr. Quayne. Cast out of his Eden, Mr. Quayne, who "loved his home like a child" (*DH*, 19), decided to remove himself from society, taking Irene out of the country in order for her to have her baby. Repeating Anna's words when talking to Portia about her parents, Matchett states that being sent away from his home was "worse than dying", for "[h]e loved his home like a child. Go? – He was sent. He liked his place in the world […] For a gentleman like him, abroad was no proper place" (*DH*, 78). Once cast out of society, Mr. Quayne made no effort to return for, as Portia comments, "he liked moving on. It was mother wanted a house, but father never would" (ibid), recognising, perhaps, the futility of "attempting to picnic in Eden".

Innocence and Society

Whilst there is no place in conventional society for Mr. Quayne and Irene, equally there is apparently no place for innocence in the Quayne household, nor, it would appear, within the circles of society in which the Quaynes, and particularly Anna, move. Portia's innocence, and the inevitability of her eventual corruption, is metaphorically represented by the rug in her bedroom; sent away to be cleaned following a spillage of varnish, Portia notes in her diary, "[m]y white rug has come back, it is fluffier than it was, fluffy like the underneath of a cat. I hope I shall not spill something on it again." (*DH*, 114). The virginal white of the rug is suggestive of Portia's initial childlike innocence as she arrives in London, an innocence that is slowly being corrupted. Her desire that she shall not soil the rug again suggests, as with the loss of keys, a wish to remain in a childlike state.

Anna, however, is uncomfortable in the presence of anyone who shows any outward appearance of innocence; contemplating the scene in her drawing room after meeting Major Brutt at the cinema, Anna is concerned by what she sees:

> She saw Portia, kneeling down by the fire, look up at Major Brutt with a perfectly open face – her hands were tucked up the elbows of her short-sleeved dress. The picture upset Anna, who thought how much innocence she herself had corrupted in other people – yes, even in Robert: in him perhaps most of all. Meetings that ended with their most annihilating and bitter quarrels had begun with Robert unguarded, eager – like that. Watching Portia she thought, is she a snake, or a rabbit? At all events, she thought, hardening, she has her own fun. (*DH*, 46)[21]

Portia's innocence unsettles Anna, but this would seem a surprising reaction in one who is so apparently sophisticated, secure and happy in her own existence. Nevertheless, Anna appears to be fearful of Portia's innocence, fearful, perhaps, that her glow of innocence may highlight Anna's own shortcomings. Portia and Anna rarely look straight at each other, deliberately refusing to make any such physical connection; Anna feels uncomfortable when Portia looks at her and "Portia had learnt one dare never look for long" (*DH*, 49). Despite her attempts to "not notice", Anna's discomfort is obvious when, during a conversation about her ex-lover, Robert Pidgeon,

> Anna had felt those dark eyes with a determined innocence steal back again and again to her face. Anna, on the sofa in a Récamier attitude, had acted, among all she had had to act, a hardy imperviousness to this. Had the agitation she felt throughout her body sent out an aura with a quivering edge, Portia's eyes might be said to explore this line of quiver, round and along Anna's reclining form. Anna felt bound up with her fear, with her secret, by that enwrapping look of Portia's: she felt mummified. (Ibid.)

While in Bowen's previous novels loss of innocence has been seen as necessary and vital for an individual to function well in society, in contrast, *The Death of the Heart* appears to suggest that society (as experienced by Anna and her friends) needs a homogeneity of experience, that, in fact, innocence is something to be feared, that the innocent are a dangerous subset of society, particularly those innocents who are no longer children. The narrator explores the dangers posed by innocent people to an inherently corrupt society:

> In love, the sweetness and violence they have to offer involves a thousand betrayals for the less innocent. Incurable strangers to the world, they never cease to exact a heroic happiness. Their singleness, their ruthlessness, their one continuous wish makes them bound to be cruel, and to suffer cruelty. The innocent are so few that two of them seldom meet – when they do meet, their victims lie strewn all round. (*DH*, 106)

Juxtaposed to this is the image of Portia and Eddie sitting "side by side at the table" (ibid), an image which suggests that they are the two main innocents in the novel, innocents whose actions will inevitably lead to destruction, not just of themselves but also of society itself. As the narrator states, "[c]hildish fantasy, like the sheath over the bud, not only protects but curbs the terrible budding spirit, protects not only innocence from the world but the world from the power of innocence" (*DH*, 294).

The presence of innocence, as Anna has discovered, can often expose the corruption prevalent in others, and the narrator in *The Death of the Heart* depicts a particular gaudiness in society, a tawdriness which would become apparent when illuminated by the innocent; describing London the narrator tells the reader, "[b]ut London, these nights, has a provincial meanness bright lights only expose. After dark, she is like a governess gone to the bad, in a Woolworth tiara, tarted up all wrong" (*DH*, 45),[22] a description which Eddie uses in connection with Anna, "[t]he thing about Anna is, she loves making a tart of another person. She'd never dare to be a proper tart herself" (*DH*, 104), a comment which suggests that Anna might not be so corrupt as she herself believes, despite her own acknowledgement that she has corrupted others, including her former lover, Robert.

The analogy of the Woolworth tiara is also suggestive of the artificial nature of the society in which Anna moves and, indeed, of the Quayne household. Contemplating her life in London as she looks towards the sea from the esplanade at Seale-on-Sea, Portia's interior monologue highlights the emptiness of life at Windsor Terrace. Outwardly the Quaynes' lifestyle appears to be fulfilling. However within Windsor Terrace, "something that should have been going on had not gone on: something had not happened. They had sat round a painted, not a burning, fire, at which you tried in vain to warm your hands." (*DH*, 149) There is a further analogy for the corrupt nature of London to be found in the description of the Quaynes' visit to the cinema where "[t]he organist still loudly and firmly playing had gone down with his organ, through floodlit mimosa, into a bottomless pit" (*DH*, 42). Whilst this is obviously an accurate portrayal of the organist's role in the cinema it can also be read as a metaphorical descent into hell, from light to dark. There are, of course, constant references to light and dark in *The Death of the Heart*; the novel opens in the "[b]ronze cold of January [which] bound the sky and the landscape; the sky was shut to the sun" (*DH*, 7), the Regency terraces are "pallid" (ibid), their windows black and the hallway of the Quaynes' house is a "well of dusk" (*DH*, 22). It is "a house to which nobody had returned yet, which, through the big windows, darkness and silence had naturally stolen in on and begun to inhabit" (ibid).[23] In contrast to the bleakness of the winter portrayed in "The World", the feelings of spring evoked in Part Two, "The Flesh"[24] introduce a more optimistic note into the novel for

> [e]arly in March the crocuses crept alight, then blazed yellow and purple in the park [...] autumn arrives early in the morning, but spring at the close of a winter day. The air, about to darken, quickens and is run through with mysterious white light; the curtain of darkness is suspended, as though for some unprecedented event. There is perhaps no sunset, the trees are not yet budding – but the senses receive intimation, an intimation so fine, yet striking in so directly, that this appears a movement in one's own spirit. This exalts whatever feeling is in the heart. (*DH*, 123).

Despite the optimism of that first spring evening, the narrator suggests that some do not, or cannot, welcome such a change. As some in Anna's society fear innocence, so others fear the force of nature for "[i]t is in this unearthly first hour of spring twilight that earth's almost agonized livingness is most felt. This hour is so dreadful to some people that they hurry indoors and turn on the lights – they are pursued by the scent of violets sold on the kerb." (*DH*, 124)

The Death of the Heart suggests that an inherently corrupt society, such as that depicted by the narrator, fears those who retain their innocence; if such people cannot be sufficiently corrupted so as to lose their innocence, there is no place for them in society and thus the innocents have to remain outsiders, outcasts. This is certainly apposite if one considers Portia, Major Brutt, Mr. Quayne and, to a certain extent, Eddie. Portia, for example, is unformed, unknowing; she is aware that society places certain constraints on people but is not fully aware of the nature of those constraints. Her childhood with Irene has been spent on the periphery of society, living a frugal, but happy, existence in hotels where "[t]hey always stayed in places before the season, when the funicular was not working yet" (*DH*, 34). Nevertheless, despite their obvious pleasure in each other's company, they exist outside society and have difficulty comprehending the rules of that society. Irene's difficulties are compounded by her feelings of inferiority, and her lack of understanding of the rules of society has had a detrimental effect on Portia. Miss Paullie's indignation when she discovers Portia surreptitiously reading Eddie's letter serves to highlight both Portia's position outside the society inhabited by Anna, and—more widely—the class divisions within the novel:

> Miss Paullie was very particular what class of girl she took. *Sins* cut boldly up through every class in society, but mere misdemeanours show a certain level in life. So now, not only diligence, or caution, kept the girls' smooth heads bent, and made them not glance again at Irene's child. Irene herself – knowing that nine out of ten things you do direct from the heart are the wrong thing, and that she was not capable of doing anything better – would not have dared to cross the threshold of this room. For a moment, Portia felt herself stand with her mother in the doorway, looking at all this with a wild askance shrinking eye […] Seldom had they faced up to society – when they did, Irene did the wrong thing, then cried. (*HP*, 56).

Whilst highlighting the differences between classes, this passage also indicates that the novel equates spontaneity with behaviour which is not acceptable to conventional society.

Portia continues to have difficulties; she "had watched life, since she came to London, with a sort of despair" (*HP*, 59), trying desperately to understand the motivation of people in London, finding particular problems in deciphering meanings in speech. It is, perhaps, not surprising that Portia should have trouble discerning meaning for, as indicated above, the novel contains multiple subtexts. This is particularly evident in Portia's inability to understand the rules of Seale-on-Sea society. Daphne's appearance, for example, belies her nature for whilst "Daphne's person was sexy, her conversation [was] irreproachably chaste […] For Portia, Daphne and Dickie seemed a crisis that surely must be unique: she could not believe that they happened every day." (*DH*, 146). However, there is a strong sense of morality which runs through those who live at Seale-on-Sea;[25] Mr. Bursley's behaviour is frowned upon by many, for example, but the strongest statement of disgust comes from Dickie who tells Portia that he doesn't like girls who smoke cigarettes, or those with "messed up mouths" (*DH*, 166). As he firmly states to Portia "Girls make a mistake in trying to be attractive in ways that simply lose them a man's respect. No man would want to give his children a mother with that sort of stuff all over her face" and claims that "that the majority of fellows, if you asked them would feel the same." (*DH,* 166-167)

Nevertheless, Portia is very aware that she does not fit in, that there would appear to be no place for her in the society which either Anna or Daphne inhabit for, as she states to Major Brutt, "I see now that my father wanted me to belong somewhere because he did not: that was why they have had to have me in London" (*DH*, 292). Portia continues,

> I suppose he and my mother did not know they were funny: they went on feeling upset because they thought they had once done an extraordinary thing (their getting married had been extraordinary) but they still thought life was quite simple for people who did not do extraordinary things. My father often used to explain to me that people did not live the way we did: he said ours was not the right way – though we were all quite happy. He was quite certain ordinary life went on – yes, that was why I was sent to Thomas and Anna. But I see now that it does not: if he and I meet again I should have to tell him that there is no ordinary life. (Ibid)

Portia appears to be a constant observer, rarely a participant in life, both in London and Seale-on-Sea, where she constantly watches Dickie, Daphne and their friends as they play golf, go ice skating, even, paradoxically, watching Daphne and Eddie holding hands at the cinema rather than engaging fully with the film. Equally, Major Brutt feels himself to be an outsider, looking in; in a draft "blurb"[26] sent to William Plomer after the end of the second world war, Bowen refers to Major Brutt as an "outlander"[27]. He and Portia live, to a certain extent, in isolation; they are both striving for understanding without realising, perhaps, that such an understanding will extract a heavy price, that of their innocence. Major Brutt's feelings of isolation are highlighted in an exchange with Thomas Quayne: "I've got a bit out of touch. [...]". When Thomas asks him to explain further,

> Some obscure hesitation, some momentary doubt made Major Brutt frown, then look across at Thomas in a more personal manner than he had looked yet. But his look was less clear – the miasma thickening in the study had put a film over him. 'Well,' he said, 'there must be something going on. You know – in a general way, I mean. You know, something you all— (*DH*, 94).

However, as Thomas points out to Major Brutt, this is a false reading of the situation; Thomas has a very bleak perception of society and his own rôle, he states "I really can't feel you are missing much. I don't think much goes on—However, Anna might know" (ibid). As Vanderbrook feels that he and his friends are "lost" (James, 1899, 37), Thomas feels equally lost in life, his belief that Anna will know highlights Thomas' own position, a position which is similar to Major Brutt and Portia, that of an outsider looking in.

In his introduction to the Penguin Classics edition of James' *The Awkward Age*, Ronald Blythe suggests that in both *What Maisie Knew* and *The Awkward Age*, "it would not be the ageing moralist who condemned the loss of standards and the new vulgarity, but uncomfortably observant adolescents, young girls who were conventionally supposed not to see or hear what was going on" (1977, xi). Equally in *The Death of the Heart* it is the adolescents, in the guise of Portia and Eddie, who observe and comment on the corrupt nature of society, a corruption that constantly threatens to betray the innocent. Eddie is, of course, more overt in his criticism whereas, arguably, Portia is expressing her incomprehension of a society in which she believes she is supposed to be able to participate.

Betrayal

Bowen's feelings of betrayal that she experienced as a result of the actions of Geronwy Rees are echoed in *The Death of the Heart*, and the betrayal of innocence is a major theme in the novel; indeed the novel opens with betrayal, the betrayal of Anna by Portia through the entries in Portia's diary for, whilst Portia is constantly betrayed by others, she too is a betrayer. The betrayal Portia feels when she discovers that Anna has read her diary is almost immeasurable and yet, paradoxically, it is Anna who feels betrayed by her portrayal in Portia's diary. As she says to St. Quentin as they walk around Regent's Park, "And I've seldom been more upset." (*DH*, 8). Anna continues "[t]hat diary could not be worse than it is. That is to say, it couldn't be worse for me. At the time, it only made me superficially angry – but I've had time to think it over in. And I haven't quite finished yet – I keep remembering more things." (*DH*, 10)

Portia's diary entries about her life with the Quaynes which, according to Anna, start with the words, "*So I am with them, in London*" (*DH*, 11),[28] is not the first betrayal that Anna has experienced in her life. Motherless from an early age and thus arguably feeling abandoned and betrayed by her mother, the ending of Anna's first love affair with Robert Pidgeon is shrouded in mystery. Keenly questioning Major Brutt about Pidgeon's whereabouts and indicating her disappointment that she has missed him during his time in London, the narrator implies that Pidgeon left Anna in order to travel, a desertion that suggests a betrayal of her love for him. Coerced by the dying wishes of Mr. Quayne into looking after Portia for a year, Anna perceives that Portia, by acting as a mirror to Anna's apparently sophisticated existence, betrays Anna and shows her, and her house, to be superficial. Windsor Terrace, and by extension Anna herself, is described as empty and soulless for "against the sky they were colourless silhouettes, insipidly ornate, brittle and cold. The blackness of the windows not yet lit or curtained made the houses look hollow inside" (*DH*, 12).

Major Brutt's emotional response to Portia's unexpected arrival at his hotel following her distress at the continuing betrayal of Eddie indicates the implications of any betrayal of trust:

> One's sentiments – call them that – one's fidelities are so instinctive that one hardly knows they exist: only when they are betrayed, or worse still, when one betrays them does one realize their power. That betrayal is the end of an inner life, without which the everyday becomes threatening or meaningless. At the back of the spirit a mysterious landscape, whose perspective used to be infinite, suddenly perishes: this is like being cut off from the country for ever, not even meeting its breath down the city street. (*DH*, 298)

This passage could be read as an interior monologue in which Major Brutt voices his own fears for the future, a future in which he will no longer be able to trust his own "sentiments" or "fidelities", where he will be "cut off from the country", evicted from his own Eden. However, the further exploration of Major Brutt's character, that "[he] had a mind that did not articulate: he felt, simply, things had changed for the worse. His home had come down; he must no longer envisage Windsor Terrace, or go there again" (ibid), suggests authorial comment, that the betrayal of trust casts one out of the metaphorical Eden with Windsor Terrace consequently becoming a metaphor for the emptiness of the life of the betrayed, a house with no "inner life".

In Bowen's fiction being cast out of Eden is equated with a loss of innocence; the betrayal of trust such as that experienced by Portia and the other "innocents" in the novel is, according to the narrator of *The Death of the Heart*, a prerequisite for loss of innocence. Portia believes trust is of great importance, as she says to Lillian "If there wasn't *something* one could trust a person about, surely one wouldn't start to like them at all?" (*DH*, 267). When Portia discovers that Anna has betrayed her trust and told St. Quentin about the diary, the realisation that Anna has deceived her provides a moment of *anagnôrisis* for Portia, a moment of recognition which causes her to re-evaluate her relationship not just with Anna and Thomas, but also with Eddie. The betrayal occupies her mind and forces her to reconsider her immediate future:

> Since the talk with St Quentin, the idea of betrayal had been in her, upon her, sleeping and waking, as might be one's own guilt, making her not confront any face with candour, making her dread Eddie. Being able to shut her eyes while he was in this room with her, to feel impassive marble against her cheek, made her feel in the arms of immunity – the immunity of sleep, of anaesthesia, of endless solitude, the immunity of the journey across Switzerland two days after her mother died. She saw that tree she saw when the train stopped for no reason; she saw in her nerves, equally near and distant, the wet trees out there in the park. She heard the Seale sea, then heard the silent distances of the coast. (*DH*, pp.256-7).

Thus the double betrayal of Portia by Eddie and Anna, "two allied betrayals [which] push up to full growth, like a double tree" (*DH*, 271), has led to a loss of innocence, a loss which manifests itself in a lack of "candour".

Betrayal manifests itself in multiple ways throughout the novel. There is of course the betrayal of trust connected with Portia's diary, and the betrayal Portia experiences at the hands of Eddie, but of equal importance in the novel in relation to betrayal and the loss of innocence is the perception of absence as betrayal; it is a betrayal felt by Anna in the absence of Pidgeon, and by Portia who feels betrayed by the death of her mother. By ostensibly describing the departure of Anna and Thomas to Capri, across the Channel, Portia's interior monologue becomes authorial comment on the pain felt when a person is left alone, perceiving that he or she has been abandoned and betrayed by the absence of the person they love:

> To look at the sea the day someone is crossing is to accept the finality of the defined line. For the senses bound our feeling world: there is an abrupt break where their power stops […] The heart may think it knows better: the senses know that absence blots people out. We have no really absent friends. The friend becomes a traitor by breaking, however unwillingly or sadly, out of our zone: a hard judgement is passed on him, for all the pleas of the heart. Willing absence (however unwilling) is the negation of love. To remember can be at times no more than a cold duty, for we remember only in the limited way that is bearable. We observe small rites, but we defend ourselves against that terrible memory that is stronger than will. We defend ourselves from the rooms, the scenes, the objects that make for hallucination, that make the sense start up and fasten upon a ghost. We desert those who desert us; we cannot afford to suffer; we must live how we can. (*DH*, 147-148)

The personal nature of this authorial comment suggests, to borrow from Lanser, an "extrarepresentational act", an authorial comment directly addressed to the reader and one within which it is possible to hear Bowen's voice. Although it is apparent from this passage that the narrator can empathise with the loss of a friend or of someone greatly loved, Bowen was aware, with hindsight, that she did not really understand the emotional devastation associated with abandonment that can be experienced when someone close dies or leaves, despite the loss of her own mother when she was thirteen years of age. Bowen's understanding of this form of grief is highlighted in a letter to Leslie Hartley dated 21st October 1952, following the death of Alan Cameron, in reply to Hartley's letter of condolence:

> Your understanding is such a comfort and such a stay to me […] I reproach myself, now, for how little I have understood loneliness – and even now, when I have such a letter as yours, I realise that I am still spared what must be worst of all, *friendless* loneliness, a complete exposure to the brutalising indifference of the world.[29]

In a further discussion of absence, Portia's diary entry highlights the physical loss felt by Eddie's absence. The entry, written following Eddie's departure from Seale-on-Sea, can also be read as a subconscious exploration of Portia's fears for the future, a future in which she will have lost innocence but not yet gained sufficient experience to enable her to function fully in society. It is a gap, a lacunae, to be feared, a place of limbo from which there is no promise of escape; she writes, "[i]t is queer to be in a place where someone has gone. It is not two other places, the place that they were in, and the place that was there before they came. I can't get used to this third place or to staying behind." (*DH*, 223).

The betrayal experienced by Portia at the hands of Anna and Eddie has thrust her into a state of mind in which "not noticing" is preferable to acknowledging that her trust and love has been betrayed in such a thoughtless fashion. The notion of "not noticing", first seen in *The Last September*, is one which is revisited throughout *The Death of the Heart.* Anna, for example, would have preferred to remain in ignorance of Portia's diary, as she tells St. Quentin: she "would far rather not know that the thing existed" (*DH*, 8). The act of not noticing is not just a deliberate attempt to negate experience; it sometimes stems from indifference or, perhaps, an inability to see beyond one's own experience, fearful that the experience of others might highlight one's own shortcomings. Sometimes, the object who is not being noticed will fail to recognise this fact: "[Anna] palpably losing interest, curled up at her end of the sofa. Raising her arms, she shook her sleeves back and admired her own wrists. On one she wore a small soundless diamond watch. St Quentin, not noticing not being noticed went on [...]" (*DH*, 30).

In contrast, Thomas perpetually appears to feel the force of not being noticed, not just by Anna but by other as well, including Portia. As Portia and Thomas sit in Thomas' study whilst Portia dwells on her life with her mother "Thomas felt the force of not being seen." (*DH*, 34). As Portia notes in her diary, however, "[a]ll Thomas's looks, except ones at Anna, are at people not looking" (*DH*, 113). Anna's father was also able to "not notice", during the time that Miss Yardes acted as Anna's governess he "felt free to form the habit of being self-protectively unobservant" (*DH*, 125). "Not noticing" therefore can be seen as a defence mechanism, deliberately "not noticing" can be read either as a means of self-protection against the innocent (as in the case of Anna in the presence of Portia) or as a protection against betrayal (as seen from Thomas' behaviour).

Allied to the notion of betrayal is the issue of the sacrificial victim. In her draft synopsis for *The Death of the Heart*, Bowen says of Portia "[e]vident victim, she is also an inadvertent victimiser – most of all in the case of the young man Eddy",[30] a distinction drawn by Roy Foster who comments "[i]t annoyed Bowen that the heroine of *The Death of the Heart* was interpreted as a victim; she saw Portia as a sensationalist, a deliberate wrecker, and she approved of this." (1993, 103) There is no shortage of people who appear to be victims in the novel but, in reality, are apparently content to sacrifice their happiness for the sake of others. Matchett, for example, would appear to be a victim of the Quaynes as she subordinates all her desires to her obligations to the Quayne family and, in particular, their furniture. It is, however, Mrs. Quayne, Thomas' mother, who gives the best performance of a sacrificial victim. However, although, as Portia says to Matchett "But Matchett, she meant to do good", Matchett is only too aware of Mrs. Quayne's true nature, "No, she meant to do right" (*DH*, 78). Matchett holds a firm opinion of Mrs. Quayne's character, one she expresses to Portia when Portia suggests that Mrs. Quayne had "made such a sacrifice" (*DH*, 74), she continues:

> Sacrificers [...] are not the ones to pity. The ones to pity are those that they sacrifice. Oh, the sacrificers, they get it both ways. A person knows themselves what they're able to do without. Yes, Mrs Quayne would give the clothes off her back, but in the long run she would never lose a thing. (Ibid)

Portia, too, becomes aware that she has sacrificed people in her attempts to be with Eddie. Her thoughts about her actions echo, to a certain extent, Matchett's thoughts about "sacrificers", for Portia "saw with pity, but without reproaching herself, all the sacrificed people [...] that she had stepped over to meet Eddie. And she knew that there would be more of this, for sacrifice is not a single act." (*DH*, 107)

Such an examination of her own actions suggests that Portia is aware of her changing situation, her loss of innocence and her transition to a world of experience. It also suggests a growing aptitude for moral judgement, an understanding of what is right and wrong; it is, however, an aptitude which is still in its infancy, as Portia's diary highlights. Recording a conversation with Matchett, Portia writes "she leaned right on my bed and said, that's all very well, but are you a good girl? I said I didn't know what she meant, and she said no, that's just the trouble" (*DH*, 121). Nevertheless, Portia's exploration of her motives and the lengths that she is prepared to go to achieve her desires suggests a further avenue for discussion: can a person truly be considered innocent if he or she has no understanding of morality? Following on from this, should Eddie be considered an innocent character? Certainly Bowen perceived him in this light; she states in her draft synopsis that "Eddy, himself of an innocence less deeply corrupted than might appear, has, in his own words, been made a monkey of by the society in which he and Portia meet: he is a jaded, unwilling playboy who has taken refuge in parodying himself."[31]

Eddie's morals are certainly open to question, the way in which he conducts his life, and in particular his love affairs and his behaviour in Thomas' advertising agency, do not adhere to an acceptable moral code.

There is no doubt that his conduct of his relationships with women is often immoral, this can be particularly seen in relation to Eddie's treatment of Portia and his betrayal of her love for him. However, his casual treatment of women is, perhaps, a defence mechanism, his apparent sophistication a mask which enables him to function in society. Aware that his behaviour could be open to question, he asks Portia if he has been unkind. He attempts to qualify his own actions by suggesting that he is not consciously aware of how his behaviour is perceived,

> I may be some kind of monster; I've really got no idea ... The things I have to say seem never to have had to be said before. Is my life really so ghastly and extraordinary? I've got no way to check up. I do wish you were older; I wish you knew more. (*DH*, 281)

However, he refuses to accept full responsibility for his own actions; rather he blames society for his lack of morality, believing that he is a victim of a corrupt society. Portia's diary entry for Thursday highlights this belief, "Eddie says our lies are not our fault" (*DH*, 118). It is a belief that is reinforced by his rather belligerent discussion with Portia, in which his comments can be read as authorial comment on the prevailing circumstances in England and Europe in the latter stages of the nineteen thirties,

> [f]or you and me there ought to be a new world. Why should we be at the start of our two lives when everything around us is losing its virtue? How can we grow up when there's nothing left to inherit, when what we feed on is so stale and corrupt? (*DH*, 275)

Despite the pessimistic view of the latter end of the thirties expressed by Eddie, and the unresolved nature of the end of the novel, St. Quentin expresses a more optimistic hope for the future both for Portia and for society, whilst decrying his rôle and that of Anna and Thomas:

> This evening the pure in heart have simply got us on toast. And look at the fun she has – she lives in a world of heroes. Who are we to be sure they're as phony as we all think? If all the world's a stage, there must be some big parts. All she asks is to walk on at the same time. And how right she is really – failing the big character, better (at least, arguably) the big flop than the small neat man who has more or less come off. Not that there is, really, one neat unhaunted man. I swear that each of us keeps, battened down inside himself, a sort of lunatic giant – impossible socially, but full scale – and it's the knockings and batterings we sometimes hear in each other that keeps our intercourse from utter banality. (*DH*, 310)

It is an optimistic view perhaps shared by the narrator. Having travelled through a dark winter and a spring which is feared by some, the novel finishes on the promise of summer and of a better life to come, a summer in which "a sort of joy would open in all hearts, for summer is the height and fullness of living" (*DH*, 318). History, of course, tells a different story.

Notes

[1] See chapter three

[2] As well as Portia's name providing an indirect echo of Henry James' views on fiction, it will be seen that parallels can be drawn between *The Death of the Heart* and James' *The Awkward Age.* It should be noted, however, that Heath suggests that Bowen did not read *The Awkward Age* until the 1950s. This supposition is predicated on a comment Bowen made at the University of Wisconsin in November 1955 when she spoke about *The House in Paris* in relation to Henry James (1961, pp.74 and 165). Nonetheless, it seems rather improbable that Bowen would not have read this novel prior to 1955.

[3] See Appendix.

[4] In his overview, Gindin includes the fiction of the Auden Generation as well as that of Elizabeth Bowen, Rosamund Lehmann, J.B. Priestley and L.P. Hartley.

[5] Kirstin Bluemel utilises the term "Intermodernism" to describe the fiction of authors and artists active in the interwar, war and postwar years (focusing particularly on the 1930s, 40s and 50s) (2009a, 7) and includes the work of writers as diverse as Margery Allingham, John Betjeman, Elizabeth Bowen, Ivy Compton-Burnett, Daphne du Maurier, Henry Green, L.P. Hartley, Winifred Holtby, Rose Macauley, J.B. Priestley and many others (2009b, 208-224).

[6] The Marx Brothers' film that the Quaynes saw could have been either *A Night at the Opera* (released in 1935) or *A Day at the Races* (released in 1937) (www.marx-brothers.org). Bowen enjoyed watching comedy films (amongst many other *genre* of film) but believed that the environment in which a film was watched, and the atmosphere within the cinema which often reflected personal taste was also important – with this in mind she gives the following parenthetical advice "(Avoid, for instance, seeing the Marx Brothers in Cork city)" (Bowen, 1937, 208). Further contextualisation is given by the reference to *Parlez-Moi d'Amour*, a very popular song recorded Lucienne Boyer in 1933; the song won the first ever Acacamie du Disque Grand Prix due Disque. (www.explore-biography.com/musicians/L/ Lucienne_Boyer.html). Ironically, although the Quaynes and Portia leave the cinema early to avoid "the Rush" (*DH*, 43), Matchett highlights the speed at which Anna, in particular, lives her life. As Matchett sets off to look for Portia, she comments "It was Mrs Thomas being all in a rush" (*DH*, 315).

[7] Pillars in the form of the female figure.

[8] Despite Bowen's inclusion in Davy's book along with other such contributors as John Betjeman, Alistair Cooke, Graham Greene, Alfred Hitchcock and Alexander

Korda, one questions why Charles Davy solicited this essay from Bowen. In the "Contributors' Who's Who" in which Davy provides potted biographies of the contributors and lists their contributions to the film industry, Bowen's entry reads thus:

> BOWEN, Elizabeth. Daughter of Henry Cole Bowen, barrister-at-law, of Bowen's Court, Kildorrey, Co. Cork. Born in Dublin. Educated at Downe House. Married in 1923 Alan Charles Cameron, now Secretary to the Central Council for School Broadcasting and a Governor of the British Film Institute. Author of *The Hotel, The Last September, Friends and Relations, To the North, The House in Paris* [...] A member of the London Film Society; has done only one piece of film criticism and has no technical knowledge of the cinema. (1937, 334)

[9] See appendix.

[10] See appendix. This is, of course, a title Bowen used in a later collection of her work.

[11] See appendix. One wonders if Bowen received this advice at an early stage in her writing career and decided to recreate the conversation in an ironic discussion of the nature of writing.

[12] It is also possible to find echoes of James' Mrs. Brookenham and Mr. Longden (*The Awkward Age*) in Anna and Major Brutt.

[13] Reprinted in The Mulberry Tree.

[14] Also reprinted in *The Mulberry Tree.*

[15] The issue of "middlebrow" fiction during the 1930s was important during that time, a decade in which Q. D. Leavis' book *Fiction and the Reading Public* was published (London, 1932).

[16] It is perhaps ironic that Daphne, who dislikes reading so much, should work in a lending library where "[h]er palpable wish never to read placed at a disadvantage those who had become dependent on this habit" (*DH*, 184). The lack of interest in reading is echoed in "Reduced" (reprinted in *Collected Stories* pp.471-480) where the library is an unwelcoming room, where "no chair invited you, the uninviting books must have been bought in lots, and looked gummed in the shelves." (*CS*, 471).

[17] The issue of class, with particular reference to the perceived morality of the upper and middle classes (and of the "hotel" class), will be discussed further below.

[18] For the purposes of this book an adult is assumed to be a person over the age of majority which at the time of publication of *The Death of the Heart* was the age of 21.

[19] A further possibility might be that the young resemble the child in "The Emperor's New Clothes", speaking truths that more sophisticated people are too careful to say.

[20] With apologies to Edith Wharton.

[21] Anna's acknowledgement of her ability to corrupt echoes James' Mrs. Brookenham's confession to Mr. Mitchett that she has corrupted Nanda; speaking perhaps in an attempt to entertain, she enlarges on her theme of sacrifice and in

answer to Mr. Mitchett's implied question of whom she has sacrificed, Mrs. Brookenham states, "Of my innocent and helpless, yet somehow at the same time, as a consequence of my cynicism, dreadfully damaged and depraved daughter." (James 1899, 63)

[22] In a letter to William Plomer dated September 24th 1945 Bowen focused her acerbic wit on governesses: "I can't stick all these little middle-class Labour wets with their Old London School of Economics ties and their women. Scratch any of these cuties and you find the governess. Or so I have always found." (1999, 207).

[23] Such a description of Windsor Terrace is an echo both of Madame Fisher's house in Paris and Pendlethwaite, the Carburys' house in Bowen's short story "Reduced", a house which "looked dedicated to a perpetual January" (*CS*, 472).

[24] Blodgett states that *The Death of the Heart* draws on Christian myth and that the "three sections of the novel are purposefully titled "The World", "The Flesh" and "The Devil" in order to establish a Christian context immediately" (1975, 114)

[25] Humble suggests that the "representation of an active lower-middle-class dislike and resentment of the upper middle class is virtually unique in middlebrow women's fiction" continuing that *The Death of the Heart* is "unusually sympathetic to lower-middle-class interests" (2001, 80).

[26] "Blurb" is the term used by Bowen in her letter to William Plomer (see undated letter to William Plomer, appendix).

[27] See appendix for the full text of Bowen's draft summary of the plot of *The Death of the Heart*.

[28] St Quentin greatly admires this sentence, particularly Portia's positioning of the comma, stating "that"s style" (*DH*, 11).

[29] See letter to L.P. Hartley, 21st October 1952 (appendix).

[30] See appendix. There are two references to "Eddy" in the synopsis, a spelling which is at odds with the spelling of "Eddie" in the 1962 Penguin edition of the novel. Is it possible that she was thinking subconsciously about her friend Eddy Sackville-West at the time of writing? An alternative source for the name could have originated from family history, specifically Bowen's mother's "youngest and dearest brother" Eddy who "had gone down with the Titanic" (Bowen 1972, 48).

[31] See appendix.

CHAPTER FIVE

HALLUCINATIONS AND INNOCENT SECRETS:
THE HEAT OF THE DAY

In an opening similar to *The Death of the Heart* (albeit in a different season), *The Heat of the Day* begins with a scene in Regent's Park one evening, specifically the "Sunday on which the sun set [which] was the first Sunday of September 1942" (*HD*, 8). Whilst Bowen might have claimed in a letter to William Plomer that the plot of the novel was uncomplicated, stating "it's so straight forward; nothing about it really needs to be explained",[1] this is an opinion with which most critics would disagree. However, as with all of Bowen's novels the plot of the novel can be described succinctly and the novel could (should one so desire) be read as a wartime novel of espionage and love.

Returning to her exploration of the innocence of adults rather than children,[2] within the novel Bowen effectively weaves three different but related strands, the "action" of the novel taking place over a relatively short period of time, some two months in 1942. The first strand is that of Stella Rodney's affair with Robert Kelway, an affair which began in 1940 at the time of the Blitz during a time of "a pure and curious holiday from fear" (*HD*, 90), and the subsequent unveiling of Robert by Harrison as a spy, an unveiling which incorporates all Stella's doubts and her confusion about her own innocence or guilt. The second strand in the novel concerns the story of Louie Lewis, a Kentish orphan, living in London while her husband is fighting in India. Roderick Rodney's inheritance of Mount Morris, with its inextricable link with the death of Cousin Francis and the life of Cousin Nettie, provides the third strand. All these strands are linked through the figure of Harrison; he is present in all three stories, as a main protagonist in Stella's story and as an observer, watching from the periphery of the lives of Louie and Roderick.[3]

In 1942, whilst Britain was embroiled in the horror of the Second World War, Elizabeth Bowen started to think about the plot of her seventh novel, eventually published in 1948.[4] Interviewed by "The Bellman" for the literary journal, *The Bell*, about the importance of "place" in her fiction,

Bowen stated, "[i]n my next novel – which I haven't started writing yet, by the way, I've already seen the Place. But I won't say anything more about it except that the story takes place between London and Ireland – somewhere in County Cork – during wartime." (Bowen quoted by "The Bellman" 1942, 424)

For Bowen, "Place" provides the necessary backdrop for her discussion of innocence but whilst, undoubtedly, Bowen's notion of place is extremely important in *The Heat of the Day*, this is just one aspect of many in the novel which helps to illuminate the theme of innocence in her work. Another is the question of epistemology within the novel, with particular reference to the loss of innocence, epistemological considerations which affect both the characters' and the reader's perception of sexual and political innocence. Consideration of the representation of espionage throughout the novel is, of course, inextricably linked with issues of epistemology, as are notions of betrayal which necessarily underpin a text where authorial manipulation of time and narrative provide a further element in the reader's experience of *anagnôrisis*.

Contexts: The "rising tide of hallucination"[5]

Whilst Bowen might have written to William Plomer that she "had such a good war" (1999b, 206), she was acutely aware of the horrors experienced by many during the Second World War. Her introduction to the American edition of *The Demon Lover and Other Stories*[6] highlights some of her emotions during this time:

> In war, this feeling of slight differentiation [experienced during peace time] was suspended: I felt one with, and just like, everyone else. Sometimes I hardly knew where I stopped and everyone else began. The violent destruction of solid things, the explosion of the illusion that prestige, power and permanence attach to bulk and weight, left all of us, equally, heady and disembodied. Walls went down; and we felt, if not knew, each other. We all lived in a state of lucid abnormality. (1945c, 48)

The short stories published in this collection serve to provide a literary and thematic context for *The Heat of the Day*, helping to portray both the everyday and the emotional lives of the British people during the war. Deborah Parsons suggests that in *The Heat of the Day* Bowen "offers an extended depiction of the effects of war on the civilian psyche and the role of women in society, and combines passages of impressionistic urban representation with comment on the political and propagandist structure of war-time society", (1997, 29-30) building on the short stories contained in *The Demon Lover and Other Stories.*

Commenting that the "stories are not placed in the time-order in which they were first written" (1945c, 49),[7] Bowen believed that the collection represented "a rising tide of hallucination", adding that the "hallucinations in the stories are not a peril; nor are the stories studies of mental peril. The hallucinations are an unconscious, instinctive, saving resort on the part of the characters" (ibid). Three of the short stories published in *The Demon Lover and Other Stories*, "The Demon Lover", "The Happy Autumn Fields" and "Mysterious Kôr",[8] have a direct bearing on the literary context of *The Heat of the Day*, each one representing the "rising tide of hallucination" and the psychological fears faced by many; the fragility of the membrane between the living and the dead can be seen both in the short stories and *The Heat of the Day*.

In a passage which contains echoes of T. S. Eliot's *The Waste Land*, the narrator explores this membrane in a London where

> [...] not knowing who the dead were you could not know which might be the staircase somebody for the first time was not mounting this morning, or at which street corner the newsvendor missed a face, or which trains and buses in the homegoing rush were this evening lighter by at least one passenger.
>
> These unknown dead reproached those left living not by their own death, which might any night be shared, but by their unknowness, which could not be mended now. [...] The wall between the living and the living became less solid as the wall between the living and the dead thinned. (*HD*, 90-91)

The thinning membrane between the living and the dead is present in each of these three short stories. Phyllis Lassner suggests that "The Demon Lover" "embeds the psychological horrors produced by a Blitzed city" (1991, 64), horrors which are returned to in *The Heat of the Day*. Mrs. Drover, on her return to her bombed London home, is haunted by the thoughts of her dead fiancé, and is terrified by the sudden appearance of a letter from him reminding her of their promise to meet. The melodrama often associated with ghost stories and the gothic is present from the very beginning of this short story, where "[i]n her once familiar street, as in any unused channel, an unfamiliar queerness had silted up" (*CS*, 661), on reaching her house, "[d]ead air came out to meet her as she went in" (ibid). There are "cracks in the structure" (ibid) that can be seen to represent the cracks in Mrs. Drover's life where the past threatens to destabilise the present. Trying to rationalise the presence of the letter from her fiancé, she tells herself that all will be well if she can find a taxi before the appointed hour referred to in the letter. However, the final taxi ride becomes, for Mrs. Drover, the culmination of all her fears, and the membrane between life and death, represented by "the glass panel that divided the driver's head from her own" (ibid, 666), is seen to be fragile. Once the drawing back of the glass panel shatters this membrane, Mrs. Drover is forced to look at the driver and realise the full horror of her situation.

Whilst "The Demon Lover" evokes the psychological atmosphere felt by Bowen and many others during the Blitz, Bowen's short story "The Happy Autumn Fields" approaches this in a more subtle fashion. Manipulating time in such a way that the reader is never sure whether the past encroaches on the present, or the present causes chaos in the past, Bowen develops her use of time shifts employed in *The House in Paris* and *The Death of the Heart* not just to delay the reader's moment of *anagnôrisis* but, in fact, to deny the reader a complete understanding of the events which take place within the story. Much as Fitzgeorge "wonders, and says he will always wonder, what made the horse shy in those empty fields" (*CS*, 685) so the reader will wonder about the cause of Henrietta and Sarah's deaths, whether it is Henrietta's malevolence or Mary's ghostly presence from the future, travelling through a slip in time. Mary is obviously aware of the approach of an horrific tragedy which has impinged upon her life, through her dreams and through the contents of "a musty old leather box" (*CS*, 677) and she is anxious to send Travis away so that she can return to her dream. Yet there is doubt as to whether it is Mary that Travis is talking to, for it would appear that for a short while Henrietta and Mary are one, and whilst there is an amalgamation of their souls and bodies in the present, her desire to return to the field in the past is overriding as she is "[f]rantic at being delayed here, while the moment awaited her in the cornfield, she all but afforded a smile at the grotesquerie of being saddled with Mary's body and lover." (*CS*, 676).

The authorial manipulation used to such great effect in "The Happy Autumn Fields" is continued in *The Heat of the Day* where Bowen manipulates the narrative and thus both the characters' understanding of their lives and reader's comprehension of the text.

The third short story which places *The Heat of the Day* within its literary context in Bowen's *oeuvre* is "Mysterious Kôr" in which the "rising tide of hallucination" reaches its climax.[9] Drawing on Bowen's own reading as a child of Rider Haggard's *She*,[10] the short story narrates one evening in the lives of Pepita, Arthur, her lover, and Callie, Pepita's flat mate whose "innocence and her still unsought-out state had brought her to take a proprietary pride in Arthur" (*CS*, 732). As in many of

Bowen's novels and short stories, the location of Pepita's story is of prime importance. However, whilst her other renderings of cities, towns and houses are usually placed on a firm grounding, the London in which Pepita and Arthur wander has a more ethereal quality, an ethereality which owes its existence to the abnormally bright moon. Although the brightness of the moon suggests an extra day, a "day between days" (*CS*, 728), it is a day with negative connotations both in a literal and metaphorical sense. The sheer brilliance of the moonlight places the city at risk, negating all endeavours to ensure the blackout is effective, the threat of German bombers becoming even more frightening in the moonlit sky. The bright moon also highlights the sense of lack to be found in the city on this particular night, the narrator tells of the "now gateless gates of the park"[11], of "three French soldiers [who are] directed to a hostel they could not find" (ibid), and people in the street who disappear quickly "as though dissolved in the street by some white acid" (*CS*, 729). The only people left in this nocturnal lacuna are Pepita and Arthur, lovers with nowhere to go to consummate their love, two people who "seemed to have no destination but each other and to be not quite certain of even that" (ibid), "homeless […] in London without any hope of any place of their own" (*CS*, 731).

The moonlight provides an hallucination for Pepita; she envisages the buildings around her in terms of her perceptions of Rider Haggard's Kôr, "a completely forsaken city, as high as cliffs and white as bones" (ibid). The moon has a similarly hallucinatory effect on her flat-mate Callie. Waiting in their flat for Arthur and Pepita to arrive, "she knew that something was happening – outdoors, in the street, the whole of London, the world. An advance, an extra-ordinary movement was silently talking place; blue-white beams overflowed from it, silting, dropping round the edges of the muffling black-out curtains." (*CS*, pp.734-735). Callie is transported by the vision of something in the street—"was it a coin or a ring?" (ibid)—to her parents' drawing-room. However, the effect of the moon is by no means benign, its malignancy suggested by the blanching of Callie's hand as it lies in the moonlight and Arthur's reaction to Pepita's vision of London as Kôr. As he says to Callie later that night, "I could have sworn she saw it, and from the way she saw it, I saw it, too. A game's a game but what's a hallucination. You begin by laughing, then it gets in you and you can't laugh it off" (*CS*, 738).

Bowen's retrospective preface for the American edition of *The Demon Lover and Other Stories* helps to place these three short stories and *The Heat of the Day* in relation to each other. Suggesting that she would not have been able to write the novel which later became *The Heat of the Day*, had she not also been able to write the short stories,[12] she states,

[d]uring the war I lived, both as a civilian and as a writer, with every pore open; I lived so many lives, and, still more, lived among the packed repercussions of so many thousands of other lives, all under stress, that I see now it would have been impossible to have been writing only one book. I want my novel, which deals with this same time, to be comprehensive. But a novel must have form; and, for the form's sake, one is always having to make relentless exclusions. Had it not been for my from-time-to-time promises to write stories, much that had been pressing against the door might have remained pressing against the door in vain. (1945c, 47-48)

Autobiographical and Historical Contexts

Whilst the short stories provide the literary context for *The Heat of the Day*, living "with every pore open" gave Bowen an empathy and sympathy for the suffering of many who lived through the Second World War, and her own experiences added colour to the narration of *The Heat of the Day*. Her essay "London, 1940" highlights the emotions felt by many Londoners following a night of heavy bombing, when the living go about their daily business, trying stoically to see a lighter side to life where "everyone laughs" after a bomb has gone off. This particular night had "been a dirty night. The side has been ripped off one near block – the open gash is nothing but dusty, colourless. (As bodies shed blood, buildings shed mousey dust.)" (c.1950, 217-218). Bowen continues:

> It is a fine morning and we are still alive.
>
> This is the buoyant view of it—the theatrical sense of safety, the steady breath drawn. We shall be due, at to-night's siren, to feel our hearts once more tighten and sink. Soon after black-out we keep that date with fear. The howling ramping over the darkness, the lurch of the barrage opening, the obscure throb in the air […] these nights in September nowhere is pleasant. Where you stay is your own choice, how you feel is your fight.
>
> However many people have crowded together, each has, while air whistles and solids rock, his or her accesses of solitude. (Ibid, 218-219)[13]

These feelings of solitude led many, including Bowen and the fictional Stella Rodney, to find company in the arms of others; the dedication of *The Heat of the Day*, which reads simply "To Charles Ritchie", hints at the extraordinary friendship between Bowen and Ritchie, a Canadian diplomat. Of all of her extra-marital affairs it was probably this relationship which was the most important to her; it was certainly the longest relationship of her life. Meeting in February 1941 at the christening of John Buchan's granddaughter, Perdita (Glendinning 1997,

134), they remained close friends until Bowen's death in 1973. Seven years younger than Bowen, Ritchie is described as "clever, gay and gallant, with a love of talk and a "sensuous perception" " (ibid, 138). Ritchie's diary, *The Siren Years*, which covers the years between 1937 and 1945, provides a great deal of information about Bowen, albeit from an increasingly biased observer who became necessarily more subjective as their affair continued. In his diary Ritchie describes their first encounter: "[m]et Elizabeth Bowen, well-dressed, intelligent handsome face, watchful eyes. I had expected someone more Irish, more silent and brooding and at the same time more irresponsible. I was slightly surprised at her being so much 'on the spot' ". (1974, 88)

His entry for 2nd September 1941 reads, "without having read a word of her writing would not one have felt that something mysterious, passionate and poetic was behind that worldly experience?" (ibid, 115-116). A later entry, dated 29th September 1941, is even more expressive, suggesting that within Bowen's writing,

> there are certain passages in which her peculiar intensity, her genius comes out, which would be hard to reconcile with this cultivated hostess. That purity of perception and compassion seem to come from another part of her nature of which she is not aware." (ibid, 117-118)[14]

Whilst Bowen's continuing relationship with Ritchie might well provide an element of autobiographical context (in particular the age difference between Stella and Robert Kelway),[15] her wartime activities provide further contextualisation. For example, her rôle as an ARP warden gave Bowen the knowledge to write about Connie's work, and Bowen's perambulation of London during her working day gave her a greater insight into the lives of other Londoners, people that would otherwise have remained outside her circle of acquaintances and friends.[16] Further, Bowen's own work in providing information on Eire to the Ministry of Information, reports which are regarded by some as an act of disloyalty, also enables a reading of *The Heat of the Day* which examines notions of espionage and betrayal within the context of Bowen's activities. In his introduction to the 1998 edition of *The Heat of the Day*, Roy Foster states "[f]amously, this is a novel about the war, spying and London" (1998, 1), an opinion with which Jenny Hartley finds accord. She notes, "[s]pying has always offered rich pickings to the novelist, with its stories of surveillance and allegiance, complicity and guilt, divided loyalties and double lives. These plots and preoccupations come together in Elizabeth Bowen's *The Heat of the Day*, one of the greatest novels of the war". (1997, 88) As Hepburn suggests, although "Bowen's knowledge of thrillers is circumstantial", her friendship with John Buchan (author of *The Thirty Nine Steps*) gave her an entrée into a world of fictional espionage, as did her enjoyment of Graham Greene's novels such as *Brighton Rock* and *The Third Man* (2005, 136-137).

Opinion differs as to the precise nature of Bowen's rôle in the gathering of information during the war, her activities being variously described as those of a "strong defender of neutrality, and an acute observer of the Irish mentality during the early 1940s" (Foster 1993, 110) or else as a betrayal of her Irish antecedents, a stance taken in a polemical attack by the Aubane Historical Society in 1999. In his introduction to this, Jack Lane states baldly that during the war, "Bowen spied on Ireland for England. That fact, more than any other, shows where her loyalties lay [...] It was the war clouds which caused Elizabeth Bowen to polish up her Irish credentials, as a means of furthering her cover for espionage." (1999a, 7)[17]

However, Bowen's reports on Irish neutrality were warmly received by Lord Cranbourne[18] who, writing to the Secretary of State for Foreign Affairs about her report of November 1940, commended her accounts as "very sensible and well balanced. The present report also strikes one as a shrewd appreciation of the position" (Cranbourne, quoted in Lane 1999a, 10). Robert Fisk describes her "astute" reports in equally glowing terms, her "gentle, sensitive dispatches from Eire are still a delight to read, a pen portrait of a nation and its people desperate to avoid involvement in a war that was not of its making" (1983, 355).

Bowen's reports provided background information for the British on the increasing fragility of the neutrality of Eire where relationships between the two countries were in an extremely delicate state following the withdrawal of British troops from the garrisons at Cobh, Berehaven and Lough Swilly in 1938 (ibid, 6) for, despite the stated neutrality, Eire was often seen to be treating Germany more favourably than Britain.[19] The neutrality of Eire was not universally welcomed, particularly by the Anglo-Irish: their attitude is explored by Bowen in her characterisation of Cousin Francis, owner of Mount Morris, who comes to London specifically to see if he can contribute to the war effort, visiting his wife at Wisteria Lodge merely as an afterthought and, rather ironically, dying on the premises.[20]

According to Sean O'Faolain, writing in *The Bell* in 1942,[21] the departure of British Troops from the three garrisons caused considerable economic problems in those particular areas (1942, 382), financial difficulties that were exacerbated by the onset of war and which were felt throughout Eire. Thousands of evacuees arrived from Britain, eighty per cent of whom were Irish citizens but there were also a significant number of British escaping conscription, some Germans and eighteen Jews (Fisk: 1983, 90). Following the British restrictions on shipping to Eire, considerably cutting levels of imports, rationing, which had already been introduced, became harsher.[22] The privations of the Irish were not necessarily well known in Britain; Stella Rodney, for example, "had assumed there to be no shortages of any kind in Eire" (*HD*, 167). This was, of course, a false assumption: "[u]p here in her bedroom, down there in the library, she was burning up light supplies for months ahead. Well on into the winter after Stella's departure [from Mount Morris] the Donovan family went to bed in the dark" (*HD*, 168).

However one would wish to interpret Bowen's actions and her reports on the neutrality of Eire during the war, whether as compatriot or betrayer, the deception required on Bowen's part provided her with an understanding of the double life led by those engaged in espionage, her experiences helping in the construction of the character of Robert Kelway and the multiplicity of the espionage activities contained within *The Heat of the Day* where Kelway spies for Nazi Germany, Harrison spies on Kelway and Stella also effectively spies on Kelway. As Maud Ellmann succinctly comments "[c]aught in these (Jamesian) wheels of surveillance – watching the watched watch the watchers – Stella has no choice but to become a spy" (2003, 3). Kelway's betrayal leads to the duplicitous behaviour of Stella; despite her work for "an organisation better called Y.X.D., in secret, exacting, not unimportant work" (*HD*, 26), it is a duplicitiousness with which she is not comfortable.

Knowledge, Betrayal, Identity and Loss of Innocence

A discussion of the multivalency of innocence in *The Heat of the* Day is necessarily complex as themes of knowledge, betrayal and identity are inextricably linked with notions of political and sexual innocence. For example, Kelway's sense of his own lack of identity leads him to betray both his country and Stella. Conversely, Harrison's espionage and betrayal of others, albeit ostensibly in the defence of his country, forces him to become rootless; when asked by Stella where he lives, where he keeps his razor, Harrison replies "in an absent tone" that he has "two or three razors" (*HD*, 140).

Louie Lewis's apparent lack of innocence and sexual morality arises from her own lack of self-knowledge, her desire for an identity fuelling her assiduous reading of newspapers. Equally, Stella's behaviour, her life as a sophisticated, experienced woman, is predicated on an unspoken accusation of guilt, an accusation which effectively provides her with a false identity and which culminates in the betrayal of her love for Kelway. Notions of loss of innocence in *The Heat of the Day* should be seen through four interrelated areas: identity, sexuality, betrayal, and knowledge.

Identity and Place

Christensen suggests that the concept of identity is a major theme in Bowen's fiction, particularly in her post-war fiction (2001, 37) and, as in Bowen's earlier novels, the sense of place in *The Heat of the Day* provides more than just a geographical location for the narration, her houses often serving as characterisations of their inhabitants, highlighting both the construction of identity and its lack. Whereas Mount Morris will, in the future, provide Roderick with a sense of identity, the depiction of Holme Dene, Kelway's family home, serves to highlight Kelway's lack of any sense of belonging. Ernestine Kelway's insistence that Holme Dene, "though antique in appearance, was not actually old [...] The oak beams, to be perfectly honest, were imitations" (*HD*, 115) provides an intimation that the house, and, by association, some members of the family, are not to be trusted.

In her portrayal of this country house, Bowen is writing against the tradition of Georgian pastoral and therefore highlights the deception inherent in the architecture, a deception which can also be read into Kelway's wartime activities. The pastoral tradition would suggest that a country house should be read as a paradigm for "Britishness", representing an Edenic, traditional, conservative way of life;[23] in contrast Holme Dene with its "CONCEALED ENTRANCE" (*HD*, 105), "betrayed garden" (*HD*, 121) mock beams, perennial unstable existence as a home, always on the market for sale, with its "swastika-arms of passage leading to nothing" (*HD*, 258) does not provide the sense of place needed by Kelway. When attempting to justify his espionage to Stella, Kelway suggests that Britain has "sold itself out" (*HD*, 268); his family life has provided him with an image of his country which he is unwilling to accept, it is a life which has not cured his ills nor, in his eyes, the ills of the country. Kelway claims

> [...] I was born wounded; my father's son. Dunkirk was waiting there in us – what a race! A class without a middle, a race without a country. Unwhole. Never earthed in – and there are thousands of us, and we're still breeding – breeding what? You may ask: I ask. Not only nothing to hold, nothing to touch. No source of anything in anything. (*HD*, 272-273)

Kelway believes that his treason has provided him with an identity which he was unable to gain from his father, his family life or his country, as he says to Stella, it "bred my father out of me, gave me a new heredity" (*HD*, 273). Had Kelway's father succeeded in buying Fair Leigh, the house on which he had set his heart before he bought Holme Dene (*HD*, 120), Kelway might perhaps have felt that life had treated him less harshly, more "fairly", and he may have found the roots which he so desired, and thus avoided the descent into betrayal, a betrayal which is not passive, rather, as Hepburn states is "in the active, Quisling manner of selling secrets" (2005, 141).

Issues of identity are at the forefront of the narrative of *The Heat of the Day*, with frequent references to its lack, and whilst it has been argued in this book that knowledge of one's own identity is important if one is to move from a childlike existence to one of experience, Kelway's lack of heredity, of identity, has more sinister connotations. Kelway's inability and unwillingness to acknowledge the truth of his own identity has left him in limbo; no longer an innocent, he turns to a life of deception and betrayal.

Whilst he might suggest that Stella is "making no impression at all" on his family (*HD*, 116), Kelway's apparent lack of substance is foregrounded by his physical appearance which is noted by Stella one October morning when she "woke to the apprehension of loss" (*HD*, 97). Travelling with Kelway to a restaurant to which she has not been before, although

> its name [was] familiar in so many stories, [it] had come to seem to be over the borderline of fiction – so much so that, making her way thither, she felt herself to be going to a rendezvous inside the pages of a book. And was, indeed, Robert himself fictitious? (ibid)

The possibility of Kelway's fictitiousness is enhanced by Stella's internal monologue in which she tries to substantiate his physical appearance; it is a monologue which highlights the thinning membrane between the living and dead explored in Bowen's short stories,

> [h]ere was the face of before she opened her eyes. Its fairness, not quite pallor, had a sort of undertone of exhausted sunburn. To this impressionistic look of alightness, hair, eyebrows gave almost nothing darker, and there was no moustache; the face had only accents of shadow [...] In the unfamiliar the familiar persisted like a ghost (*HD*, 98).

It is, however, not just in London that Kelway's identity seems to lack substance, its lack is also apparent at Holme Dene. Much as Louie Lewis constructs herself whilst reading the newspapers, Kelway's identity is apparently constructed by both the photographic montage and contents of his room which appear as a shrine to his childhood; the "[g]lass cases of coins, birds' eggs, fossils, and butterflies that he must once have fancied or been supposed to fancy" and the collection of some "sixty or seventy photographs" (*HD*, 116) attest to an apparently idyllic Edenic childhood and adolescence. However, these images are at odds with Stella's second glance around the room when she notices a "narrow glacial bed, which, ends and all, had been draped in a starched white cover" (*HD*, 117), a vision which, in this instance, suggests death; it is a room which, despite its contents, Stella feels to be empty. Robert does not disagree with this, stating, "It could not feel emptier than it is. Each time I come back again into it I'm hit in the face by the feeling that I don't exist – that I not only am not but never have been" (ibid).

Thus Robert is aware that his character, his identity, lacks substance; the photographs on the wall, which should represent his childhood, in fact create a false image of his early years and he suggests that the photographs capture moments in his life which are mere "imitations", a "pack of lies" (*HD*, 118). However, Ernestine's statement that the photographs "in their own way recall the past" (*HD*, 124) suggests that, whilst the photographs may well capture an imitation of life, they accurately portray the lack of identity and heredity as experienced by Kelway.

In contrast, Roderick acknowledges that he needs to acquire self-knowledge before he can truly enter into a world of experience and is very aware that he will have to search for this element in his character for, "[h]e searched in Stella for some identity left by him in her keeping. It was a search undertaken principally for her sake. Only she made him conscious of loss or change" (*HD*, 48). Whereas Kelway's belief that he has no heredity, that he cannot identify himself with his country, leads him to betrayal, by acknowledging that he has yet to make this journey and recognising that there is an element of his character and understanding that is yet to be formed, Roderick is able to continue to fight for his country.

Louie's lack of identity and self-knowledge arises, arguably, from the loss of her parents and her family home. Her perceptions of innocence are very much bound up in knowledge, in particular a lack of knowledge of her own identity and an understanding of Stella's virtue. A "child of Kent" (*HD*, 16) who later moved to Seale-on-Sea with her parents, she has been orphaned and abandoned by the war, surviving unhappily on her own while her husband fights in India, feeling isolated in London, "like a day tripper who has missed the last night train home" (*HD*, 145). In her unhappiness and loneliness, Louie is eager to strike up conversations with anyone who will talk to her even, as on that afternoon in Regent's Park, with those who are unwilling to talk, such as Harrison. Having been displaced by the war, Louie has no rôle model and desperately seeks someone against whom she can measure herself,

> [h]er object was to feel that she, Louie, *was*, and in the main she did not look willingly at what might have been said or done in pursuit of that ... Left to herself, thrown back on herself in London, she looked about her in vain for someone to imitate; she was ready, nay eager, to attach herself to anyone who would seem to be following any one course with certainty (ibid, 15).

It is not until she meets Connie, an ARP warden with fixed notions of what is right and wrong, that she is able to identify with a rôle model and, through Connie's collection of newspapers, Louie is able to begin to construct herself in the rôle which she believes is right for her.

Connie, however, despite her Herculean efforts to acquire newspapers without payment, is suspicious of all that she reads in them, looking behind the pictures and the propagandist attitudes of many of the newspapers published during World War Two, thus echoing the suspicious nature and cynicism of Harrison. Louie starts to imitate Connie's quest for newsprint, at first trying to follow the stories. However, "[o]nce Louie had taken to newspapers she found peace" (ibid, 151); she begins to construct herself from the stories for,

> Louie, after a week or two on the diet, discovered that she *had* got a point of view, and not only a point of view but the right one. Not only did she bask in warmth and inclusion but every morning she was praised ... Dark and rare were the days when she failed to find on the inside page of her paper an address to or else account of herself. Was she not a worker, a soldier's lonely wife, a war orphan, a pedestrian, a Londoner, a home- and animal-lover, a thinking democrat, a movie-goer, a woman of Britain, a letter writer, a fuel-saver and a housewife? (ibid, 152)

Thus Louie, in her innocence, constructs herself by reading newspapers, which provide an identity and a sense of belonging which has been missing from her life. Whilst the question of Louie's innocence is based on her lack of self-knowledge, it is a lack which is contributed to by her inability to construct herself without the questionable editorial content of the newspapers she reads. This lack, in Lacanian terms, keeps Louie in the imaginary stage. A child or person cannot enter the symbolic stage until they have acquired the necessary language tools for such a progression but, as the narrator states:

> [i]t was the blanks in Louie's vocabulary which operated inwardly on her soul; most strongly she felt the undertow of what she could not name. Humble and ambiguous, she was as unable to name virtue as she had been, until that sudden view of Harrison's companion, to envisage it. (*HD*, 306)

Louie's return to Seale-on-Sea, away from the temptations of London, allows her to remain in the Lacanian imaginary stage; arguably, despite her age, she never enters the symbolic stage and a meaningful existence within the world of experience and adulthood.

As Kelway is defined, in part, by his family home, Stella's flat acts as a personification of her character; initially she is presented by the narrator as transient, superficial and artificial, living in a rented flat with rented furniture, a person with no apparent roots. It could be argued, however, that Stella's sense of identity was, in fact, stolen from her, much as the false accusation of adultery stole her good name. Forced from Mount Morris as a young woman, Stella has to leave the ancestral home which belonged to her husband's family; her return to Ireland provides some clarity for her:

> [n]ow she seemed to perceive on all sides round her, and with a phantasmogoric clearness, everything that for the eye the darkness hid. The declivities in the treads of the staircase, the rounded glimmer of its Venetian window (ever wholly extinguished only by blackest night), the creak of the lobby flooring under the foot, and the sifted near-and-farness of smells of plaster, pelts, wax, smoke, weathered woodwork, oiled locks and outdoor trees preceded themselves in her as she followed Mary. Knowledge of all this must have been carried in her throughout the years which in these minutes fell away (*HD*, 166)

However, Stella is aware that it is impossible to return to the Edenic existence promised by Mount Morris, as the path that she has taken has shaped her life irrevocably, "her gloves, shaped by her hands, her bag, containing every damning proof of her identity, were still, always, there on the centre table where she had put them down" (*HD*, 164). Of course, Mount Morris is not necessarily a benign house; Cousin Nettie, "pressed back, hour by hour, by the hours themselves, into cloudland" (*HD*, 174), has to seek refuge at Wisteria Lodge in order to escape the obligations of both the house and marriage to Cousin Francis.

Whilst Kelway, Roderick, Stella and Louie may well be confused as to their own identities for differing reasons, authorial manipulation adds to the confusion a reader might experience over the physical identity of the characters. Although neither Stella, nor the reader, is initially aware that Harrison and Kelway share the same first name, a retrospective reading of the novel suggests that the two men could be read as being both binary opposites or two halves of the same person. Indeed, following Kelway's confession of his guilt to Stella, "[i]t seemed to her it was Robert who had been the Harrison" (*HD*, 275).

The naming of Roderick Rodney, with its alliteration, adds to this narratorial confusion, a confusion which is felt by Colonel Pole as he refers to Roderick as Robert, a mistake which could be read as a "Freudian slip". Whilst there are no overt Oedipal overtones in the novel, this confusion suggests a jealousy on the part of Roderick of his mother's relationship with Kelway. However, whereas Roderick's alliterative name and similarity to the name of Stella's lover might well provoke a Freudian reading of the novel, Louie's name has different connotations. Her name sounds as a repetition, the androgynous nature of the name "Louie" adding, perhaps, to the reader's perception of her lack of sexual experience and, it could be argued, her ultimate lack of desire for the relentless parade of servicemen. That her identity is really only conferred on Louie when she becomes a mother, rather than a lover, adds to the notion of her asexuality.

Sexual Innocence

Consideration of Louie's innocence presents a dichotomy; although married and therefore possessing, one would presume, a certain amount of sexual experience, it is her naivety which leads others to question her sexual innocence, particularly given her predilection for servicemen. At a time when "it came to be rumoured about the country, among the self-banished, the uneasy, the put-upon and the safe, that everybody in London was in love", (*HD*, 94-95), in a place where the "very temper of pleasures lay in their chanciness, in the canvas-like impermanence of their settings" (*HD*, 94), Louie tries to fill up her lonely days with work, the cinema and walks in the park, usually in the company of a steady, but varying, flow of servicemen.

The narrator states that "it was a phenomenon of war-time city night that it brought out something provocative in the step of most modest women. Nature tapped out with the heels on the pavement an illicit semaphore" (*HD*, 145). However, although her behaviour could be construed as immoral, Louie apparently retains her innocence, naïvely taking servicemen to places that she visited with her husband, Tom, before the war, and in particular, to a certain part of Regent's Park for "[t]o this spot, to which Tom had been so much attached, a sort of piety made her bring any other man: she had thus the sense of living their Sundays for him" (*HD*, 18). The unnamed serviceman on the afternoon of the concert, applying a double standard to her behaviour in comparison to his own, is cross with Louie when she rejects his sexual overtures: "You make me sick […] Starting off by saying you were lonely. Wasting my afternoon." (*HD*, 19)

As Louie wryly thinks, whilst listening to the concert later that afternoon, "all men [seemed] to be one way funny like Tom – no sooner were their lips unstuck from your own than they began again to utter morality" (*HD*, 17). The narrator in *The Death of the Heart* tells us that the innocent "exist alone; when they try to enter into relations they compromise falsifyingly – through anxiety, through desire to impart and to feel warmth. The system of our affections is too corrupt for them" (*DH*, 106), and this is particularly apposite when one considers Louie. Her main desire is to "feel warmth"; starved of affection because of the death of her parents and the absence of Tom, her desire to fill this emotional lacuna leads to misunderstanding and condemnation.

Louie's faith in respectability and virtue, and her trust in Stella, is shattered when Louie reads accounts of Robert Kelway's inquest. The knowledge that Stella is not the person that she thought, that Stella "had other men friends; there had nearly been a fight […] there was no refinement" (*HD*, 306) provides a moment of *anagnôrisis* for Louie:

> For Louie, subsidence came about through her now knowing Stella not to be virtuous. Virtue became less possible now it was shown impossible by Stella, less to be desired because Stella had not desired it enough. Why Louie should have attached her own floating wish to be a face watched for an hour cannot be said: there must be faces which attract aspiration just as others focus sensuous dreams – what else had happened originally in the case of Harrison? Louie had felt herself to be in a presence. For her, therefore, now it was Stella who had fallen into the street. (*HD*, 305-306)

Louie's reading of Stella's evidence during the inquest into Kelway's death has proved to be a "crack across the crust of life", a moment of recognition, which might thrust Louie from her world of innocence and ignorance. Ironically though, it is her rejection of her former life and her apparent imitation of Stella's lifestyle that allows her to return to a form of Eden, represented by Seale-on-Sea with her son. These are "the long term effects on Louie of Stella's fall from grace" (*HD*, 307). It is her own fall from grace into pregnancy which provides Louie with a *raison d'être*, as the war ends and travel becomes easier, to return to Seale-on-Sea "an orderly mother" (*HD*, 329), having found her own rôle in life, that of a mother of a son (named Thomas Victor) who will, in his own innocent state, love her unquestioningly and unconditionally. Having found this rôle and the knowledge of who she is, Louie is able to attempt to recapture her own "virginal inner dream" (*HD*, 8).

Her confusion about Stella's virtue is shared by the reader. Through the narratorial manipulations within the novel, the reader first perceives Stella as a true representative of those living in London during the war, living life to the full in a hedonistic society in which neither the past nor the future are considered. According to the newspaper reports of Robert Kelway's inquest that Louie reads, she is also a woman who leads an immoral life; "[s]he had not been too good. Here, and not in one paper only, was where it said about her, the bottles, the lover, the luxury West-End flat. She had had other men friends; there had nearly been a fight" (*HD*, 306). Stella's physical appearance however belies this account of superficiality and artifice. Whereas Louie's naturalness (which could be associated with childlike innocence) is apparent in "the profuse softness of hair on her bare legs [which] showed these to have been never pumiced or shaved" (*HD*, 11), Stella's physical naturalness highlights the dichotomy which is present both in her own, and the reader's, perception of her innocence; a dichotomy which is apparent in her hair, for "[n]ature had kindly given her one white dash, lock or wing in her hair; and that white wing, springing back from her forehead, looked in the desired sense artificial" (*HD*, 25). This suggests that one should not take Stella's apparent guilt at face value, that although her hair appears dyed, this results from nature rather than artifice. However, as the narrator states, Stella "was not wholly admirable; but who is?" (*HD*, 26). There is therefore narratorial ambiguity, and a binary opposition is established between naturalness and artificiality, innocence and guilt.

The perception of Stella's guilt is based on the falsehood that it was she who was the guilty party in the break up of her marriage and she allows Roderick, Harrison and others to believe in this deception. Many of her husband's family and friends in Ireland also believe in Stella's guilt although Colonel Pole, a friend of Cousin Francis and attendee at his funeral, is not so certain for "[h]e dared not decide whether [Stella's] eyes, with their misted askance look, were those of the victim or of the *femme fatale*" (*HD*, .83). Through Colonel Pole, the narrator relates one version of Stella's story which suggests that, after two years of marriage, Stella asked her husband, Victor, for a divorce. Contemporary rumour suggested that Stella wanted to live with another man and Victor "quixotic to the last" (ibid), had granted her a divorce. In the eyes of the family in Ireland, Stella was "ever detestable […] Her worthlessness had lost [Victor] wife, son and home" (ibid). Victor's apparent innocence remains with him even after his death which occurs soon after the decree absolute is granted.

This account of the events is, however, at odds with the explanation given to Roderick by Cousin Nettie, when she tells Roderick that it was Victor who asked for a divorce so that he could live with the woman who nursed him back to health after the 1914-18 war. Despite her lack of guilt, Stella has persisted in promulgating the lie because of her desire not be considered naïve. As she tells Harrison in the café, whilst she believed herself to be in love with Victor, Victor told Stella that if she "imagined [she] loved him […] that was simply proof that [she] had not, as he'd for some time suspected, the remotest conception what love was" (*HD*, 223), that he had given her "a very fair trial" (ibid). In her innocence and youth, and in an attempt to salvage some pride, Stella decides not to fight the accusation of guilt. As she asks Harrison, "[w]ho, at the age I was, would not rather sound a monster than look a fool?" (*HD*, 224). Shunned by those connected with Mount Morris, the family home later inherited by Roderick, Stella subsequently builds her life on this premise of guilt. It therefore causes Stella considerable distress when Cousin Nettie tells Roderick the truth, as she tells Harrison:

'[…] Cousin Nettie talked – she told him I'd been the innocent party.'
'Surely,' said Harrison blankly, 'That's always rather to the good, on the whole, useful? But innocent party when?'
'Years and years ago,' she said impatiently, 'in the divorce. You know all about that, you've got my dossier. Yes, I divorced Victor, I was officially innocent. But nobody for an instant supposed I was.' (*HD*, 222)

Although in the eyes of many Stella is guilty of adultery and sexual impropriety, her reaction to Harrison's blackmail attempt belies this assumption. Initially Stella is unwilling to believe Harrison's allegations about Robert Kelway, seeing them merely as a device to blackmail her into an affair. Her disbelief and further interrogation of Harrison raises issues of both morality and epistemology. Having laid his plan before her, Harrison asks Stella if she understands she replies "Perfectly. I'm to form a disagreeable association in order that a man be left free to go on selling his country." (*HD*, 36)

Knowledge, Secrets and Betrayal

Whilst Louie may well naively believe that she knows and speaks "the truth every time" (*HD*, 13), Stella can be seen to be on an epistemological journey as she accepts the truth of her own past and seeks to discover the truth about Kelway's betrayal of his country. As discussed in the introduction to this book, epistemological theory can be condensed into three main questions—what is knowledge, what can we know and how do we know what we do know—questions which are of paramount importance throughout the novel, for as Connie states, "we must live and learn" (*HD*, 155). However, the novel highlights the difficulties of being certain that what one knows is true, a question voiced by Kelway when he asks Stella "[h]ow do you expect me to know what's true?" (*HD*, 191). Roderick, in his naivety, might well assume that if one knows a person well, all secrets are known, nothing about them is a surprise,

> ' [...] If I properly knew the person I'd already know the thing – I should imagine. If I knew what I was told was true, it would not be news to me. If it was both news to me and then did turn out to be true, I suppose I should take it that after all you never had properly known the person.' (*HD*, 64)

Harrison, too, has a surprisingly similar approach to the truth, believing that things are "either downright impossible or [...] a fact" (*HD*, 131). He suggests that Stella's inability to see his point of view is a fault of her gender, however, it could be argued that this arises from her own situation and her awareness that situations can be read in different ways.

Whilst Louie's state of innocence is, of course, an important element in *The Heat of the Day*, it is, perhaps, the narrator's construction of Stella's innocence upon which the discussion of the epistemological elements of the novel turns. The main question to be asked, of course, is how does one know the truth. Although Roderick might suspect that Cousin Nettie has a "*malade imaginaire*" (*HD*, 215), she provides the *caveat* for anyone who presumes they know the truth as she asks, "[b]ut what story *is* true?" (*HD*, 215). This is particularly apposite in relation to Stella, both with regard to her own innocence (or lack of it) and the guilt of her lover, Robert Kelway. Frederick Karl's statement that "the novel [...] works on a double plot in which Stella's activities find duplication in those of Louie Lewis" (1964, 126) gives weight to any argument suggesting that Stella should be considered as retaining a certain amount of innocence or, rather, that she should not be considered the guilty party.

Louie's acquisition of knowledge, her epistemological journey, is predicated on other people's perceptions of her and the opinion pages in the popular press. She appears as a blank canvas at the beginning of the novel but arguably never entirely acquires self-knowledge, her acquisition of peace in Seale-on-Sea apparently due to her newly constructed rôle as a mother. In contrast, Stella's acquisition of knowledge arrives from an acceptance of her own innocence. Bowen's manipulation of the reader, however, delays the instance of *anagnôrisis*, the moment of recognition, for both the reader and Stella. Thus the narratorial and epistemological considerations of the novel are bound together as the reader and Stella seek the truth both in relation to Stella's innocence and the question of Kelway's guilt.

Stella's entire adult life has been predicated on a deception that was practised on her when she was young, naïve and innocent. However, a further dichotomy in her character emerges from this deception, for whilst Stella's predominant motive for being a party to this duplicitous arrangement may well have been a form of self-protection, it can be argued that her intent was, in fact, altruistic in the apparent exoneration of Victor and, by continuing with the deception, she allows Roderick to believe in his father's innocence. The deception has far-reaching consequences, not least in her feelings of detachment and rootlessness. However, this emotional vacuum is shared by many who live in London during the Blitz where "life-stories were shed as so much superfluous weight" (*HD*, 95)

It is within this vacuum that Stella and Kelway meet, and it is both a metaphorical and a literal vacuum for, at the time of their meeting, a bomb detonates nearby:

> It was the demolition of an entire moment: he and she stood at attention until the glissade stopped. What they *had* both been saying, or been on the point of saying, neither of them ever now were to know. Most first words have the nature of being trifling; theirs from having been lost began to have the significance of a lost clue. What they next said, what they said instead, they forgot: there are questions which if not asked at the start are not asked later; so those they never did ask. (*HD*, 96)

Stella, it should be noted, "never had asked much, from dislike of being in turn asked" (*HD*, 26) and although this trait suggests that Stella would prefer not to explain herself to others, it is a characteristic which would have found favour during wartime with the Government's instruction to avoid gossip as "careless talk costs lives". Stella's desire not to know, not to notice, highlights her reluctance to travel on her own epistemological journey and, whilst Kelway becomes "a habitat" (*HD*, 90) for Stella, an oasis of calm in the horror of the London Blitz, providing her

with feelings of safety, nevertheless she remains reluctant to ask questions.
As their relationship progresses,

> [h]is experiences and hers became harder and harder to tell apart;
> everything gathered behind them into a common memory – though singly
> each of them might, must, exist, decide, act; all things done alone came to
> be no more than simulacra of behaviour: they waited to live again till they
> were together, then took living up from where they had left off. Then their
> doubled awareness, their interlocking feeling acting on, intensified what
> was round them – nothing they saw, knew, or told one another remained
> trifling; everything came to be woven into the continuous narrative of love;
> which, just as much, kept gaining substance, shadow, consistency from the
> imperfectly known and the not said. For naturally they did not tell one
> another everything. Every love has a poetic relevance of its own; each love
> brings to light only what is to it relevant. Outside lies the junk-yard of what
> does not matter. (*HD*, 99)

According to Harrison, Kelway's "junk-yard" consists of his spying
activities for Germany. Through Stella's reluctance to question others for
fear of having to reciprocate and provide answers about her own past, it is
possible for Harrison to sow the seeds of doubt as to Kelway's patriotism.
In their discussion of Kelway's guilt or innocence and following
Harrison's admonition that she should not warn him about the investigation,
Stella questions the nature of knowledge asking "[w]ho is to know – still
more, how would anyone know?" (*HD*, 37)

Stella in fact questions the very concept of knowledge and raises the
issue of how a person can truly "know" something. Although some time
elapses following Harrison's accusation, Stella remains reluctant to
uncover the truth. Before approaching Kelway, she feels she must
determine the veracity of Harrison's accusations but she delays this
examination, and her interior monologue is an attempt to clarify the
situation. Arguing that it is a question she could only safely ask of the
deceased Cousin Francis:

> She understood, with a shock, that here was a question she would be
> prepared to put to the dead only – why? Because the answer could mean
> too much. She had not yet, in London, made one move towards checking
> up on Harrison. *Was* he what he had made himself out to be? Was he in a
> position to know what he said he knew, to act as he told her he could? She
> could have come at all three answers: what evasion to tell herself she could
> not! She was not, as she had indeed told Harrison, a woman who did not
> know where to go; these late years she had lived at the edge of a clique of
> war, knowing who should know what, commanding a sort of language in
> which nothing need be ever exactly said. Now she looked back at that

Sunday – how many weeks ago? – when Harrison had come to her with the story. 'Who are you, to know?' she had in so many words said (*HD*, 171-172).

It could be suggested that Stella has an evasive attitude to the truth, particularly when the truth is buried. Discussing the implications of the truth being revealed, she tells Harrison that to "dig up somebody else's truth for them would seem to me sheer malignancy; to dig up one's own, madness" (*HD*, 229).[24]

As Harrison protests that his accusations against Kelway can be proved, Stella turns on him, saying that she would sooner believe Kelway than Harrison. Nevertheless, Harrison has sown a seed of doubt in Stella's mind, and this doubt then colours her relationship with Kelway. Returning from Holme Dene, Robert's family home where his mother (Muttikins), his elder sister and the children of his younger sister live, Stella

> began to feel it was not the country but occupied Europe that was occupying London – suspicious listening, surreptitious movement, and leaden hearts […] The physical nearness of the Enemy – how few were the miles between the capital and the coast, between coast and coast! – became palpable. Tonight, the safety-curtain between the here and the there had lifted; the breath of danger and sorrow travelled over freely from shore to shore … she found some sort of comfort in asking herself how one could have expected to be happy. (*HD*, pp.126-127)

Harrison's accusations gradually erode Stella's belief in Kelway's innocence, her original thought that she knew he would not betray his country corroded by Harrison's continuing presence in her life. She believes herself to be constantly watched and haunted by Harrison even when she is in Eire staying at Mount Morris, where Donovan, the servant, tells her that someone stayed with Cousin Francis, a "chap or gentleman with a very narrow look, added to which he had a sort of discord between his two eyes …" (*HD*, 170).

As Jenny Hartley notes, "[t]o spy on is to betray" (1977, 101). By spying on Kelway and asking questions, Stella betrays both herself and her love for Kelway. Harrison's accusations of Kelway's betrayal forces Stella to become a spy and hence intensely aware of the action of watching. That Kelway feels betrayed by Stella is apparent in his reaction to her interrogation. By spying on Kelway and by her deception, Stella has, in Kelway's eyes, become the very worst kind of betrayer. Whilst he can, in his own eyes, justify his betrayal of his country, he cannot accept that Stella has betrayed him,

[…] All I can see now is, how well you hide things – you may have been having another lover all this time for all I know; and I'm not sure I wouldn't rather it had been only that. This other thing seems colder, more up against me. This thing locked up inside you, yes; yes, but always secretly being taken out and looked at – and how without going mad am I to let myself imagine at what moments? (*HD*, 191).

Stella's innocence, it can be argued, is therefore lost when she too becomes a spy. However, she is only too aware of the corrupting nature of secrets, both Kelway's secrets and her own. Whilst it could be perceived that her innocence was corrupted when she accepted the guilt foisted on her by her husband, Victor, and his family and despite the fact that she was, in fact, the innocent party in the divorce, both in a legal and a moral sense, Stella believes that she has been corrupted by this secret that she has kept from Roderick and others. As she says to Harrison,

[…] Oh, I should doubt,' she exclaimed, 'whether there's any such thing as an innocent secret! Whatever has been buried, surely, corrupts? Nothing keeps innocence innocent but daylight. A truth's just a truth to start with, with no particular nature, good or bad – but how can any truth not *go* bad from being underground?' (*HD*, 228)

Stella's belief that an innocent secret will be corrupted by being buried is echoed when the boat at Mount Morris, sunk whilst Cousin Francis was still alive, is brought back to the surface on Roderick's instructions. As Donovan tells Roderick, "[w]e raised the boat for you, sir, but she isn't much; she's decayed" (*HD*, 313)

Narrative, Time and Authorial Manipulation

Bowen's narrative constantly manipulates the reader's moments of *anagnôrisis* and understanding of the text. Whereas the narrative pattern in *The Death of the Heart* returns to the teleological form of Bowen's early novels, time in *The Heat of the Day* is manipulated in similar ways to *The House in Paris*. Whilst *The Death of the Heart* does not provide the closure associated with the teleological novel of the nineteenth century, the ending of *The Heat of the Day* to some extent does do so in terms of marriage, motherhood and death; however Bowen's manipulation of time subverts this paradigm.

Through the many references to time throughout the novel the reader is made conscious of the importance of time in the narrative. In an echo of Leopold's place in Karen and Ray's marriage in *The House in Paris*, for example, the narrator states that Robert Kelway and Stella "were not alone, nor had they been from the start, from the start of love. Their time sat in the third place at their table" (*HD*, 194), time in Stella's flat is marked by the falling of rose petals (*HD*, 24), watches seem to "belie time" (*HD*, 97), some clocks in London have been "shock-stopped" (*HD*, 99) and Kelway sees Stella's betrayal in terms of a ticking clock beneath her pillow (*HD*, 199). Each reference to time reinforces the notion that it is of paramount importance.

The novel apparently begins, effectively, in the present (in this case the present is "the first Sunday of September 1942" (*HD*, 8)). Authorial manipulation is, however, present at the very beginning of the novel; as the text focuses on Louie and Harrison, the narrator suggests that Louie is the main female protagonist in the novel.[25] By means of analepsis, the focus of the narrative then turns back to the funeral of Cousin Francis in May 1942; this is an occasion which could lead the reader to question Stella's sexual conduct, an interpretation which is reinforced by the second major episode of analepsis in the novel which foregrounds the circumstances of the first meeting between Stella and Robert Kelway. Following a sustained focus on 1942, the narrative experiences a proleptic shift to 1943 and 1944, the novel's ending coinciding with the end of the Second World War.

Whereas the chronological manipulation in *The Death of the Heart* serves to illuminate elements of Anna's character and helps to provide the reader with an understanding of her behaviour, the manipulation of time in *The Heat of the Day* delays the reader's moment of *anagnôrisis* and thus manipulates the reader's epistemological journey. The doubling of names and the alliterative names of Roderick and Louie (with its attendant androgynous associations) also serve as a manipulation of the reader's understanding of the text. Further authorial manipulation is to be found in the latter stages of the novel when the narration changes from a third person narrative with an omniscient narrator to a first person narrative. There is a startling change to "we" when relating the events of 1943 when "[t]he day after Christmas we sank the *Scharnhorst*" (*HD*, 308) and of 1944 when "[a]s early as January we broke the Gustav Line … February, we encircled ten enemy divisions" (ibid). Such a significant change in the narrative voice involves the reader more closely both in a shared experience and in the epistemological journey to discover the truth.

Despite the themes of betrayal and loss of innocence which permeate the novel, the narrative ends on a positive note, although it is one which should not, given the authorial manipulation throughout the novel, perhaps be accepted at face value. Through his inheritance of Mount Morris

Roderick achieves a sense of his own identity together with a sense of his own mortality and is thus prepared to enter into adulthood and a world of experience. The birth of her son confers identity on Louie, and Stella has hopes of closure through her impending marriage, although not before she offers Harrison the opportunity to spend the night with her, which is rather ironic given Harrison's implied part in Kelway's death.

Louie's Eden is probably to be found at Seale-on-Sea, her childhood home. When Eve bit into the apple she lost her innocence and her place in the Garden of Eden: if it can be assumed that a loss of innocence equates to eviction from Eden then it can be argued, perhaps for Stella, Mount Morris is her Eden. However, it is Roderick who gains this particular Eden through the inheritance from Cousin Francis and Stella realises that it is inevitable that Roderick will one day take a wife to Mount Morris, a wife who will supplant Stella not just in Roderick's affections but also in Stella's own version of Eden. Although, as Bowen wrote, once we have lost innocence "it is futile to attempt to picnic in Eden" (1946, 265), she was also aware that for some it was necessary to try to regain the sense of security which is to be found in that person's Eden. Writing to Charles Ritchie about Hythe, the town in Kent on which she based Seale-on-Sea, where she had once lived with her mother and to which she returned later in life, Bowen wrote "[i]t is a nice little town – reassuring and right-and-tight and sound. One of the few places that make me love England and Englishness. But I think that apart from Englishness there's a peculiar quality of Kentishness that I like. The Hythe people are flamboyant and hardy and unmawkish". (Bowen quoted in Glendinning 1977, 222)

Realising the inevitability of the loss of Mount Morris and thus the loss of a secure existence, Stella eventually seeks refuge and security in a marriage to a brigadier, "a cousin of a cousin" (*HD*, 321). The experiences of Bowen and many others throughout the Second World War would suggest that the safety represented by childhood and innocence has been lost for ever and both Stella and Louie should however be aware of the *caveat* which provides a chilling warning to all those who may seek to regain their Eden, "[y]ou may imitate but cannot renew safety" (*HD*, 159).

Notes

[1] See letter to William Plomer, 22nd September 1948 (appendix).
[2] There are relatively few references to children in *The Heat of the Day*. The most disturbing image of childhood can be seen in the inherent violence of children which is depicted in the pictures in Cousin Nettie's room where "there was a bevy of tinted pictures of children; all, it seemed, engaged innocently in some act of

destruction – depetalling daisies, puffing at dandelion clocks, trampling primrose woods" (*HD*, 209-210), an image which takes a more literal and sadistic form in Bowen's short story "The Inherited Clock" (1944).

[33] Lassner (1998, 150) describes the novel as a "story of wartime dispossession [… which] turns domestic fiction inside out. Not only does it portray the end of private life at this historic moment, but its heroine's psychological divorce from domesticity shows how the war enabled women to resist its ideologies." Lassner's exploration of Bowen's wartime fiction helps to locate *The Heat of the Day* within its literary context. This context is further explored in Allan Hepburn's study *Intrigue: Espionage and Culture* (2005) and in Eibhear Walshe's essay "A Time for Hard Writers" (2009).

[4] Despite Clune et al's assertion that "Elizabeth Bowen, indeed, failed to produce anything at all" during the Second World War (1997, 62), in fact, not only did Bowen start to write *The Heat of the Day*, she completed her short autobiography *Seven Winters* and the history of her home, *Bowen's Court*. She also wrote and published two collections of short stories, *Look at all Those Roses* (1941) and *The Demon Lover and Other Stories* (1945), a survey of English fiction, *English Novelists*, published in 1942, and many essays and reviews. Glendinning notes that Bowen had written a draft of the first five chapters of *The Heat of the Day* by the summer of 1944 and gave this work to Lady Tweedsmuir (wife of John Buchan) for safekeeping (1977, 149).

[5] Bowen 1945c, 49.

[6] Published as Ivy Gripped the Steps.

[7] *The Demon Lover and Other Stories* contained the following stories in this order: "In the Square" (originally published September 1941), "Sunday Afternoon" (July 1941), "The Inherited Clock" (January 1944), "The Cheery Soul" (December 1942), "Songs My Father Sang Me" (November 1944), "The Demon Lover" (November 1941), "Careless Talk" (Originally published as "Everything's Frightfully Interesting" in October 1941), "The Happy Autumn Fields" (November 1944), "Ivy Gripped the Steps" (September 1945), "Pink May" (October 1942), "Green Holly" (December 1944) and "Mysterious Kôr" (January 1944). (Sellery and Harris, 1981, pp.58, 110-111, 138-141). When reference is made to Bowen's short stories the parenthetical reference will be to *Collected Stories*, referred to as *CS*.

[8] These three stories are reprinted in *Collected Stories* pp.661-666, 671-685 and 728-740 respectively.

[9] Clare Hanson states that this short story "is a *tour de force*, catching the atmosphere of the forced conjunction of three people whose nerves have been frayed by the war. It is a short fiction which illustrates almost perfectly what Elizabeth Bowen meant when she wrote that for her 'the short story is a matter of vision, rather than of feeling' " (1985, 124).

[10] In a broadcast on 28th February 1948 (reprinted in *The Mulberry Tree*) Bowen spoke about the influence *She* (published in 1887) had on her as a child of 12, stating "I read *She*, dreamed *She*, lived *She* for a year and a half […]" (1948a, 250).

[11] The iron gates would have been removed to provide metal for the war effort.

[12] In her preface to *Stories by Elizabeth Bowen* (reprinted in *The Mulberry Tree*) Bowen indicates that, for her, her novels and short stories acted as counterbalances (1959, 130).

[13] There is some doubt as to when Bowen wrote this essay. Hermione Lee states it was written in 1950. A manuscript of a longer version of the essay exists at the University of Texas at Austin within the Arthur Ransom Humanities Research Collection, this is dated 24th April 1950 (Sellery and Harris 1981, 222) but Sellery and Harris suggest that the essay, published in *Collected Impressions* and *The Mulberry Tree*, was prepared for the Ministry of Information, an organisation which was dissolved following the war (ibid, 71).

[14] Despite Bowen's marriage to Alan Cameron (which is believed by some to have remained unconsummated) and Ritchie's later marriage to his cousin and his return to Canada, their affair lasted over 33 years until Bowen's death. Bowen would meet him when she went to the United States to lecture and Ritchie would visit her, frequently staying at "Carberry", her house in Hythe. It was an "intimate friendship" (Lee 1999, 149) to which the dedications to *The Heat of the Day* and *Eva Trout, or Changing Scenes* attest.

[15] Jenny Hartley suggests that Robert Kelway was based on Charles Ritchie and also shared some of Bowen's own characteristics (1997, 102). The choice of names of the two male protagonists may have some autobiographical bearing (should Elizabeth have been a boy, her parents had decided to name the baby Robert) and whilst the age difference between Kelway and Stella may well mirror that between Bowen and Ritchie, the high esteem that Bowen had for Ritchie would necessarily preclude any comparison made between the two men with regard to their war time activities, for whilst Ritchie represented the Canadian Government and would, no doubt, have reported on the situation in Britain, there is no suggestion that he ever betrayed his own country, or compromised the British war effort.

[16] This aspect of the novel is specifically discussed by Deborah Parsons. Drawing on the work of Rachel Bowlby, Parsons examines Bowen's rôle as a *flâneuse*, walking the streets of London, her insights into the lives of London resulting from her acts of voyeurism, much as the Baudelairian model of the *flâneur* walked the streets of Paris in the nineteenth century (1997, 24-25).

[17] Lane's introduction also indicates his dislike of Bowen's fiction, suggesting that the reports reprinted by the Aubane Historical Society are "far more readable than her literary works" (1999a, 7). In the conclusion to his introduction, Lane is vitriolic in his opinion of Bowen, stating that "[l]ike all spies, Bowen basically despised those she spied on, and made that clear towards the end of her life when she told Hubert Butler that she hated Ireland, and said so with a vehemence that shocked him and his wife" (ibid, 9). This last comment is not referenced and therefore it is difficult to ascertain its veracity.

[18] Secretary of State for Dominion Affairs, 1940-1942.

[19] An indication of this can be seen in the differing treatments of the flying of flags, Eduard Hempel, the German Minister in Dublin, was permitted to fly the Swastika flag outside the German Legation (Fisk 1983, 136). In contrast, Sir John

Loader Maffey, the "United Kingdom Representative in Eire" (ibid, 90) was not allowed to fly the Union Jack.

[20] Clair Wills' *That Neutral Island: A History of Ireland During the Second World War* (2007) provides a valuable history of this period in Irish history.

[21] Foster notes that O'Faolain and Bowen had a "brief love affair" whilst in Salzburg in 1937 (1993, 111), although Wills states that the affair ended in the summer of 1939 (2007, 80).

[22] The tea ration was halved from two ounces per person per week to just one ounce in January 1943 and then to three quarters of an ounce in the summer of 1943 (this compares with the ration of two ounces per person per week in Britain). Domestic coal was no longer available for householders, gas supplies were restricted to just six hours a day and each household was only permitted half of ton of peat a month (Fisk 1983, 254 and 271).

[23] Although specifically referring to the "great country house" such as Chatsworth or Longleat, Malcolm Kelsall suggests that such a house is "a natural excrescence. It has not been built so much as grown by organic process from the English soil. It is not a social phenomenon, but gives the impression of being out of time, 'as if it had always been there'. Thus, it is as much part of England as the rocks and stones and trees." (1993, 6)

He further suggests that this reading of the country house is artificially replicated in the "Barrett" house of the 20th century (ibid, 8).

[24] She is, of course, specifically referring to her own secret, that of her innocence.

[25] This is a narrative ploy, of course, utilised by Bowen in several of her novels and can be seen, for example, in *The Death of the Heart.*

CHAPTER SIX

BURIED TREASURES, HIDDEN SECRETS:
A WORLD OF LOVE AND *THE LITTLE GIRLS*

Writing to L. P. Hartley on 15th September 1954, Bowen stated that she had finished her seventh novel, *A World of Love* (published in 1955),[1] continuing "J. Cape peevishly complain [it] is rather *short*. But myself I like it."[2] Her satisfaction with the novel was shared by others; Charles Ritchie, for example, wrote "Elizabeth's new book, *A World of Love*, is marvellous, a masterpiece of her own genius" (1981, 79). Bowen was equally happy with *The Little Girls* (1963), stating to William Plomer in a letter dated 1st June 1963 that the ending, in particular, "does now please me".[3] Whilst eight years separate the publication of the two novels, similar themes run through both texts, themes such as the importance of the past and the haunting effect the past can have on the present, the innocence of children, notions of identity and the epistemological issues which surround identity and, specifically, authorial manipulation of time both intra- and extra-textually.

Described by Bennett and Royle as "her most intense and compact" novel (1995a, 104), the novel is set in 1950s rural Ireland, the "heroine", Jane, whilst searching for Edwardian dresses in the attic, discovers a bundle of letters tied up with white ribbon which were written by her mother's dead fiancé, Guy. As an impressionable young lady she falls in love with the ghost of Guy, and, in turn forces her mother, her aunt and her father to re-examine their own lives in relation to the myths that surround Guy. Within this narrative the reader is exposed to Maud, Jane's younger sister, a child with an obsession with the chimes of Big Ben, religion and her imaginary friend. The emotions stirred within Jane by Guy's letters enable her to fall in love with Richard Priam, a discarded lover of Lady Latterly.

A quotation on the back cover of the Penguin Twentieth Century Classics edition (1982) from *The Times* states that *The Little Girls* is "the funniest of all Miss Bowen's novels"; whilst this is a debatable point, it is a novel which explores the childhood and middle age of three women. Charles Ritchie noted in a diary entry dated 19th January 1957 that

> Elizabeth says that her next book is to be called *A Race with Time*. She says that she knows its title but not yet exactly what it is to be about. There will be a "star-shaped" plot with characters and events converging on a point in time. She is working very hard at her present book, writing all morning on most days and in the early afternoon. She says that when a woman becomes a widow she goes back to the arts and crafts of her youth in attaching friends and combining people and, in order not to be lonely, returns to her early gregariousness. (1981, 112-113)

Whilst changing the title of the novel, Bowen retained the concept of the "star-shaped" plot; utilising a time frame similar to that in *The House in Paris*, Bowen frames the story of the girls' apparently idyllic childhood with the story of Dinah in her middle age with the other two women acting in a supportive rôle. The narration of their school days revolves around the burying of a casket complete with secret treasures within the grounds of their school in Southstone. This episode is recounted after the reader learns of Dinah's attempts to get in touch with her childhood friends and her re-enactment of the burial of treasures, albeit containing different artefacts. The third section of the novel narrates their attempts to recover the past and Dinah's decline following the disinterment of the original casket. However, as is always the case with Bowen's fiction, such brief synopses belie the complexities of the novels.

Historical Context

A World of Love and *The Little Girls* were written when the West was embroiled in the Cold War with the East. Fears of another world war, but one fought with hydrogen bombs and therefore potentially more cataclysmic than the Second World War, were rife, but this world of fear and its politics are implicit rather than overt in *A World of Love*. Equally implicit in this novel is the continuing estrangement between Roman Catholics and Protestants within Ireland and the continuing threat of violence both in Eire and beyond. The narrator tells us, for example, that

> [n]ot since Montefort stood had there ceased to be vigilant measures against the nightcomer; all being part of the hostile watch kept by now eyeless towers and time-stunted castles along these rivers. For as land knows, everywhere is a frontier; and the outposted few (and few are the living) never must be off guard. (*WL*, 79)

Further allusions to the turmoil of world politics can be read into Jane's attitude to the concerns of the world for, like Lady Naylor (*The Last September*) who deliberately chooses not to notice the events taking place outside the demesne of Danielstown,

> Jane was without emotional curiosity; her lack of it was neither failure nor chance but part of a necessary unconcern. She had grown up amid extreme situations and frantic statements; and, out of her feeling for equilibrium, contrived to ignore them as far as possible. Her time, called hers because she was required to live in it and had no other, was in bad odour, and no wonder. Altogether the world was in a crying state of exasperation, but that was hardly her fault: too much had been going on for too long … The passions and politics of her family so much resembled those of the outside world that she made little distinction between the two. It was her hope that this might all die down, from lack of recruits or fuel or, most of all, if more people were to take less notice. She did what she could by adding no further heat. (*WL*, 34-35)[4]

The early Fifties was an era of austerity with shortages of food, coal, tobacco, clothing and, particularly in Britain, housing; and there was also high taxation. Eire and Britain faced similarly dire financial situations; as Cronin notes, the political difficulties faced by the Republic created a "moribund state" (2001, 223), difficulties which were exacerbated by the country's continued reliance on agriculture in comparison to the move towards industrialisation and urbanisation exhibited by much of Europe. Of equal significance were the continuing high levels of emigration as the economic problems faced by the Republic led to some eighty per cent of those born in the 1930s emigrating in the 1950s; further, such emigration devastated large areas of the country, a situation for which the various governments of the 1950s seemed unable to provide a solution (ibid).[5] In charting the inequalities inherent in British society within the period 1920-1970, John Atkins suggests that *The Little Girls* "is completely and unquestionably post-war in spirit" (1977, 74) and whilst the ramifications of the shortages common throughout both Ireland and England can be identified in *A World of Love*, *The Little Girls* can be seen to portray a post-war, post-austerity world in which Clare's chain of shops known as "Mopsie Pye" can flourish, a world where, although living in reduced circumstances, Dinah is still able to employ the services of Francis, her Maltese houseboy, and "alternate widows" for the housecleaning (*LG*, 56).

Autobiographical Context

Bowen's husband, Alan Cameron, died on 26th August 1952 (Glendinning 1977, 183) and she felt devastated by her loss. Writing to L. P. Hartley from Rome on 1st April 1953 she stated that when

> in Venice for two days more or less by myself, except for a few social occasions, I became so melancholy, so much a prey to the feelings of vacancy that I do my best to evade, these days, that I wept from a small bridge into one of the small canals.[6]

However, whilst missing his physical presence she appears to have felt a spiritual awareness of her husband; writing in 1958 Bowen states, "Alan never seems dead, in the sense that he never seems gone: I suppose that if one has lived the greater part of one's life with a person he continues to accompany one through every moment." (1999, 209)[7] Despite her great loss, Bowen apparently enjoyed the 1950s; in the same letter to William Plomer she writes, "I wonder how you feel in the 1950s? Personally I am enjoying this epoch – it is really the first one, it seems to me, in which I've enjoyed being "grown-up" as much as I expected to when I was a child." (Ibid)

Whilst autobiographical elements can be read in the two novels, particularly in relation to the locations of both Montefort in *A World of Love* and the school in *The Little Girls* (which bears more than a passing resemblance to her own school, Downe House), Bowen was concerned that the novels should not be read as instalments of autobiography. Writing to Plomer in 1963 she states,

> *The Little Girls* as I feel that you saw, though others may not, is not autobiographical. I myself was not one of those 3. But it is what Americans would call "a recall of sensory experience" book. I've taken some liberties with the Folkestone landscape, but as it's called Southstone I suppose that doesn't matter.[8]

Bowen was, however, very concerned with the accuracy of the historical facts within her novels. In the same letter to Plomer she writes "I have a horror of anachronisms, real or apparent. This was – I could still swear – apparent; but in so far as it is apparent must be explained." Within this letter she writes particularly about her reference to two photographs in Sheila's bedroom which "was surely the prettiest in Southstone?" (*LG*, 108)[9] where on "the chimneypiece was a signed – how obtained? – photo of Pauline Chase flying in at the window as Peter Pan, and an unsigned,

more frantic photo of child tennis prodigy Suzanne Lenglen." (Ibid)[10]
Bowen's stated desire to ensure that her novels were historically correct
provides, in this instance, not only a historical context but, despite her
statement to the contrary, also an autobiographical contextualisation for
her novel, writing into the lives of Sheila, Claire and Dinah elements of
her own childhood.

Innocence and Corruption

Within the two novels Bowen portrays two opposing aspects of
childhood innocence. In *A World of Love*, Jane's adolescent innocence is
contrasted sharply with that of her sister, Maud, one of Bowen's most
malicious children.[11] Dostal views Maud as an "innocent and a destroyer
of innocence in others" (1964, 91) who "combines, it seems, the innocence
of Miss Bowen's Cordelia which brings others to knowledge without
being affected itself" (ibid, 96). Dostall continues, in a comparison with
Anna and Leopold (*The Death of the Heart* and *The House in Paris*), that

> Maud is a much more complex innocent than they, for in her Cordelia-like
> destructive quality she has a wider scope, reaching out to more people and
> touching them personally, and in her own destruction, unlike Anna and
> Leopold, she lacks pathos, the most natural characteristic [in one] whose
> innocence has been blighted (ibid).

Her malevolence is alluded to early in the novel when she is found in
the kitchen collecting eggs. Her mother finds this consumption of eggs
quite abhorrent, a disgust which she voices to her daughter, berating her
for "sucking them like a serpent" (*WL,* 22), an allusion, perhaps, to the
serpent in the original Garden of Eden. Not only does Maud like to suck
the contents of the eggs, she collects the "chipped-off drippings" from
candles which she states are "useful for images" (*WL,* 23), a pastime
which suggests the making of wax voodoo dolls and the practice of
sticking pins in the dolls in order to cause pain. Her interest in the
supernatural, highlighted by her constant, but invisible, companion Gay
David[12] and adherence to rituals, in particular the ritual of hearing Big Ben
on the radio, and her fascination with the Bible from which she quotes at
length when upset with her father, add to the Gothic elements of the novel.
In contrast to Maud, who is not averse to physical violence at school or
on the "Protestant Van", the bus on which she is transported to school
everyday (*WL,* 109), nor to resorting to a mercenary attempt to extort
money from her father in return for Guy's letters, Jane appears to be a girl
of a gentler temperament. Like many of Bowen's "heroines", Jane is on

the cusp of adulthood, seeming at times to be almost a woman and then, at others, reverting to childhood both in her dress and in her actions. The narrator alludes to this transitional state when Jane is introduced to the reader at the beginning of the novel and at the beginning of the day when,

> [k]indled by summer though cool in nature, she was a beauty. […] her height and something half naïve half studied about her management of the sleeves and skirts made her like a boy actor in woman's clothes, while what was classical in her grace made her appear to belong to some other time. Her brows were wide, her eyes an unshadowed blue, her mouth more inclined to smile than in any other way to say very much – it was a face perfectly ready to be a woman's, but not yet so, even in its transcendency this morning. She was called Jane and was twenty years old. (*WL,* 10)

Just before lunch, however, Jane reverts to her normal mode of dressing, "back again into gingham showing her limbs" (*WL,* 35), thus providing a portrait of a child rather than a woman. This portrayal of Jane is, however, somewhat at odds with the fact that she has been sent to a finishing school, and is further complicated by her choice of clothing for Lady Latterly's party which is dictated by the clothes Jane has with her for, as the reader is told in parenthesis, "(Jane wore the morning's dress, skirts pressed, top hastily cut out and sleeves away, for she had nothing better with her at Montefort.)" (*WL,* 60).

Blodgett states that *A World of Love* "puts far less emphasis on the shaping of its young heroine's moral will and far more on her desire and capacity for love" (1975, 45) but, whilst Maud may well appear to be the embodiment of malevolence at Montefort, Jane could be perceived as the harbinger of bad luck, acting as a catalyst in the explosion of emotions which occurs once Guy's letters have been discovered in the attic; as Antonia says to Jane, "You have an igniting touch" (*WL,* 40).

Antonia's accusation reiterates Bowen's premise in *The Death of the Heart* that the innocent cause chaos as Jane discovers the letters amongst the many objects in the attic which are described by Lilia as "not only dirty but so inflammable day and night up there over our heads" (ibid). Jane acknowledges that it is she who has caused the ignition of a metaphorical rather than a literal fire,

> '[…] I am the one,' Jane easily said. 'But if I'd started a fire, you'd know by now.'
> 'We think we do,' said Antonia. 'That's what's the matter. We think we can smell burning; or at any rate the beginning of burning, smouldering. What have you done?' (ibid)

The narrator alerts the reader to the possibility of a physical fire at the very beginning of the novel; referring back to the title of Bowen's previous novel,[13] the narration indicates a heat which is almost oppressive, a heat which does not die down when the sun sets at the end of the day, where "[t]he sun rose on a landscape still pale with the heat of the day before" (*WL,* 9),[14] it is a landscape which is parched and where water supplies run low. It would therefore seem almost inevitable that some sort of fire will occur, however it is the emotions of the main protagonists which are set alight rather than the grounds in which Montefort stands. The narrator's description of Jane adds weight to this argument; her "kindled" appearance suggests inflammation, a lighting of fires and a lighting of passion. The novel resounds with recurring images of fire which include both the everyday occurrences of candles and fires and the implicit imagery associated with Jane's ability to blush, and the naming of Lady Vesta Latterly, a first name which conjures up images of both a proprietary brand of matches and her namesake, the Roman goddess of the hearth.[15]

Bowen also utilises the heat of the summer, suggestive of a passion to come, in *The Little Girls.* The summer of 1914 (the last summer, perhaps, of innocence) appears oppressive, for

> [t]oday, the heat was a little less, which insofar as it was to blame for the disturbances of yesterday was as well. The weather continued to be set fair: Tuesday's nervy little hot breeze or breath having died at sunset, Wednesday's great warmth was extremely still. (*LG,* 85).

In both novels, much as a very hot day will precipitate a meteorological thunderstorm, psychological storms follow the oppressive heat inherent in the emotions of the protagonists. Such a dramatic change, which could be read as the movement from innocence to experience, is alluded to in *The Little Girls*: the narrator discusses the swinging techniques of Dinah, Clare and Sheila, techniques which can be seen not only in their ability to master a crooked swing but also to describe their personalities. The narrator states that "[t]hose were the days before love" and continues, "[t]hese are the days after. Nothing has gone for nothing but the days between" (*LG,* 56), a comment which highlights the notion that an element of innocence was lost when the Great War began. This is an opinion shared by many including Philip Larkin who, whilst describing the lines of men queuing to enlist to fight in the First World War in his poem "MCMXIV", concludes "Never such innocence again." (132)

The poetry recited during Class IVa's "poetry time" by Clare and Sheila whilst pupils at St. Agatha's also harks back to an earlier time of innocence. Clare's first attempt at recital is William Wordsworth's "Intimations of Immortality" from *Recollections of Early Childhood*; this does not meet with her teacher's approval and Clare is told to sit down for she is "[r]uining that beautiful poem" (*LG,* 68). Sheila's recital, "The Fairies" by William Allingham, also suggests the death of innocence (albeit rather differently), however, Sheila's understanding of the poem, and the understanding of her classmates, is cut short when she is unable to complete the fourth line of the third stanza and her inability to recite the line "He's nigh lost his wits" (line 20) injects a farcical note into the proceedings. These two poems, together with the poem recited by Clare following the disinterment of the coffer, ("The Woods of Westermain" by George Meredith) also highlight Victorian attitudes to childhood and innocence through the poems that tell stories designed to alert children to the vagaries of human nature, vagaries which include childish malevolence and cruelty.

There are other references within Part Two of *The Little Girls* which can be read both as analogies for the inevitability of the corruption and loss of childhood innocence, and the innocence of a whole society which will be lost with the onset of a world war. The cutting of a privet hedge at the bus stop where Dinah and Clare wait for a bus following their shopping expedition in town for fetters is one such example. Whilst narrating what could be read as an everyday occurrence in the summer time, the narration is given added resonance by Bowen's selection of vocabulary and the juxtaposition of the hedge with a pillar box, the hedge which "protected a corner garden" and was "just into bloom, had been clipped today – perhaps rather cruelly? It gave off a knife-freshened but injured smell. Here, too, was a scarlet pillar-box." (*LG,* 110). The colour of the pillar-box could, of course, be suggestive of the blood that will be shed during the war to come. A line drawing of Olive's birthday cake also serves to highlight the demarcation between the innocence of childhood and the horrors associated with the First World War. Acting almost as a punctuation mark in the narrative, the drawing of the cake supplies the date of Olive's party, July 23rd 1914, just twelve days before Britain declared war on Germany. The extinguishing of birthday candles also indicates the chaos and destructive forces which were to affect Britain over the following four years for "[s]omething about the destruction (or so it seemed) of the moment of the candles let loose not exactly disorder but an element of scrimmage about the party" (*LG,* 22).

Portrayals of two gardens associated with Dinah also provide analogies for the loss of innocence both of the young girls and society. Described in contrast to the "unenchanted" garden of the Burkin-Jones' rented house

(*LG,* 112), the pre-war garden of Mrs. Piggott, (Dinah's mother) is represented as a garden of Eden, but one which has gone, literally, to seed,

> [t]he neglected grass of the lawn, already growing up into seed, created a sort of pallor about [... Major Burkin-Jones'] feet: nothing splashed anywhere with colour, except where a meagre delphinium leaned through ferns or ungirt cabbage roses burned purple-pink. This came to be a garden like none other – or was it always, perhaps? The moment could, at least, never be again. Or, could it – who knew? Happy this garden would be to have such a revenant, were he ever dead. Though who would be there to see, were they all gone? (*LG,* pp.84-85)

This passage is more complex than a superficial reading would suggest as the subsequent meeting between Major Burkin-Jones (Clare's father) and Mrs. Piggott at Olive's party implies undertones of a love affair, though not necessarily a sexual relationship. There is no direct reference to any relationship between them other than that of parents of friends, indeed Dinah's comment to Claire that "the non-sins of our fathers—and mothers—have been visited upon us" (*LG,* 186) suggests that the relationship was not consummated; however, the manner of their parting is tender and suggestive of the parting of lovers. The narrator implies that the Major is in love with Mrs. Piggott and thus his walk through her garden is given, with hindsight, an added resonance, one which suggests that Major Burkin-Jones realises that life is about to change irrevocably and that he may only return to this garden in his dreams and, perhaps as ghost following his death in the coming war.

Dinah's cottage garden at Applegate is also suggestive of an Eden "growing up into seed". The very name of the cottage is synonymous with Eden, the apple being the fruit that Eve ate before she and Adam were cast adrift. Once an orchard, the garden still retains vestiges of its past with trees that are "[t]wisted, old but only too fruitful still" (*LG,* 17). As a result of the hard work of Dinah and Frank, the garden is beginning once more to bear fruit, although rather than the fruits of the past, the garden now provides "Provençal and other exotic vegetables, the 'musts' of the better cookery book" (*LG,* 17-18). Whilst their cultivation can be seen to reflect a desire to become self-sufficient, such labour could be read as an attempt to recreate Eden, a lost childhood, as does Dinah's recreation of her childish burial of artefacts.

Whereas Dinah's gardens provide a sense of place within *The Little Girls*, in contrast the location of both Montefort and Clonmore are seen as places in abeyance, places which could, perhaps, be seen as sites of either limbo or hell. Montefort can be perceived as a house which is totally isolated both in geographical and chronological terms: the house presents "a blind-end to the nearby gorge" (*WL*, 9), the stranger who drops Lilia and Maud off at the gates of Montefort confesses "No idea there was anyone living here" (*WL*, 30) and, in discussion with Jane at Lady Latterly's party, a guest says of Jane's home, "Montefort? Pity that place has gone." (*WL*, 64). Whilst Montefort is a forgotten place, Clonmore, with its hairdressing *salon* whose proprietor disappears whilst in the middle of styling a customer's hair, lacks cafés and,

> not only provided no place to be, it provided no reason *to* be, at all. So, but for the heat, was the place at all times – but the glare today stripped it of even its frowsty mystery, flattened it out, deadly glazed into a picture postcard such as one might receive from Hell. Gone was third dimension; nothing stood behind anything (*WL*, 88-89)

A reading of *A World of Love* which suggests a metaphorical geographical location within a state of limbo is informed by one which is aware of the notions of corruption evident in the novel, where "[t]he early wasp was already probing at last year's jam" (*WL*, 49-50). It is, however, specifically the secrets of the past that have the capacity for corruption in the present. Echoing Stella's comments about buried secrets (*The Heat of the Day*), Antonia believes, unlike Dinah, that the past should not be uncovered for re-examination. Talking about Jane's visits to the attic, and following Jane's comment that everything in Montefort belongs to Antonia, she states "I've no idea what *is* in the house" continuing "I can't help wondering what you've unburied – there may be much (I should think there probably is) that we should all do far better to leave alone." (*WL*, 37-38)

There is a narratorial inference in *A World of Love* that it is the past which has the power to corrupt both youth and post-war society. Equally, there is a suggestion that the sacrifices of so many leave a hole in society and, by extension, that the death of the contemporaries of Fred, Lilia and Antonia have left society incomplete. Written following Alan Cameron's death, the narrator's deliberations on the nature of death and its effect on the living can be read as authorial comment, an attempt to make sense of what can be seen as a senseless event. The narrator first suggests that denial of love for the dead is, in some sense, a self-defence mechanism for "[t]heir continuous dying while we live, their repeated deaths as each of us die who knew them, are not in nature to be withstood" (*WL,* 44). However, the narrator continues that the death of the young is not so easy to accept for "it is hard, for instance, to see a young death in battle as in any way the fruition of a destiny, hard not to sense the continuation of the apparently cut-off life, hard not to ask, but *was* dissolution possibly so abruptly, unmeaningly and soon." (ibid)

Although Bowen may well have believed it "unethical – for some reason? – to allow the supernatural into a novel", a reluctance which, she suggests "may be one of my handicaps as a sincere novelist" (1965b, 9), there is no doubt that *A World of Love* is, in effect, haunted by the ghost of Guy through the medium of his letters and the memories of Lilia and Antonia. Reiterating a narratorial comment in *The Heat of the Day* which indicates that there is a fine division between the living and the dead, the narrator indicates that mere doors and locks cannot protect the present from the past. Antonia might attempt to protect Montefort from the night but

> the ceremony became a mockery: when Antonia had done bolting and barring she remained, arms extended across like another crossbar, laughing at the door. For the harsh-grained oak had gone into dissolution: it shut out nothing. So was demolished all that had lately stood between him and her … (*WL*, 79)

Erica Johnson suggests that "[h]aunting can be seen as a vital means of access to memory and history that is available through no other mode of recall" (2004, 111) and it can be seen that Antonia's inability to fully accept the fact of Guy's death has serious implications for herself, Fred and Lilia; unable to think of him in any form other than living, Antonia condemns the trio to a life in which "[t]hey were incomplete" (*WL*, 45). Echoing Bowen's "The Demon Lover"[16] there is the inference that Guy's ghostly presence is not benign, his last words to Antonia, *"You'll* never see the last of me!" (*WL*, 96) suggests a malignancy. Much as Leopold becomes the third person at Karen and Roy's table in *The House in Paris*, Guy too is narrated as third man, a ghostly guest who has a place laid for him at Lady Latterly's table (although, of course, ostensibly this place is laid for a guest Lady Latterly allegedly forgets to invite). Death hangs over the dinner table in other guises, for example roses which "outraged [following Mamie's depetalling of a fellow rose] and candle scorched, began to shed petals over the salted almonds" (*WL*, 66) and a moth which, having flown through a candle, is "pinched […] to death" by Terence (*WL*, 67).

Having spoken Guy's name, Jane is aware of the effect that she has had on the gathering, an effect which adds weight to the reading of Jane as a catalyst. The result of Jane's statement continues to affect the other guests for "not a soul failed to feel the electric connection between Jane's paleness and the dark of the chair in which so far no one visibly sat" (*WL*,

67). However, despite Jane's ability to conjure up images in the imaginations of Lady Latterly's guests and her propensity for causing a metaphorical fire and considerable emotional disruption in the lives of her family, Jane's innocence appears to be untouched. Although it could be argued that her discovery of Guy's letters has opened up the possibilities of a place within a world of love, equally it would appear that she remains uncorrupted by the events of the past. This is particularly so at Lady Latterly's party; having lit the touch paper Jane retires, viewing the other guests' reactions from a distance,

> "[s]he experienced the absolute calmness, the sense of there being almost no threat at all, with which one could imagine fighting one's way down a burning stair-case – there *was* a licking danger, but not to her; cool she moved down between flame walls." (*WL*, 65)

As Christensen argues (2001, 174-185), doors and entrances play a significant rôle in many of Bowen's novels and their importance to Bowen's narrative is particularly apparent in *A World of Love.* In addition to the many doorways enumerated in the novel, the narrator mentions in the second paragraph of the novel a "stone archway, [which] leading through to the stables and nobly canopied by a chestnut tree, sprang from the side of the house and was still imposing" (*WL*, 9). By its very presence at the beginning of the novel the reader could, with hindsight, attach a certain amount of importance to this particular archway. It reappears later in the novel as the place of Jane's viewpoint as she watches her mother and father. The two have been in deep conversation, discussing their lives which have been overshadowed by the death of Guy and although they both realise that Guy will always be a presence in their lives, their very act of talking "had been an act of love" (*WL*, 105), an act which will allow them to re-evaluate their marriage and their future life together; Lilia has, of course, already signalled her willingness to change by the symbolic act of having her hair cut short in Clonmore. Thus the archway has an important rôle within the novel; much as the long shadow of the obelisk can be felt throughout the novel,[17] the archway resonates with symbolic meaning for Jane for, arguably, it becomes the doorway to adulthood. However, having perceived the two adults sitting through the archway as being her parents, Jane is unwilling to join them. Whilst this could be read as a desire to leave her mother and father alone, it could also be read as an unwillingness to cross the threshold from adolescence to adulthood. It is, however, Jane's act of reading Guy's letters which not only forces Fred and Lilia to re-evaluate their marriage but also opens up the possibility of Jane falling in love with a living person, rather than the rather romanticised image of her mother's dead fiancé, falling in love, in fact, with Richard Priam.

Sexuality and Love

Whilst Jane's possible entry into adulthood is predicated on the emotions stirred by the hidden letters, the division between childishness and the promise of womanhood is clearly demarcated in *The Little Girls* by the onset of menstruation. In an episode narrated ostensibly through the focalisation of an eleven year old, the reader is made aware of the physical differences between the younger and older girls which become apparent when the schoolgirls go down to the beach to bathe in the sea. All should, according to the rules of the school, bathe except "some of the bigger ones, who were for some reason debarred. The mystic smugness with which they bore their exclusion made such girls as ludicrous to their juniors as did, already, their bulging forms" (*LG*, 86). The teachers also bathe with the girls with the exception, on this occasion, of "Miss Kinmate, herself *unwell* today" (ibid). Further reference to the physical transformations which are inevitable, a reference which also alludes to the changes facing society, can be read into the narration of the changing tide on the day when the schoolgirls bathe in the sea when "shoes being higher up than when they'd been left was the one sign that there was a tide at all – it was going out" (*LG*, 87).

Despite the coyness of the narrator relating the division of girls whilst bathing in the sea, it would seem apparent that Dinah, Clare and Sheila are aware of the imminent changes to their bodies with the onset of puberty, if not the precise details of such a change, and, like Maud, they are not reticent in using information as a tool for blackmail. They demand that Trevor—later to become Sheila's husband—should pay for the hire of a carriage to take them back to Sheila's house following their shopping trip to town. Trevor asks why Sheila is "clanking" (this is, of course, due to the fetters being wound around her waist) to which Sheila replies "Trevor, I don't think *you* ought to ask", following this answer Trevor, in his embarrassment, first goes pink and then "bright scarlet" (*LG*, 105).

Maud Ellmann states that " 'Proust without sex' more or less sums up *The Little Girls*. […] Memory, rather than desire, stokes the action of *The Little Girls*" (2003, 191-192).[18] However, Jane Rule provides a different reading of *The Little Girls*, suggesting that there is an "indication of overt sexual tension between women, […] the primacy of their need for each other in adolescence and early womanhood and again in widowed middle age is candidly explored" (1976, 115). She further identifies Clare as "the only overt lesbian among all the characters created" (ibid, 119). Issues of sexuality are indeed raised in the novel; for example, Dinah questions the sexuality of Sheila and Clare. Dinah, is of course, the only one of the three to have both married and have children of her own; Clare did marry, as she tells Sheila at their first adult meeting, "Mr Wrong came along, all right. That was a mess." (*LG*, 32) He was a man who gave her "but scant chance to show my form" (*LG*, 44). Sheila inherited two children on her marriage to her husband, Trevor Artworth. Of course, not having children does not equate with lack of sexual experience, but Dinah does wonder about both Sheila and Clare's sexuality. When Dinah learns that Sheila married relatively late in life she asks Clare, "Why did she marry so late, too? What happened first? She *could*, I suppose, have not been anything more than "a fair but frozen maid", but I deeply doubt it." (*LG*, 147). Dinah's second question regarding sexuality is also made to Clare. Dinah and Clare are discussing Frank and following exchange takes place,

> '[…] What am I doing, when he's so dear and good to me, as you see? And apart from that, also, I often bore him – nor, I may say, is he the first I've bored. But then, boredom is part of love.'
> 'That I deny!'
> 'Well, of affection.'
> '*That* I doubt.'
> 'Then you've got no affections. – Mumbo, are you a Lesbian?'
> 'Anything else, would you like to know?' (*LG*, 197)

This exchange suggests that Dinah might well have had various lovers in the past, however, as Clare does not answer Dinah's question, the reader is left in doubt as to Clare's sexuality. Various commentators have suggested that there is a sexual attraction between Clare and Dinah. Wyatt-Brown, for example, interprets Clare's silence as a sign that she has sexual feelings for Dinah (1993, 176), Christensen suggests that Clare's "words and actions leave little doubt about her unarticulated same-sex leanings" (2001, 55) and Rule concludes her reading of the novel by stating that Clare and Dinah "will now deal with the relationship the one has longed for, the other longed for but dreaded." (1976, 121)

Issues of sexuality are more explicit in *A World of Love*. These present in a variety of ways throughout the novel from Lady Latterly's ability to take up and then discard lovers, to the implication in the text that Fred's love for his daughter, Jane, is too intense. His reaction to Lilia's suggestion that Jane might have fallen "in love with a love letter" (*WL*, 39) suggests jealousy and the narrator implies that Fred's love for Jane is very strong, when she states that "[i]t was when Jane took form as herself that her father entered upon his first and last, devouring, hopeless and only love" (*WL*, 19).

Christensen identifies an "undertone of sexual attraction between Jane and Antonia that lasts until the end of the book, when Jane simultaneously frees herself from the domination of the long-dead Guy and that of his living counterpart, Antonia" (2001, 55). Certainly Antonia experiences feelings of jealousy when she considers the relationship between Fred and Jane, but, rather than this jealousy resulting for any sexual attraction she might feel for Jane, it could be argued that the jealousy arises from her own emotions surrounding her earlier relationship with Fred or her perception that Jane is a rival for Fred's affections. Following Antonia's day trip to the sea, and whilst looking down on Jane and Fred, Antonia considers their relationship,

> what went on in the hall down there was more and more assuming a grotesque cast: there had been a race between herself and Jane into Fred's arms, and the girl had won. Antonia counted the times when he and she could have been lovers: could one continue what was never begun? Tonight the answer could have been, yes. Everything was magnified and distorted; everything had its way with the unpent senses – the stone cast from the sandal spat like a shot on the floor; the lamp chimney around the urged-on lamp flame gave warning by an earsplitting crack, and the flame itself, spurting threads of itself and smoke stinkingly upwards towards the ceiling, crimsonly stuttered inside the gloom it made like an evil tongue. Watching the scene being played out at the foot of the stairs, she saw at work in Jane, as in herself, the annihilating need left behind by Guy. (*WL*, 76)

Like the archway to the stable yard, the obelisk also plays an important rôle in *A World of Love* providing an overriding symbol of male sexuality. References to the obelisk permeate the novel, its presence and its shadow hinting at a possible Freudian interpretation of the text. It could be argued, for example, that the obelisk represents patriarchal society, even if the name of the person who constructed the obelisk (the name of the father, perhaps) has been forgotten by most people. This is a society which Jane is keen to escape; the narrator tells us that Jane "stepped out slowly towards the obelisk" (*WL*, 10), stepping "slowly" suggests, perhaps, a reluctance to remain within the restrictions of patriarchal society. Neil Corcoran examines this aspect of the novel and states that

> the symbolic obelisk which casts its shadows on the house in the novel's opening pages and figures prominently throughout [...] is redolent of the different passions and yearnings of the novel's characters, and it has a

phallic insistence which appears to verge on the parodistic in a way consonant with Bowen's attitudes to Freud elsewhere in her writings (2003, 127)

One should be aware, however, of the *caveat* included in *The Little Girls,* a statement which could be read as authorial comment. Writing to Clare to ask for the butter knife she saw in "Mopsie Pye", Dinah comments "[...] And you need not worry if it is a symbol, as practically everything is, as we now know" (*LG*, 152). Whilst being aware of Bowen's apparent cynicism about Freudian symbolism in fiction, two further metaphors relating to innocence and sexuality should be examined in the two novels. The first relates to the shedding of tears by Dinah in *The Little Girls.* The narrator records two specific instances of Dinah's tears, the first when Dinah cries at her first lunch with Clare where "[d]own her white face a tear made its bewildered way. One forgets that each tear is shed for the first time" (*LG*, 59). The second episode occurs when Sheila is looking after Dinah during Dinah's illness: "Dinah had raised herself on an elbow. Down her white face, under the ignominious bruise, a tear made its bewildered way" (*LG*, 212). It could be argued that the juxtaposition of the tears against the white face could be a metaphor for the loss of innocence. This is, however, a very tenuous connection, but Bowen's reiteration of the phrase "a tear made its bewildered way" is suggestive of a connection between the two events, each time, perhaps, representing Dinah's mourning for the past and the loss of childhood innocence. Bowen's use of the colour white, in this instance to describe Dinah's face on these two separate occasions and which suggests a virginal appearance in relation to her tears, is also apparent in *A World of Love* where the white of the satin ribbon which ties Guy's letters together is linked to Jane's "re-whitened" sandals (*WL*, 133) and Jane's appearance, dressed "in white", for her trip to Shannon Airport. The virginal colour of Jane's clothes and the satin ribbon can be considered in juxtaposition to the tiles in Lady Latterly's "black-and-white" drawing room (*WL*, 58) which suggest the presence of innocence in the midst of corruption. Jane's decision to discard the ribbon which constrained both the letters and, metaphorically, the past could suggest that she is willing to move from a world of innocence to one of experience. Further, Jane's departure from Montefort is somewhat akin to a bridal "going away" following a wedding as the bride is waved off by her parents. Such an allusion is reinforced by the narration of the event where,

> Jane [...] appeared in the door of Montefort saying 'Father?' at which Fred
> half-comprehendingly turned. The girl said: 'Only, I'm off. Goodbye,' and
> ducking her head, made a blind bridal rush past him into the van [...]
>   Watching the van drive away, bearing the children, the three stood –
> Antonia outside the fence, Fred and Lilia framed in the doorway. This was
> an echo, a second time – second time of what? Wedding afternoon. All was
> repeated almost exactly (*WL*, 138-139)

The repetition of Fred and Lilia's wedding day brings the novel to a
chronological full circle, for, having acknowledged that Fred "was never
Guy" (*WL*, 103) and turning to him following Jane's departure, Lilia is
now ready to open herself up to the possibility of loving Fred. Equally, by
her symbolic departure from Montefort to Shannon Airport, Jane is
released to find both love and her own identity.

Identity and Knowledge

As with much of Bowen's fiction, notions of identity permeate both *A
World of Love* and *The Little Girls*[19] and in both instances identity is
predicated on the past. However, it is the interpretation of the past which
leads to both success and failure in the construction of identity, Dinah's
acquisition of identity in particular raises epistemological concerns. For
Jane, identity is inextricably linked with the discovery of Guy's letters but
the three women who were once schoolgirls together have built their
identities in differing ways.[20] Clare's notion of identity is defined by her
business; following a question from Sheila

> Clare's expression became uplifted. She looked round her at the emptying
> tables like a big speaker deprecating a small audience. The eyes she at
> length returned to her friend were dedicated and abstract – not, it seemed,
> to be focused merely on one face. 'I am MOPSIE PYE,' she made known.'
> (*LG*, 41)

It would appear, therefore, that Clare has poured all her energies into
her chain of shops and, in so doing, constructed an identity that does not
rely on relationships or friendships and thus becomes a barrier which
protects her from emotional upheaval, a barrier that she attempts to
maintain even against Dinah.

Sheila's identity is also apparently constructed by her surroundings.
Answering Clare's question about her marriage, Sheila explains that she
married "Mr Artworth's second son [...] The elder was killed." (*LG*, 33).
However, it transpires that she married Trevor Artworth whilst she was in
her thirties; better clues to the way she has constructed her identity is

perhaps to be found both in the relationship she had before she married Trevor and in her abandoned dancing career, a career which was cut short when she was told at an audition at "[*t*]*he* place in London" that her dancing was "vulgar" and she "had too much to unlearn" (*LG*, 172). The bombardment of Dinah's advertisements threatens to destabilise the image and identity she has so carefully constructed for herself and she considers that her reputation in Southstone might be irretrievably damaged by Dinah's campaign.

Whereas Clare and Sheila's identities have been based on something relatively tangible, Dinah's self-knowledge and identity is predicated on the act of the interment of the coffer in the gardens of St. Agatha's. Her decision to attempt a second burial of artefacts from friends, albeit on a larger scale, is her bid for immortality; her re-enactment of her childhood burial is not, as Frank suggests, for "a laugh" (*LG*, 11), but rather, "a clue for posterity. Or, poser." (Ibid). Not wishing to be thought of in the future merely as part of a race, Dinah wishes people to be remembered as "personalities" and that "[o]ne should give posterity a break. One must leave posterity some clues!" (*LG*, 14.) In her exposition to Mrs. Coral, the deliverer of the parish magazine, of the value of the contents of the cave Dinah states her belief that clues are needed for those in the future to

> [r]econstruct *us* from. Expressive objects. What really expresses people? The things, I'm sure, that they have obsessions about: keep on wearing or using, or fuss when they lose, or can't go to sleep without. You know, a person's only a *person* when they have some really raging peculiarity (*LG*, 15).

Writing in 1951[21] Bowen paints a picture of childhood memories which can be read as forming the bedrock of Dinah's identity. Referring to the contemporary trend and "prevailing mood" of nostalgia (1951a, 54), Bowen comments on the importance of childhood to some adults,

> [f]or the child (or so it appears now) everything was an adventure or a drama; at the same time, there were spaces of lyric happiness. Nothing – so our re-awakened memory tells us – nothing in childhood went to loss. The semi-mystical topography of childhood seems to be universal, for all who revisit it find the same: the stream, the woods, the thicket hideout, the beach or estuary, the attic or the old barn, the toyshop, the grandmother's treasure box, the 'haunted house', and so on. [...] Best of all, there was emotional simplicity – rebellions perhaps, but (we think) no conflicts. And, framing the whole picture, we see security. (Ibid, 55)

Of course, Dinah's childhood is not as secure as she, perhaps, would have wished. Lacking her father, who committed suicide by "going under that train", rather than with the revolver which Dinah subsequently placed in the coffer (*LG*, 193), Dinah and her mother were financially dependent on Cousin Roland, who, as Dinah tells Clare, "[...] paid my school bills I *think*; but also, which was still nobler, all those years he kept Mother in flowers and new novels" (*LG*, 193). However, the security promised by Dinah's recollections of the past, the security which she has associated with the contents of the coffer, prove false and the identity which she has so carefully constructed for herself is found to be based on emptiness once the coffer is recovered.

Both Jane and Dinah's identities are inextricably linked with the past. However, such identities are not based on the facts of the past, rather, in Jane's case, a reconstruction of the past and, in relation to Dinah, a false reading of the events of her childhood. Bowen states in her essay "The Mulberry Tree", "[m]emory is, as Proust has it, so oblique and selective that no doubt I see my school days through a subjective haze" (1935, 193); Dinah too sees her childhood through a similar haze and as she learns the truth of the contents of the buried coffer she finds the edifice of her carefully constructed life crumbling away. The disinterment of the coffer should, from Dinah's point of view, reinforce both her memories of her childhood and the structures that she has placed in her life which give her identity and, perhaps, a *raison d'être*. Although she may not know what each of the other two girls placed in the coffer,[22] its very being appears to have provided a structure, albeit one based on a misconception, on which she has built her life. The bald statement with which the narrator describes the discovery of the coffer—"It was there. It was empty. It had been found." (*LG*, 158)—does not truly express the horror Dinah feels. Whilst Sheila might view the whole ludicrous episode as "[...] *what* a laugh, after all!", Dinah's reaction suggests that she alone has found the disinterment very distressing and the realisation that the coffer is empty proves a moment of *anagnôrisis* for her. Responding to Dinah's statement that she must return to Applegate, Sheila states "Your home, [...] won't run away" (*LG*, 163) but, as Dinah replies forlornly

> 'That's what it *has* done, Sheikie. [...] Everything has. *Now* it has, you see. Nothing's real any more. [...] Nothing's left, out of going on fifty years.'
> 'Nonsense!'
> '*This* has done it,' said Dinah. 'Can't you see what's happened? This us three. This going back, I mean. This began as a game, *began* as a game. Now – you see? – it's got me!'

'A game's a game,' Sheila averred, glancing down her nose.
'And now,' the unhearing Dinah went on, 'the game's collapsed. We
saw there was nothing *there*. So, where am I now?' (*LG*, 163)

Following collapse of "the game", and Clare's later rejection of
Dinah's offer to stay the night at Applegate, Dinah falls into a nervous
breakdown in which "[t]he one sign she gave of sickness was […]
indifference, but it was an indifference so great as to be a sickness in
itself" (*LG,* 199); in Frank's opinion, however, Dinah is not ill but
"unstuck" (*LG*, 220).

As the past has been utilised by Dinah to construct her identity,
however false its foundations might prove to be, so too is Jane's identity
predicated on the past. Bowen's "treasure box" of childhood to which she
refers in her essay "The Bend Back" contains, in this instance, the bundle
of letters from Guy which Jane uncovers in the attic of Montefort.
Although Christensen argues that Jane's identity is only established once
she has broken away from Antonia's, and by association, Guy's
dominance (2001, 64), it is the fact of Guy's letters which enable Jane to
begin to consider her own identity. At the age of twenty arguably it is
appropriate that Jane should move from adolescence to adulthood, from
innocence to experience, indeed Bowen's epigraph to *A World of Love*
suggests this possibility; taken from Thomas Trahernc's *Centuries of
Meditations* the epigraph reads that "[t]here is in us a world of Love to
somewhat, though we know not what in the world that should be […] Do
you not feel yourself drawn by the expectation and desire of some Great
Thing".[23] Jane, it could be argued, is ready to experience such a desire.
However, whilst Guy's letters may well prove to be the catalyst in Jane's
self-knowledge, it is the perceived loss of her father to her mother, Lilia,
allied to the loss of the letters which provides the main instance of
anagnôrisis for Jane, a moment of recognition which leads Jane to re-
evaluate her life and her relationships with both her parents and Guy,

Jane […] put her fist to her forehead and lay back. She had been robbed,
too short a time ago to have yet taken the measure of her loss. First it had
been the letters: their being gone had been a mystifying shock. Wakened
by the sounds of Maud in the afternoon, she had set out to visit them […]
In the sultry-scented inside of the elder, there the stone was, nothing at all
to show it had been disturbed until she came to lift it – then, so completely
no trace was to be found on the crushed-down, whitened roots of the grass
that her first fear was, *had* they ever been there at all? Or had they conjured
themselves into nothingness? – or stolen away by evaporation? Where,
though, in that case, was her solid ribbon? No, no way out of it: she had
had to know – vilely, the letters had been taken! But that, though bad, had

been nothing more than the start, the foreshadowing of the robbery to
come. For the worst of loss is, when it at the same time is an enlightenment
– that is what is not to be recovered from; ignorance cannot be made good.
She had lost her father, and twice over – lost him in not having known him
until she lost him, lost him in the instant of beholding. Yes, and in that
comprehensive view through the arch she'd not only blundered upon a man
and woman but perceived the packet upon her mother's wanton lap. Guy
too, then, had finished his course there. (*WL*, 120)

However, whilst the discovery of the letters may well assist Jane on
her journey of self-knowledge, their effect on the other inhabitants of
Montefort is equally striking, forcing Fred, Lilia and Antonia to re-
evaluate the last twenty years of their lives, for example their presence
forces Lilia to relive the departure of Guy from the railway station and the
fact of Guy's betrayal with Antonia (although, of course, Lilia is not aware
that it is Antonia to whom Guy exclaims "*You!*" (*WL*, 96)). This
knowledge has, in fact, corrupted her life; unable to love another and
trapped in an apparent loveless marriage, it is the recognition of the fact of
Guy's betrayal (some twenty one years after the event), together with the
acceptance that Fred is not a substitute for Guy which will, perhaps, enable
Lilia to open herself up into a "world of love". It is, however, ironic given
the effect that the letters do have, that the reader is never aware of the
identity of the recipient of the letters, an element of authorial manipulation
that will be discussed further below.

Authorial Manipulation

As has been discussed briefly already, one of the ways the narrator
and, by extension, the author, manipulates the reader's own moments of
anagnôrisis in both novels is related to names, or in some cases, to the
lack of names, thus delaying the reader's acquisition of knowledge. In *A
World of Love*, for example, there is the similarity between the names of
Guy Danby and Gay David, Maud's familiar.[24] This is, however, not the
main element of narratorial manipulation in this novel; this arises from
two main instances, the first being the identity of the addressee of Guy's
letters. The reader might assume on a first reading of the novel that the
letters were sent to Antonia for, as Lilia comments, "[e]verything up there
[the attic] belongs to Antonia", to which Jane responds, "[b]ut so does
everything in this house" (*WL*, 37). However, Lilia is firmly of the
opinion, and hope perhaps, that they are her love letters; her reaction to the
letters when Fred eventually thrusts them at her in the stable yard suggests
that she no longer believes that they are hers, that indeed she does not wish

to read them. Although she tells Fred that she no longer cares about the letters and tells him to return them to Jane, this could well be a protective mechanism to prevent the dashing of her dreams. Jane learns of the name of the addressee from Kathie, but to her it is an "unknown name" (*WL*, 137). Having asked her aunt about the name, Antonia claims that she does not remember the person and in a moment of altruism tells Lilia that Jane has burnt "[…] the letters from Guy to you." (*WL*, 139). Whilst Antonia deceives Lilia from the best of motives, she also deprives the reader of the knowledge of the recipient of the letters, all one can infer is that they were addressed to neither Lilia nor Antonia but to a third woman, the woman, perhaps, that Guy looks for at the station after he has said his farewells to Lilia; how the letters came to reside in the attic at Montefort, however, remains a mystery.

The name of the man who caused the obelisk to be built also provides narratorial manipulation in relation to nomenclature and thus poses a further mystery for the reader. The obelisk, which casts such a shadow over the novel and the inhabitants of Montefort, was erected by an apparently long-forgotten resident of the house. As with Guy's letters, Antonia knows his name and supplies the details to the gathering on the lawn of the house as they wait for Jane to depart to Shannon Airport but the manner in which she imparts this information once again denies the reader knowledge and understanding.

Names in *The Little Girls* provide an opportunity for the narrator to manipulate and defer moments of *anagnôrisis* for the reader. Throughout the novel, the narrator alternates between the names of the three women as children and their given names; added to this confusion is Dinah's change of name from Diana. Dinah's desire to use childhood names continues even after her collapse, a desire which Clare constantly attempts to thwart. Indeed it is Clare who, by the act of saying, "[g]oodbye, Dicey, […] for now and for then" (*LG*, 236), indicates her desire to put her childhood behind her. It is, however, a habit which is difficult to discard for when Dinah, stirring asks "Who's there?", Clare reverts to naming herself "Mumbo" but, as Dinah states, "[n]ot Mumbo. Clare. Clare, where have you been?" (*LG*, 237), thus echoing Dinah's cry at the end of Olive's party when "[a]lone in the middle of the empty sands wailed Dicey 'MUM-BO-O-O!'" (*LG*, 133).

Of course, it is not just the narrator's vacillation between the adult and childhood names which can be seen to manipulate the reader's understanding of the text; echoing Bowen's use of clothing to denote a person in *A House in Paris* in which Karen's travelling companion on the ship from Ireland to England is known only as "Yellow Hat", the narrator of *The Little Girls* variously describes the three main protagonists in the novel by either items of their clothing or their physical actions at a particular point in the narration. Hence Clare is first introduced as "Black Turban" and Sheila as "Pink Roses" (*LG*, 30), a device which continues from the time the two women meet in the "tea room at the top of a Knightsbridge department store" (*LG*, 29) until tea is ordered and "Pink Roses deliberately turned her head and said: 'Well, Clare …' " (*LG*, 31). Having been called "Nonchalance" (*LG*, 101) when the girls are debating whether they should use one of Sheila's coffers, Sheila is later referred to as "the local girl" (*LG*, 157) and "the settee's owner" (*LG*, 162), Dinah is "the late-comer" (*LG*, 162) and Clare "the magazine addict" (*LG*, 161).[25] Christensen suggests that this constitutes "non-naming" and that "being nameless, the women have now lost one of the foremost signs of their identity" (2001, 46), but it could also be argued that this is a narrative ploy designed to add to the confusion of identity for the reader.

Whilst the narratorial manipulation in relation to names throughout the two novels is of interest, the manipulation of time also warrants discussion. As has been argued above, in both novels the past has an overwhelming effect on the present. In *A World of Love* consideration of the past will eventually enable Jane to pass through the archway from adolescence to adulthood. Equally, reconsideration of their varying relationships with Guy force Antonia, Lilia and Fred to re-evaluate their own lives. Dinah's misunderstanding of her past does not have such a positive outcome and her sense of identity is demolished once the empty coffer is disinterred.

In her essay "Notes on Writing a Novel" Bowen explores the use of time within a novel. She states that,

> '[f]or the sake of emphasis, time must be falsified. But the novelist's consciousness of the subjective, arbitrary and emotional nature of the falsification should be evident to the reader. Against this falsification – in fact, increasing the force of its effect by contrast – a clock should be heard always impassively ticking away at the same speed. The passage of time, and its demarcation, should be a factor in plot. The either concentration or even or uneven spacing-out of events along time is important.' (1945b, 259-260)

Seven years later Bowen reiterated the importance of time in her novels in the "Preface" to the American edition of *The Last September*, stating "I am, and am bound to be, a writer involved closely with place and time; for me these are more than elements, they are actors." (1952, 96). This can certainly be seen in *A World of Love* where time does, indeed, become an "actor" within the fiction. Although the novel is not as time-specific as, for example, *The Heat of the Day*, the time frame within which the novel is set is structured in such a way that the reader can accurately reconstruct the passage of time over the four days which pass between Jane's discovery of Guy's letters and her trip to Shannon Airport to meet Richard Priam; Maud's fascination with Big Ben and Lilia's use of the clock as a hiding place all add to the notion of time as an agent in the novel. A reconstruction of the time frame is equally possible with *The Little Girls* although, of course, the novel is set over a longer period of time.

It is this narratorial manipulation of time which can be seen to have the greatest effect on the reader's understanding of the two novels; in *A World of Love* such manipulation is experienced in the opening pages of the novel. Much as the opening of *The Last September* suggests that the novel is set in an earlier time (as, indeed, it was), so too do the first few pages of *A World of Love*. After placing Montefort within a geographical location, the narrator then suggests that the temporal setting is that of the early part of the twentieth century, rather than that of the post-war era of the 1950s. There is reference to "the sweep for the turning carriage" (*WL*, 10) and the girl (who the reader subsequently learns is called Jane) "[w]earing a trailing Edwardian muslin dress" (*WL*, 10). Of course, the narrator quickly points out that the "cut of her easy golden hair was anachronistic over the dress she wore" (ibid), an anachronism which highlights the importance of the past throughout the novel. Bowen adds to this temporal confusion by the frequent references to the Gothic, suggesting by implication that this is a novel which could have been read in the dying days of the nineteenth century. David Punter's description of the Gothic fiction of this period as "peopled with stock characters, who discoursed in predictable ways" (1980, 11) could easily be ascribed to *A World of Love*. He continues that

> the shy, nervous, retiring heroine, who was nevertheless usually possessed of a remarkable ability to survive hideously dangerous situations; the heavy-handed, tyrannical father; the cast of comic extras and servants who, like in fact many of the other characters, often seem to be lifted wholesale out of Jacobean drama; and above all the villain. (ibid)

However, the inclusion of contemporary events, in particular, Jane's journey to Shannon Airport, places the novel firmly in the second half of the twentieth century.

Further authorial manipulation arises from Bowen's use of analepsis within *A World of Love*. Although mostly narrated as a teleological novel, there are four major episodes of analepses. The first is a flashback of some twenty-one years; the second is the narration of the day of the fete, the day on which Jane discovers Guy's letters. The third instance is a flashback of approximately thirteen years and the fourth returns to a period some twenty-one years earlier. Genette, in his study of Proust's *A la recherche du temps perdu*, states that it is not sufficient merely to identify the temporal sequences of a novel, it is necessary "to define the relationships connecting sections to each other" (1972, 39); it is within these relationships that Bowen manipulates the understanding of the reader. Without a completely linear structure, the reader is only able to understand the relationships within the family at the discretion of the narrator. This is particularly so with the third occasion of analepsis in the novel; although the reader is aware of the complicated circumstances of Fred and Lilia's marriage and, indeed, Antonia's rôle at Montefort, until Lilia begins to explain her engagement to Guy as she and Jane sit waiting in Miss Francie's *salon* the reader is unable to comprehend fully the difficulties faced by Lilia and Fred. Further understanding is aided by the narrator's discussion of Lilia's "bolt for London" (*WL*, 92) and Fred's subsequent trip to collect her, a trip in which he "re-wooed" (*WL*, 93) Lilia.

Following her revelations to Jane, Lilia finds herself reviewing her last meeting with Guy. This further act of recollection provides a moment of *anagnôrisis* for both Lilia and the reader; the reader is more fully conversant of the facts (having been presented with a similar story from two different points of view, that of Lilia and Antonia[26]) and Lilia finally recognises that she has it within her to love her husband.

Time also appears as an "actor" in *The Little Girls*, but whilst episodes of analepses occur throughout *A World of Love*, there is only one major moment of analepsis in Bowen's later novel, although the recollections of Dinah, Sheila and Clare also provide analeptic narration. Utilising a framework similar to that of *The House in Paris*, Bowen frames the past between two sections which narrate the present, "Part Two" providing information about Dinah's childhood, a narrative which, in turn, provides recognition for the reader, the narrator utilising, to borrow from Genette, a "completing" analepsis (1972, 51).[27] Such a reading of the time frame of the novel, however, does not fully explain the authorial manipulation of chronological time in the novel. Basing his work on that of Tzvetan Todorov and Gunther Müller, Genette discusses the "temporal duality", "the opposition between erzählt Zeit (storytime) and Erzählzeit (narrative time)" (ibid, 33); such a distinction is particularly apposite when one considers the chronological manipulation inherent in *The Little Girls*. As Bowen states in "Notes on Writing a Novel", she believes the "spacing-out of events" to be extremely important in a novel, a narrative ploy she utilises to great effect in *The Little Girls*. Initially Bowen is relatively regimental in her treatment of time in the plot in relation to the pagination of the novel; in Part One the four chapters cover three months (September to October in the present). The following seven chapters in Part Two narrate the events of the summer of 1914 and thus represent a slowing down of the narrative. Reverting back to the present (an unspecified year in the early 1960s), the following five chapters continue with the narration through to November. However, it is the final chapter which particularly highlights Bowen's manipulation of time in the novel: this is the longest chapter in the novel, running to just over thirty seven pages, yet it deals with only a single day in the lives of Dinah, Sheila and Clare, thus significantly slowing down the narration.

Such spaces within the text also leave the reader questioning the meaning of the narrative and a telephone conversation between Dinah and Sheila whilst in a branch of "Mopsie Pye" acts to confuse the reader further. Playing very effectively with the concept of a literal, verbal narratorial space, Bowen utilises the actual spaces between sentences to add to this confusion as Dinah apparently relays questions and answers from Sheila to Clare in a conversation peppered with ellipses,

> … Oh, *Sheikie*, hullo! … Why yes, of course I am me! (She knew my voice) … I was just telling Mumbo, you knew my voice … Yes, of course she is here. Or rather, I am with her … In a Mopsie Pye shop … A garden of all delights. (She wants to know what your shop's like.) … I was telling Mumbo you want to know what her shop's like … She's very well. (You are, aren't you?) … (*LG*, 149).

Despite the apparent fullness of the conversation, the inclusion of so many ellipses might lead the reader to wonder whether Dinah is faithfully recording the conversation or if she is being economical with the truth; as a narratorial device this further adds to the opaque nature of the text.[28]

Thus it can be seen that Bowen manipulates narrative, nomenclature and chronology, and effectively delays and defers the reader's own recognition and understanding of the plot. Her choice of narrators also adds to this manipulation. Although *A World of Love* contains some major moments of analepsis, and despite the frequent use of a syntax which bears more than a passing resemblance to Henry James,[29] the novel is superficially a very straightforward novel, narrated in the main as a teleological novel with an omniscient third person narrator. However, Bowen was eager to find a new form of narration for *The Little Girls*, one rejecting the notion of omniscience for her narrator. In his foreword to

Pictures and Conversations, Spencer Curtis Brown recalls a discussion he had with Bowen whilst she was writing the novel, stating

> [i]n *The Little Girls*, she for the first time deliberately tried, as she said when discussing with me the writing of it to present characters entirely from the outside. She determined never to tell the reader what her characters were thinking or feeling. She recalled that once when she had remarked to Evelyn Waugh that he never told his characters' thoughts, he had replied, "I do not think I have any idea what they are thinking; I merely see them and show them." In a way vastly different from Waugh's, she set herself the technical puzzle of writing a book "externally" (1975, xxxviii).[30]

This, of course, has a significant effect on the reader's understanding of the plot, but whilst Bowen may well have decided that omniscience was not to be a feature of her narrator for *The Little Girls*, she substitutes knowledge with questions. Bowen interposes questions to the reader throughout the novel, this use of the interrogative within the narration implies a complicity with the reader and suggests that the reader has as much knowledge, if not more, than the narrator. Yet, obviously this is not the case but, much as the reader might feel superior to the child narrator of James's *What Maisie Knew*, it also has the effect of denying the reader complete understanding. An omniscient narrator also chooses to present the narration in such a way that limits information for the reader; both types of narrator therefore affect the reader's understanding and knowledge in differing ways.

Endings

The final pages of the two novels continue to highlight the differences in narration. The reader of *A World of Love* is told that when Jane and Richard meet "[t]hey no sooner looked but they loved" (*WL*, 149), an ending that provides closure at least for Jane, if not for all the protagonists of the novel. In contrast, much as the reader has been posed questions throughout the novel, the ending of *The Little Girls* leaves many questions unanswered. In fact, such an open ending is not uncommon in Bowen's *oeuvre*, as has been discussed in earlier chapters; it is, however, an ending that could provoke even more questions. Whereas *A World of Love* can be seen as exorcising "the ghost of her former fiction" (Ellmann 2003, 189), *The Little Girls* can be seen as one of Bowen's more experimental novels, a novel in which as Atkins suggests, "[t]here are no signs of an aging writer trying to appear up-to-date by superficial tricks" (1977, 74). Both novels, however, highlight the importance and relevance of the past and each, in its own way, provide the foundations for the narrative technique utilised in *Eva Trout, or Changing Scenes*, her tenth novel and last published work of fiction.

Notes

[1] When reference is parenthesis is made to *A World of Love* "WL" will be used. Similarly, *The Little Girls* will be referred to as "LG" in parenthesis.

[2] See letter to L.P. Hartley, 15th September 1954 (appendix).

[3] See letter to William Plomer, 1st June 1963 (appendix).

[4] Clair Wills highlights the novel's relationship with the Cold War noting Jane's reluctance to involve herself with the "passions and politics of her family" and those of the "outside world" (*WL*, 34):

> Jane feels 'forbidden to enter' this arena but lingers on the threshold—it appears that there is no space for her. The room is overcrowded, filled up with the 'passions and politics' of previous inhabitants who won't go away. Guy and his contemporaries have not yet left the room, and the legacy of the First and Second World Wars ensues that the siege-like state of war continues. Jane's attempt to assuage the rising tensions by adding 'no further heat' is designed to maintain the cool temperature of a war which is already quite overcharged enough. (2009, 135)

[5] See Clair Wills' essay "Half Different: The Vanishing Irish in *A World of Love*" (2009) for a further discussion about concerns over emigration in the 1950s.

[6] See letter to L.P. Hartley, 1st April 1953 (appendix).

[7] This letter is reprinted in *The Mulberry Tree*.

[8] See letter to William Plomer, 1st June 1963 (appendix). Bowen would appear to have been fond of Folkestone, a fondness to which her essay "Folkestone: July, 1945" attests.

[9] Bowen's use of the interrogative in this novel will be discussed further below.

[10] Suzanne Lenglen was born on 24th May 1899 in Compiène, France. In 1914, aged 14, she competed in the final of the French Championships, losing to Marguerite Broquedis. Later that year she won the International Clay Court Championship held in Sainte-Claude. During her career Lenglen won 81 singles titles, 73 doubles titles and 8 mixed doubles titles. (http://www.tennis.co.uk/player/suzanne-lenglen/index.shtml). Pauline Chase first appeared as Peter Pan in 1905 and gave an estimated 1,400 performances as Peter Pan between 1905 and 1913 (http://www.collectorspost.com/Actors/pauline_chse.html). *Peter Pan* is, of course, the story of the child who cannot grow up.

[11] Maud's treatment of others can be compared to the actions of Paul, the older brother in Bowen's short story "The Inherited Clock", who forces his sister's hand into the mechanism of a clock; a full discussion of this story can be found in chapter three.

[12] Maud's familiar, Gay David, is similar to familiars that can be found throughout Irish Gothic literature. Patricia Coughlan, for example, notes the use of such

characters in many of the short stories of J.S. LeFanu (1989, 20), an author who can be seen as a literary influence on Bowen. Indeed, McCormack suggests that by naming Lilia's fiancé Guy, Bowen is referring to LeFanu's *Guy Deverill* (1994, 406-407).

[13] This is not the only intertextual reference to Bowen's earlier fiction in these two novels; there is a reference to Browning's poem "The Last Ride Together" in *The Little Girls*, a poem which is also mentioned in *To the North*. Corcoran suggests that Jane's journey to Shannon Airport can "be regarded as a benign version of the final suicidal and murderous drive of *To the North*" (2003, 134). Equally, references to fire in *A World of Love* provide a point of comparison to *The Last September* where the fear of the future of Danielstown, that it might suffer the same fate of death by fire as its neighbours, causes great concern. Neil Corcoran particularly highlights the many implicit references which link *A World of Love* to *The Last September* (ibid, 129-130). Intertextual references are made throughout Bowen's fiction and recurring references are made in *The Little Girls* to *Macbeth*.

[14] Whilst this chapter briefly discusses the many references to heat and fire, Toni O'Brien's article focuses specifically on Bowen's use of light and dark in both *A World of Love* and *The Last September*.

[15] An alternative reading could suggest an authorial comment on the issue of class in Irish society for, Lady Latterly "was *nouveau riche*; but, as Antonia said, better late than never" (*WL*, 57). Alternatively it is possible, of course, that Bowen adopted the name from D.H. Lawrence's eponymous heroine, Lady Chatterly.

[16] See chapter five for a full discussion of "The Demon Lover".

[17] The symbolism of the obelisk will be discussed further below.

[18] Bowen would, presumably, have been very happy about this comparison having used a Proustian epigraph for *The Last September*, she also translated parts of *Le Temps Retrouve;* the typescripts of her translations are held at the Humanities Research Center at the University of Texas at Austin (Sellery and Harris 1981, 235), and she published at least one article about Proust, "The Art of Bergotte" reprinted in *Pictures and Conversations.*

[19] Referring to both *The Little Girls* and *Eva Trout, or Changing Scenes*, Anne Wyatt-Brown states that "we can read these final novels as part of Bowen's search for identity" (1993, 166).

[20] The narrators of both novels actively confuse the issue of identity for the reader and such authorial manipulation will be discussed further below.

[21] There would appear to be some confusion about the original date of publication of Bowen's essay, "The Bend Back" which was first printed in *Cornhill* in 1951, although an earlier version, "Once Upon a Yesterday" appeared in *Saturday Review of Literature* on 27th May 1950. (Sellery and Harris 1981, 163). Despite the body of the text of the essay as reprinted in *The Mulberry Tree* stating "[t]his is 1951" (p.54), the date given there for the essay is 1950.

[22] It is eventually revealed that the contents of the coffer included Dinah's revolver (*LG*, 192), Clare's volume of Shelley's poetry which she had "given up" (*LG*, 188) and Sheila's sixth toe (*LG*, 234).

[23] *Centuries of Meditation*, Thomas Traherne's unfinished prose work, is presumed

to have been started in 1669; however, it was not published until 1908 after its discovery in a London bookstall. In his work, Traherne discusses, *inter alia*, the innocence of childhood and his own philosophy of religion based, in part, on the beliefs of Pelagius, a British monk during the fourth and fifth centuries. (Davis 1980, 7-15).

[24] This confusion is added to by the typographical error in the 1999 Vintage edition of the novel which erroneously refers to the geographical location after which Maud's familiar is named as "Guy David's Hole" (*WL*, 47)

[25] It is not just the narrator who tries to confuse with the use of names, Dinah also uses this device when the three women are discovered by the householder as they disinter the coffer; in a deliberate attempt to disguise their identities Dinah shortens Clare's surname, referring to her simply as "Miss Jones" (*LG*, 159).

[26] Genette names such moments of analepsis as "repeating analepses" (1972, 54)

[27] Genette describes a "completing analepses" as "retrospective sections that fill in, after the event, an earlier gap in the narrative" (ibid, 51).

[28] A longer discussion of Bowen's use of spaces within the text of *The Little Girls* can be found in Darwood, 2009, pp11-20.

[29] Such Jamesian syntax can be found throughout the novel (and Bowen's work as a whole), the most quoted example can be found within the description of the kitchen at Montefort where "[m]ush for the chickens, if nothing else, was never not in the course of cooking" (*WL*, 21). Ellmann suggests that the narrative style within *A World of Love* "seems frozen and febrile at the same time" (2003, 189).

[30] Spencer Curtis Brown states that he holds the last chapter ending to *The Little Girls*, but that he "will never print them, for that was not her wish". He continues, however, "[m]aybe some day a thesis-writer will compile a learned, but I hope not dull, comparison of the two versions." (1975, xxxix). Wyatt-Brown suggests that Bowen faced difficulties in writing *The Little Girls* which arose from unresolved issues surrounding the death of Bowen's mother when she was thirteen: she states,

> [t]he novel's conceptual problems resulted from its emotionally charged content. Not only was her heroine, Dinah Delacroix, attempting to reconstruct the severed strands of her past life experience and to understand her own emotion, but the author was engaged in the same task as well. As a result she could not be confident about the direction that the work should take. (1993, 177)

CHAPTER SEVEN

"A CONCATENATION OF CIRCUMSTANCE": EVA TROUT, OR CHANGING SCENES

Since its publication in 1968, *Eva Trout, or Changing Scenes*[1] has received a mixed reception from the critics: Hoogland, for example, praises the novel for its "conscious subversion of the ideology of narrative itself" (1994, 210) but, conversely, Lee believes it to have a "preposterously haphazard plot [which] culminates in a farcical melodrama on Victoria Station" (1999, 200). Austin regards the novel in an ambivalent light stating, "[t]he book is very entertaining [...] But in retrospect we wonder if it adds up to much" (1989, 68). However, like *A World of Love* and *The Little Girls*, Bowen was very satisfied with *Eva Trout* and was particularly pleased that William Plomer enjoyed the novel; writing to him on 27th February 1968 she states:

> I'd been on tenterhooks to know what you'd think of EVA – what *you'd* think, I mean. Thank you very much, indeed, for writing as you did. One – or I – so easily could begin to believe an entire book has been a hallucination. It means more than I can say to know that you like it, that you have enjoyed it.[2]

Charles Ritchie noted Bowen's excitement in his diary; having met her in London his subsequent diary entry dated 6th October 1967 highlights her joy, "Elizabeth is approaching the last chapter of *Eva Trout*. God knows how it will be received. Her delight in it is catching" (1983, 85).[3] Contemporaneous reviews from America were very encouraging according to Ritchie, the book received a "chorus of praise", a fact about which he took particular pleasure (ibid, 106).

Like her earlier novels, the plot of Bowen's last completed novel can be retold simply. It tells the story of Eva Trout, heiress to her father's fortune, and her attempts to survive in a society that is alien to her. Having lived a rootless existence following the death of her mother, Eva eventually tries to find a place in society for herself at school and then, some years later, by staying as a paying guest with her former teacher,

Iseult, and her husband, Eric. This is not a success and Eva runs away to set up her own home only months before she is due to receive her inheritance. Having reached the decision that she would like a child, Eva travels to America and adopts a young boy who, it later transpires, can neither speak nor hear. Eva and her son, Jeremy, remain in America for eight years until Eva decides to return to England. Jeremy is subsequently abducted by Iseult under the misapprehension that he is the son of her former husband. Having been reunited with Jeremy, Eva flees to France where she places Jeremy in the care of Monsieur and Madame Bonnard who Eva believes will be able to help Jeremy in his search for speech. This decision has disastrous consequences for Eva as she and Jeremy lose the ability to communicate. As Eva prepares to leave with her lover, Henry Dancey, on a journey purporting to be for the purposes of marriage, Jeremy shoots Eva and she dies in the throes of extreme happiness.

Bowen creates an intricate web in this novel, a web which draws the reader into the world of the eponymous heroine and one which raises many questions in relation to knowledge, innocence, sexuality, passion and identity, taking the discussion of these issues found in her earlier novels a step further. Of course, although Hoogland comments that *Eva Trout* "represents Bowen's last novelistic effort to explore the constitution of (female) sexuality/subjectivity" (1994, 207), it is important to recognise that Bowen did not intend it to be her last work of fiction for, at the time of her death, as well as writing an autobiographical work, she was working on a new novel, *The Move-In*.[4] Indeed Bowen was very wary of treating a person's last published novel as the culmination of all their work. This is particularly apparent in her essay on Virginia Woolf, in which she states

> [b]ecause *Between the Acts* is Virginia Woolf's last book, the reader may search it for some touch of finality. Of this I find, as I expected to find, none. The form and the combination of elements are, as always, new; she never used any combination or form twice. When the book ends it is, as at the end of the other books, as though a lamp had been switched off at its base, but the current is still waiting along the flex. *Between the Acts* in no sense completes her work, which is incapable of being completed. One envisages or desires completion only upon a level upon which she neither wrote nor lived. (1941, 74)[5]

Hoogland further suggests that the novel "perpetuates a line of exploration running through and connecting all the author's previous works" (1994, 208). It is obviously the case that the novel shares many common themes with her earlier novels and in this last published work Bowen again plays with these in such a way as to constantly manipulate the reader's own understanding of the narrative. By discussing these themes together with issues such as *anagnôrisis* and epistemological concerns and by drawing on other sources such as the autobiographical elements of *Pictures and Conversations*, Bowen's only children's book, *The Good Tiger*, as well a short story, "Her Table Spread", this chapter explores Bowen's narrative treatment of these issues, a treatment that might well provide a "concatenation" (*ET*, 268) of her earlier novels.

Now widowed and having sold Bowen's Court, Bowen travelled in Europe and America extensively, lecturing in American universities and for the British Council. In the mid-sixties she decided that she needed a more permanent base. Moving to Hythe, a town which had many childhood associations for her, she bought a house known as Wayside, which she renamed Carbery, the name of a house that once belonged to her mother's family. Many of her friends lived near Hythe and she entertained frequently, her friends either staying with her at Carbery or at the White Hart Hotel in Hythe where Bowen paid for their rooms in advance (Glendinning 1993, 223, 225). Her friendship with Ritchie continued to be of great importance to Bowen: following her purchase of Carbery she wrote to Ritchie saying "[t]he west bedroom which will be yours is the larger of the two, and is over the living room" continuing "when you are not there I shall probably use it as a room to write in, as it's so pleasant" (Bowen quoted in Glendinning 1993, 223). Her deep affection for Ritchie was one which was reciprocated and two of Ritchie's diary entries particularly highlight his feelings for Bowen: on 21st April 1968 he wrote "[i]t is time Elizabeth returned. What if she never did? Some day she won't." (1983, 92). A later entry dated 24th January 1969 asks "God! how will it be if I outlive her" (ibid, 111). His dedication "to the memory of Elizabeth Bowen" in his last volume of diaries (published in 1983) attests to the affection in which he held her.[6]

In his introduction to *Pictures and Conversations*, Curtis Brown quotes from a letter written to Bowen by John Bayley in which he states:

> What I find especially stimulating and devastating about Eva and her whole ambience is the *modernity*. The sense of burning one's fingers with the present moment, which so many novels now try – with what fatiguing laboriousness – to give one, is yours from page one. Your "intouchness" is indeed marvellous. (Bayley quoted in Curtis Brown 1975, xxv)

Indeed, the novel resounds with modern touches as Eva's purchases for Cathay (the house she initially rents following her flight from Iseult) demonstrate. Her drawing-room contains "[o]utstanding examples of everything auro-visual on the market this year" (*ET*, 118) and space is provided in the dining room for her computer (*ET*, 119). However, it is not merely the evidence of high consumerism which places the novel firmly within its historical context but also its references to homosexuality. The novel was written in a period that is often perceived as one of sexual liberation, a liberation which encompassed discussions not just of heterosexuality but also homosexuality and the growing number of cases of those who underwent re-gendering operations.[7] Whilst there is no mention of any such case in *Eva Trout*, certainly the effect of the liberalisation of the laws in relation to homosexuality might well be read into the novel. Jeffrey Weeks notes that there had been "an evolution of attitudes which can be traced back to the 1950s and early 1960s" (1990, 156), a sea change which may well have led to the decriminalisation of private male homosexual acts between consenting adults in 1967 (ibid, 11).[8] According to John Atkins, Bowen's fiction kept pace with such changes; he states, "Bowen is aware as anyone else of the decadence of modern society" (1977, 72), continuing

> Miss Bowen was keeping up, and not much escaped her sharp eye. In 1964 and again in 1969 she produced works which, despite all the evidence, still surprised by their contemporaneity […] In *Eva Trout* again one notes the open-minded acceptance of a new world and a new people (ibid, 74-75).

Changing attitudes to homosexuality can be seen particularly in Bowen's characterisation of Eva's father and of his lover, Constantine, Bowen's only overt male homosexual characters in her fiction. Whilst opinion may well have been changing in relation to homosexuality, it was not widely accepted by the general public, nor were the growing numbers of single parents. Eva herself seems only too aware of this as is shown by her eagerness to suggest that she has been married and that the marriage was not a success: this imaginary marriage gives legitimacy to Jeremy's existence.

Despite the general perception that the 1960s was a decade of sexual freedom, love and peace often associated with the hippy movement, Britain and the western world were overshadowed by the Cold War and the threat of an apocalyptic war fought with the atom bomb. This period of the 1960s was, according to Hoogland, a time in which "the epistemological crisis marking the middle of the twentieth century was already well underway" (1994, 214), a "world in which the likelihood of emotional and cultural amputation [was] strong" (Deane 1996, 26). This was a crisis feared by many and Henry articulates this fear as he and Eva contemplate the (im)possibility of a future together. Discussing his turbulent emotions in relation to Eva, Henry asks Eva if she has any notion of his predicament:

> 'I wonder,' he said, 'whether, in spite of all I was telling you this morning, you can conceive what a state I am in and how chaotic it is. *Feel?*—I refuse to; that would be the last straw! There's too much of everything, yet nothing. Is it the world, or what? Everything's hanging over one. The expectations one's bound to disappoint. The dread of misfiring. The knowing there's something one can't stave off. The Bomb is the least. Look what's got to happen to us if we do live, look at the results! Living is brutalizing: just look at everybody! We shan't simply toughen, Eva, we shall grossen. We shall be rotted by compromises. We shall laugh belly-laughs. We—' (*ET*, 235).

However, whilst it incorporates characterizations of homosexuality and the fears of many for the future, the novel, like much of her fiction, never explicitly discusses the economic situation of Britain, in this instance that of the 1960s with its high levels of poverty. Granted, Eva's inheritance is discussed; described by Constantine as "fabulous wealth" (*ET*, 40) it was a wealth which would have been considered exceptional at a time when many children were living in households whose income was not sufficient to meet the basic needs of the family and when unemployment figures were rising, a fact that would surely have been noted by Eric Arble as he sought to find suitable employment but one that does not appear to fully register in the world of Eva Trout. Eva's wealth is seen in contrast to the relative poverty of the Danceys and the Arbles; the reader is told, for example, that "Henry stood out: topmost intelligent one of a family all rendered to a degree intelligent by poverty, breeding and the need to get on" (*ET*, 14) but the Danceys would have been well off by comparison with many families during that period. [9]

Eva

Bowen's novels are complex structures in which narrative themes are interwoven and this is particularly so in *Eva Trout* where issues of innocence, sexuality, identity and knowledge are intertwined in a multifaceted construction which can be difficult to disentangle. Any discussion of innocence within the novel also necessitates an exploration of Eva's and other protagonists' sexuality, as notions of identity and knowledge are equally relevant to the question of innocence and its loss.

The notion of innocence is foregrounded by the title of the first section of the novel, "Genesis"—the first book of the Old Testament in which

Adam and Eve are cast out of the Garden of Eden after they have eaten the fruit of the "tree of the knowledge of good and evil".[10] Eva Trout is, like so many of Bowen's "innocents", a protagonist who exists outside society but who desperately seeks understanding and knowledge of that same society, "an outsider in a gender-divided and heteronormative environment, who struggles to understand the dominant culture" (O'Toole 2009, pp.163-4). Like Valeria Cuffe in Bowen's short story "Her Table Spread",[11] Eva has not, at the age of twenty-five, yet made her entrance into adult society. As with many of Bowen's protagonists, Eva's unusual childhood has delayed such an entry. Eva is an orphan whose mother died in a plane crash when she was only two months old and of whom Eva has no memories. As a child, Eva travelled throughout the world with her father, Willy Trout, periodically being left with, amongst others "a Baptist missionary family in Hong Kong [… and] some relations of his chiropodist's" (*ET*, 57). Her nomadic lifestyle can certainly be seen as one contributing factor to her sense of herself as outside society, a stranger to the world.

Henry's subsequent observation of a thrush trapped in his father's parish church can be read as an analogy for Eva: the thrush

> was adolescent; though full-grown still hardly more than a bloated fledgling. Barely yet fit to fly, it did so with arduousness and terror, hurtling, hoping, despairingly losing height, not knowing where it was to land, if it ever did, or how to take off, if it ever could. Here or there, it beseechingly came to rest, wings widespread, head twisted over its back, beak agape, a palpitation in its speckled throat. (*ET*, 250)

Eva could be considered similarly unqualified for life, "[b]arely yet fit to fly", lacking direction and knowledge of what she could and should do with her life. A "giantess" whose profile shows "the still adolescent heaviness of the jawline" (*ET*, 12), Eva shares many physical and emotional characteristics with Valeria Cuffe. A guest staying at Valeria's Irish castle, for example, "recollected having heard that she was abnormal – at twenty-five, of statuesque development, still detained in childhood" (*CS*, 418). Valeria is a young woman who continues to live in a childish world of fantasy; she is "impulsive" according to Mrs. Treye, another of Valeria's guests. Having discarded Mr. Alban as a potential husband, Valeria sets her heart on marrying a British naval officer, Mr. Garrett, an ambition which is never realised. Like Eva, Valeria is an heiress to a considerable fortune. However, her aunt despairs of her inability to find a suitable suitor and voices her fears that Valeria "would die of a chill, childless, in fact unwedded; the Castle would have to be sold and where would they all be" (*CS*, 420). There are of course differences between the two girls; nevertheless Valeria can be read as a prototype for Eva, an heiress who does indeed die legally childless and "unwedded".

Eva's place outside society echoes not only that of a number of Bowen's previous protagonists but also the central character in her earlier children's story *The Good Tiger*. First published in 1965, this short book tells the story of a tiger who refuses to act like the other animals who live in the same zoo who "ate all the meat they were given and wanted more" (*GT*, 1); instead the tiger only wants to eat cake. Lonely without another tiger with whom he can be friends, he is befriended by two small children, Bob and Sarah. Invited to tea at Sarah's house the tiger, naturally, is not aware how to behave in this new society. As the narrator states, "[h]ow should he act at a party? The tiger did not know, for no one had told him." (*GT*, 10). After running away from Sarah's house, the tiger falls asleep in a car and dreams of his own version of Eden, a place where "he was a baby tiger once more. All round were trees, bright green trees, and the sun was hot. In his dream, the tiger knew where he was. This was the forest, his own forest." (*GT*, 17-18). Once left in the wood by the owner of the car in which he has fallen asleep, the tiger realises that the wood is not as Edenic as he might have dreamed and that he desperately wants to see his two young friends, Bob and Sarah, again; reunited with them again the tiger regains a sense of happiness. Eva, too, acts like the good tiger; unable to find her own niche in society she runs away to America to acquire a child and then continues to live outside society as she and Jeremy share a world without speech. Her decision to return to England and to seek out her former friends, in particular Henry Dancey, indicates that she realises that she cannot live forever outside of society and, like the good tiger, she too needs friends in order to live in that society.

Eva's nomadic childhood and her orphan state, combined with the knowledge of Willy's total obsession with Constantine, has a great effect on Eva as she tries to find her true place in society and gain self-knowledge for, as the narrator states, "*her* existence had gone under a shadow: the shadow of Willy Trout's total attachment to Constantine" (*ET*, 17). Eva's journey towards knowledge and understanding of her own identity does not begin until, at her own insistence, she returns to England at the age of fourteen to attend school. Her first experiences of school life are, however, disastrous. Situated in the castle which Eva will later tell the Danceys was to be the place of her honeymoon, the school is actually financed by Willy with the express intention of keeping Constantine away from Kenneth, the head teacher and lover of Constantine. The school is, according to Eva, "experimentary" in nature (*ET*, 13) and lacking in authorial control; it is ultimately a failure. However, despite its shortcomings the school brings Eva into close contact with other children of similar age, "juveniles – a species known to her so far only in parks or in hotels fleetingly" (*ET*, 49).

Eva gains a greater understanding of societal rules at her second school, Lumleigh. Relying on the daily routine as "a conveyer-belt, smooth and ceaseless" (*ET*, 63), Eva initially tries to conform in matters of appearance but, despite the initial efforts of her "co-existers" (ibid) she still stands apart and, anticipating Jeremy's future existence, she is "unable to speak – talk, be understood, converse" (ibid). Her inability is visible in her "countenance with its look of subjection, bewilderment, fatalism" (*ET*, 64) and, as she continues to stumble through life towards the concatenation which leads to her death, Eva remains bewildered by society and its rules. There is, however, one redeeming feature of this school for Eva: the presence of Iseult Smith (later to become Iseult Arble), a teacher at the school. Their relationship continues throughout Eva's time at Lumleigh and for some years after when Eva goes to stay with Iseult and her husband, Eric, as a paying guest. Here the relationship flounders and Eva ultimately feels betrayed by Iseult; in turn she appears to betray her former teacher.

Without doubt Eva can be considered an "incurable stranger to the world" (*DH*, 106) and she shares the innocent's ability to cause chaos. The narrator of *The Death of the Heart* explores the dangers posed by innocent people whose "singleness, their ruthlessness, their one continuous wish makes them bound to be cruel, and to suffer cruelty" (ibid). Eva might well perceive that she has suffered cruelty at the hands of her father, Constantine and, later, the Arbles (although, there is an element of adolescent resentment against figures of authority) but her ability to cause chaos and cruelty to others cannot be in doubt. Certainly Constantine recognises that Eva is quite capable of causing trouble. Talking to Iseult over lunch in a London restaurant he states, "We must face this: Eva's capacity for making trouble, attracting trouble, strewing trouble around her, is quite endless. She, er, begets trouble – a dreadful gift" (*ET*, 44). Henry, whilst not being as harsh as Constantine, shares this view. Comparing her to Browning's poetic character Pippa in the poem "Pippa Passes", he tells Eva, "[i]n a way you're a sort of Pippa – though in reverse" (*ET*, 179). Henry clarifies his statement, continuing:

> Pippa diverted people from lust and villainy, and exactly one or the other of those two things, or both sometimes, do rather seem to spring up where you set foot. Don't feel I feel this reflects on you. Ethically perhaps you're a Typhoid Mary. You also plunge people's ideas into deep confusion; that is so far as they ever had any […] You are artless; that is the awful thing.

> You roll round like some blind indeflectible planet. *Sauve qui peut*, those
> who are in your course. (*ET*, 179-180)[12]

But is the chaos that surrounds Eva of her own making or the result of
her circumstances? Austin suggests that it is inevitable that Eva should
become a victim, she is a "child of violence … [who] comes full circle to
her true inheritance of violence" (1989, 63). The narrator of *The Death of
the Heart* states that when two innocents meet, "their victims lie strewn all
around" (*DH*, 106) and whilst Eva's actions can seen to result in chaos for
others, it is, perhaps, the meeting of two innocents, Eva and Jeremy, which
results in the most violent episode in the novel, Jeremy's act of matricide,
an act which may be caused ultimately by Eva's prolonged state of
innocence and her lack of understanding of twentieth century society.
When she receives her inheritance at the age of twenty-five Eva puts in
motion a chain of events that will lead, eventually, to her premature death.
Desiring a child, but deciding not to follow the traditional route of
marriage and children, she acquires a child illegally by a method that is
never fully discussed in the novel with the exception of a mysterious
telephone conversation in which Eva and an unnamed voice exchange
cryptic messages. In another genre this telephone call would be considered
a humorous element in the novel, the exchange "[d]og in the ditch" and
"[c]at on the wall" (*ET*, 143) is clearly ludicrous and one which would not
be out of place in a spoof spy novel. Bowen's sense of humour in her
novels is, according to Barreca, usually "hidden and subversive" (Barreca
1994, 117). Here, however, the humour is overt but its effect is subversive;
by ridiculing the conversation Bowen also highlights the absurdity of the
situation in which Eva finds herself.[13] Barreca suggests that Eva, like
many of Bowen's characters, "remains outside the realm of the expected"
(ibid, 114). Such characters have a residual strength which

> lies in the fact that they remain on the periphery of social and cultural
> structures, undermining those structures by their very presence. They are
> unassailable. Yet they remain the central characters of Bowen's comedy,
> never actually the creators of vicious humor, but still the catalysts initiating
> recognition of the absurdity of the absolute (ibid).[14]

In this instance the absurdity of the conversation contrasts sharply with
the seriousness of the result. The consequences associated with the illegal
trade of children are discussed by Mr. Anapopoulis and his exposition,
although aimed at warning Eva about the possibility of kidnapping,
highlights the precariousness of her situation, as he states:

But there's a racket more deadly [than kidnap] – are you aware? There's a black market in infants, unknowing babies: are you conscious they can be purchased, they can be traded? *Are* you aware, those who cannot by law adopt, due to ineligibility, become buyers? Are you aware that this is a market in which demand has come to exceed supply? Have you ever conceived, ma'am, the means resorted to that demand may be met? (*ET*, 139).

Although the scene in which this speech is delivered could be considered somewhat clumsy in terms of the general plot of the novel, it does serve to highlight the precarious path that Eva treads in her desire to acquire a child, an acquisition which leads to a child being traded illegally, a trade in which, as Henry points out to Eva, she was "sold a pup" (*ET*, 152).

A Sense of Eden

When innocence is lost a person is cast out of his or her Eden. With no childhood home with which to associate an Edenic existence, Eva's place of safety, her Eden, is arguably represented by the castle in which her first school is housed. Apart from its one-time status as a school, the castle appears on two other occasions in the novel. Its first appearance is in the opening scene when Eva tells Mrs. Dancey and her children, "[t]his is where we were to have spent our honeymoon" (*ET*, 11). The honeymoon to which Eva alludes has never taken place because, as both Iseult Arble and Constantine suspect, Eva's intention to marry was always fictitious. She later returns to the castle with Henry where he hints at his love for Eva (although denying this when Eva directly asks him about his emotions) and concludes by "asking … [her] intentions" (*ET*, 234). It is at the end of this visit to the castle that Eva asks Henry to take part in the pretence of a wedding journey at Victoria Station, a request that Henry grudgingly agrees to although he is initially unwilling to be part of an apparent charade.

Eva's fascination with the castle and her desire to return to it and claim it as the place in which she would have spent her honeymoon suggests that she might have considered it her particular Eden, a place in which she felt relatively safe and secure. It was, after all, the first place in which "after the malicious lying of her misleading dreams in which she was no one, nowhere, she knew herself to be *here*" (*ET*, 53). Following Hoogland's argument, the castle could be seen to symbolise the safe haven of a womb, surrounded by amniotic fluid, which will cushion her from a larger society of which she has no understanding. As Iseult discovers, Eva is fearful of her lack of understanding and self-knowledge, apparently seeking comfort in not knowing. Using the extended metaphor of the safety of water, a metaphor which can be seen to draw upon the image of the castle's lake, Iseult questions Eva about her fears:

> 'Are you coming nearer the surface, I wonder?' her voice asked. 'I want you to.'
> 'Yes. I am.'
> 'Yet there are sometimes times when I think you would rather go on being submerged. Sometimes you cling to being in deep water. What are you afraid of?'
> Eva might have said: 'That at the end of it all you'll find out that I have nothing to declare …'
> 'You are dragging me up from the bottom of a lake, Miss Smith?'
> 'Nobody's "dragging" you. Come up of your own accord, or stay where you are.' (*ET*, 64-65)

Hoogland suggests that the notion of being drawn back to the womb in the novel represents a "fictional recreation" of Bowen's unconsciousness which highlights her desire to return to her own particular Eden (1994, 278) Bowen, of course, recognised that an insistence on staying in such an existence, in Eva's case at the bottom of the metaphorical lake, can preclude knowledge and understanding of society. The notion that Eva has been cast out of her Eden is explicitly revisited in Professor Holman's letter in which he refers first to the apple Eva eats and then to the loss of her apple, "[e]scaping from others in the bag it cleared the edge of the seat the bag was on and symbolically bounded towards me across the aisle" (*ET*, 125); Eva's propensity for eating apples can, of course, be directly associated with Eve's act in the original Garden of Eden.

In an attempt to live in a wider society, combined with her search for self-identity, Eva eventually exchanges the promise of the womb-like security of the castle for life in America but, in fact, enters the equally womb-like silent world which she shares with Jeremy. Their apparently Edenic life in America, whilst arguably unnatural, nevertheless gives Eva, and Jeremy, a feeling of security, for "[h]is and her cinematographic existence, with no soundtrack, in successive American cities made still more familiar by their continuous manner of being in them, had had a sufficiency which was perfect. Sublimated monotony had cocooned the two of them, making them near as twins in a womb." (*ET*, 188)[15]

Eva and Jeremy are not, of course, the only ones to have a sense of a place of Eden. For Iseult, however, Eden is not represented by a geographical location but by her profession. When she first meets Eva she is a young teacher:

[...] at that time, that particular spring at Lumleigh, the young teacher was in a state of grace, of illumined innocence, that went with the realisation of her powers. They transcended her; they filled her with awe and wonder, and the awe and wonder gave her a kind of purity, such as one may see in a young artist. No idea that they could be power, with all that boded, had so far tainted or flawed them for her. About Iseult Smith, up to the time she encountered Eva and, though discontinuously, for some time after, there was something of Nature before the Fall. There was not yet harm in Iseult Smith – what first implanted it? Of Eva she was to ponder, later: 'She did not know what I was doing; but did I?' (*ET*, 61).

Constantine, some years later, acknowledges that Iseult is no longer an innocent; discussing Eva's propensity for causing and attracting trouble, he comments on Iseult's "blinker[ed]" approach to Eva stating, "You and I, Mrs Arble, are wicked people. We know, at least, what the form is. You and I cut ice. We effect *something*, and—do you know?— it's not always quite for the worse. Don't blinker yourself."(*ET*, 44)

Sexuality, Passion and Identity

A "wonderful teacher" (*ET*, 58), Iseult holds her pupils at Lumleigh in thrall, "[t]hroughout a lesson, her voice held a reined-in excitement— imparting knowledge, she conveyed its elatingness. The intellectual beauty of her sentences was formed by a glow" (ibid). Her teaching therefore provides her not just with an emotional outlet, it also provides her with a sense of identity. Iseult's delight in her occupation is in stark contrast to Miss Murcheson, the teacher in an early short story by Bowen, "The Daffodils".[16] She desperately tries to get her pupils to appreciate beauty and not to rely on second-hand experiences. She concludes "[w]hat a responsibility teaching is—But is it? They'd believe me, but they wouldn't care. It wouldn't matter really" (*CS*, 23).

Iseult's love for teaching is, in her view, stolen from her when she falls in love with Eric; she is, of course, aware of the far-reaching consequences passion can have and this is apparent in the diary entry written on the night that Eric goes to visit Eva and she blames her passion for Eric for her own loss of identity:

The passion I had for Eric was becoming less than a memory, now its more than one. That kind of passion at its height can wipe out anything that's an obstacle. In this case, the obstacle was my life, as it was – and was to have been, and the "I" I had been. So ... I did not implicate him in the crime; he was not aware of it, he would not have approved it. What he has had to do is, live with its outcome. I now see, he had wanted me as I was. He wanted me because I was *not* his kind. I was beautiful, the death of me dulled that out. I'd excited him because I seemed set apart. My bookishness and my being a teacher fascinated him like a Pythic mystery. Therefore, I murdered for nothing. Not so good. (*ET*, 91)[17]

Whilst Eric may have subdued Iseult's former identity and her sexual fervour, her gluttonous nature has not deserted her as she continues to find food "seductive" (*ET*, 41). This is particularly evident when she is taken to luncheon by Constantine: here her "enjoyment of her oysters was at once methodical and voluptuous", and she "gave herself up, untainted, to this truest sensuality that she knew" (ibid).

Iseult's fervour for Eric, food and language are not the only passionate elements in the novel since notions of sexuality and passion underpin much of the narrative of *Eva Trout*. There is, of course, Willy and Constantine's homosexual relationship and the implication that Eva's mother was involved in an affair when she died in an airplane over the Andes. In contrast, Eva's sexuality is initially in doubt. When asked by her fellow pupils at Lumleigh whether she is a "hermaphrodite" Eva can only reply "I don't know" (*ET*, 51); in fact her sexuality remains undiscovered until the day Henry discovers her passion. Eva's decision to acquire a child through an illegal adoption adds weight to an argument that she could be asexual, homosexual or that she has no real understanding or knowledge of her sexuality, preferring perhaps, "to be like Joan of Arc" (ibid), who according to the schoolchildren was always supposed to be a "hermaphrodite" although it was "never established" (ibid). To a twenty-first century reader, the use of the term "hermaphrodite" instead of, perhaps, lesbian, suggests an equal lack of understanding on the part of the Lumleigh pupils; however, it was a common term in the earlier part of the twentieth century. Writing in 1920, Arabella Kennealy states that "[i]n aiming at Hermaphroditism, feminism is continuing not only a frustration of all that Evolution has achieved in Life and Faculty, but is making for the extinction of Life itself. The Hermaphrodite is incapable of parenthood" (Kennealy, quoted in Weeks 1990, 106).

Although such a term would have been archaic even in the second half of the twentieth century, it might still have been employed in certain sections of society. Eva may well have had grounds for considering herself a "hermaphrodite" as her first two experiences of passion are for Elsinore and then Iseult, but the reader is left to wonder what the outcome might have been had Elsinore not been removed from the school in the castle, following her near-drowning in the castle lake. Eva remains in the "octagonal vaulted chamber with a balconied window and lake outlook" (*ET*, 52), the room she occupies in deference to her position as "the donor's daughter" (ibid) and shares with Elsinore, "a fairylike little near-albino" (ibid). In the secluded room which is irregularly visited by the doctor, Eva's fancies take flight as she becomes caught up in her intense emotions:

> The octagonal chamber, outlook gone from its window, seemed more locked-up round its consenting prisoners than if a key had been turned in the door, and, made medieval by the untimely dark, began in a cardboard way to belong to history. Though set in the middle of the castle, whose unreal noises could be heard, the place was as though levitated to a topmost turret. What made Eva visualize this as a marriage chamber? As its climate intensified, all grew tender. To repose a hand on the blanket covering Elsinore was to know in the palm of the hand a primitive tremor – imagining the beating of that other heart, she had a passionately solicitous sense of this other presence. Nothing forbad love. This deathly yet living stillness, together, of two beings, this unapartness, came to be the requital of all longing. An endless feeling of destiny filled the room. (*ET*, 56)

Her love for Elsinore is curtailed when Elsinore is removed from the school but Eva's love is not forgotten. Fortuitously meeting Elsinore once more in America when she goes to buy her child, Eva recalls her devastation when Elsinore was removed from the castle: "[*t*]*he dark: the unseen distance, the knowing nearness. Love: the here and the now and the nothing-but. Don't take her away, DON'T take her away. She is all I am. We are all there is*" (*ET*, 133). The two women have one last moment together and Elsinore's continued love for Eva comes to the fore as she says goodbye to Eva for the last time. Turning to Eva in the lobby of the Anapoupolis's apartment, Elsinore "flung herself against Eva: the bottomless, nocturnal sobbing began. '*Take me with you, Trout!*' The ungainly tear-wetted fur slithered and heaved between their two bodies. '*You never left me, you never left me before!*' " (*ET*, 142). Elsinore then realises the impossibility of her going with Eva and, despite Eva's protestation that she will return, waves her goodbye.

Eva's second experience of passion for another person comes when she meets Iseult at Lumleigh. Envied by her contemporaries for her close relationship with Iseult, Eva is slow to recognise her feelings for her teacher:

> Then, through one after another midsummer night, daylight never quite gone from the firmament, cubicle curtains round her like white pillars, she was kept amazed and awake by joy. She saw (she thought) the aurora borealis. Love, like a great moth circled her bed, then settled. Air came to her pillow from hayfields where, not alone, she had walked in a trance, or

the smell of the rushy and minty and earthy wetness of moments at the
fringe of the stream returned. (*ET*, 63).

It is, of course, a platonic relationship but the reader might suspect that
this was due rather to circumstances than as a result of a conscious
decision when Father Clavering-Height (Constantine's new friend and
platonic replacement for Willy Trout) asks Eva:

'Had you a sapphic relationship?'
'What?'
'Did you exchange embraces of any kind?'
'No. She was always in a hurry.'
'Good,' he said, ticking that one off. (*ET*, 184)

Eva's attachment to Iseult continues after she has left Lumleigh. Iseult
"remained an influence—all the more so by having incurred, it seemed, a
lifelong devotion" (*ET*, 17), and her desire to live with Iseult is a testament
to Eva's love for her former teacher. It is, however, a love which is tested
and one from which Eva later desires to be set free; her belief that Iseult
has abandoned her forces her to seek a house in which she can, perhaps,
begin her search for her own sense of identity.

Her third, and last, passion for another person is her love for Henry,
despite the age difference between them. Although (chronologically) an
adult when they first meet and, at that stage, twice Henry's age,[18] Eva's
relationship with Henry is immediately different to any relationship she
has encountered in her life. This is due, in part, to Henry's apparent
maturity and strength of character for "[a]lready he was qualified to deal
with Eva: she could not boss him and he could mortify her […] treating
her, on the whole, as he might an astray moose which when too
overpowering could be shooed away" (*ET*, 14). It is to Henry that Eva
turns when she decides to sell the Jaguar to finance her move to Cathay;
she seeks him out on her return from America with Jeremy and it is Henry
whom she asks to accompany her on her fictional marriage journey. She
finally recognises her love for Henry when she visits him in Cambridge.
Having taken "up one of the more trickily balanced yet authoritative of his
standing attitudes" (*ET*, 179), and discussed Eva's propensity for causing
trouble, Henry questions her ability to love, " 'I shouldn't think there's
anybody you've ever gone *out* for, is there […] Unless me,' he said – as
though in parenthesis" (*ET*, 180). His question rings true with Eva and
"[l]ooking with fervour, with passion almost, into the geometry of the
mobile, Eva uttered no word. She nodded, however" (ibid). Travelling in a
taxi to the train station, Eva agonises over the future:

she sat locked in an anguish nobody could explain […] across her the other two played cat's cradle with the cord off a cake box. She could not endure this day's being over. Fixedly looking ahead, past the driver's ears, she cast no backward glances; she could not bear to. Nor did she need to; the beautiful agonizing mirage of the university was escapable from. This was a forever she had no part in. The eternity was the more real to her for consisting of fiery particles of transience—bridges the punt slid under, raindrops spattering the Cam with vanishing circles, shivered reflections, echoes evaporating, shadows metamorphosizing, distances shifting, glorification coming and going on buildings at a whim of the sun, grass flashing through the arches, gasps of primitive breath coming from stone, dusk ebbing from waxen woodwork when doors opened. Holy pillars flowed upward and fountained out, round them there being a ceaseless confluence of fanatical colours burningly staining glass. Nothing was at an end, so nothing stood still. And of this living eternity, of its kind and one of its children, had been Henry, walking beside her. (*ET*, 180-181)

This moment in time represents a significant episode of *anagnôrisis* for Eva, a realisation that Henry has always walked with her since they first met. The last instance of *anagnôrisis* occurs when she prepares to leave on her wedding trip with Henry from Victoria Station and recognises that her love is returned, a realisation which might have occurred whilst she was in France. Had she received Henry's letter in which he discusses his feelings for her, then, perhaps, the false wedding trip would not have taken place— and consequently Eva might not have become Jeremy's victim. However, in a moment of narratorial manipulation, Eva does not receive Henry's letter and therefore remains unaware of his love for her until they meet at Victoria Station. Henry informs Eva that he has placed all their luggage on the train, telling her that he has no plans to leave the train:

Something took place: a bewildering, brilliant, blurring filling up, swimming and brimming over; then, not a torrent from the eyes but one, two, three, four tears, each hesitating, surprised to be where it was then wandering down. The speediest splashed on to the diamond broach. 'Look what is *happening* to me!' exulted Eva. […] 'What a coronation day…' (*ET*, 267).

The moment of recognition finally catapults Eva from adolescence into adulthood and into a state of ecstatic happiness, a happiness which culminates when she sees Jeremy running up the station platform. Unaware that her life is about to end, she stretches out her arms to her son; her resulting death is, indeed, a "concatenation of circumstances" (ibid) but not the favourable concatenation Constantine had hoped for in his farewell speech.

Identity and Language

As in all of Bowen's novels, questions of identity are of paramount importance in *Eva Trout* and Eva's search for her identity is a quest which permeates the pages of the novel. It is, however, a mission on which Eva believes she has failed, a failure which she blames on Iseult's withdrawal. As she angrily states to Father Clavering-Haight, "I resent my teacher [...] she abandoned me. She betrayed me." (*ET*, 184) When pressed for further details, Eva continues,

> 'She desisted from teaching me. She abandoned my mind. She betrayed my hopes, having led them on. She pretended love, to make me show myself to her – then, thinking she saw all, she turned away. She –'
> 'Wait a minute: what were your hopes?'
> 'To learn,' said Eva. A long tremble shook her. 'To be, to become – I had never been.' She added: 'I was *beginning* to be.'
> He remarked, with enthusiasm: 'A gifted teacher.'
> 'Yes. Then she sent me back.'
> 'Sent you away?'
> 'No; sent me back again – to be nothing [...] I remain gone. Where am I? I do not know – I was cast out from where I believed I was.' (*ET*, 184-185)

Cast out from the safety of Iseult's sphere of influence, Eva's subsequent actions prove to be the final destructive blow for Iseult, one which effectively destroys Iseult's marriage.

After Eva's return to England with Jeremy, she has a telephone conversation with Iseult which forces her to question the notion of identity. Although she believes that she has spoken to Iseult on the telephone in Box 3 at Paley's Hotel, Eva has doubts about the identity of the caller, "[h]ad this *been* Miss Smith, or was she dead and somebody impersonating her? [...] Something—who was to say what—had not rung true" (*ET*, 193). However, Eva attempts to apply reason to her argument, "[b]ut she had given an impression of dissolution. Or, if not of that, of a volatility amounting to it" (ibid). Eva eventually reaches the following conclusion, a conclusion which has a resonance for all of Bowen's fiction:

> what a slippery fish is identity; and what *is* it besides a slippery fish? [...] What *is* a person? Is it true, there is not more than one of each? If so, is it this singular forcefulness, or forcefulness arising from being singular, which occasionally causes a person to bite on history? All the more, in that case, what *is* a person? (*ET*, 193-194).

Eva endeavours to resolve her dilemma by visiting the National Portrait Gallery. This is not, however, a success and "the less clear she became as to what that [aim] had been, the more systematically she stood by it" (*ET*, 195). Eventually Eva decides that "they *were* all 'pictures'. Images. 'Nothing but a pack of cards'?" (ibid)[19], a belief that leads her to the stark and "malign" conclusion that "every soul that Eva knew become no longer anything but a Portrait. There was no 'real life'; no life was more real than this. This she had long suspected. She was now certain" (*ET*, 196).

As Corcoran notes, issues of both personal and maternal identity are debated in the novel (2004, 129), and Jeremy's disappearance throws into question Eva's rôle as a mother. Her visit to the National Portrait Gallery has forced Eva to realise that she does not have a place in conventional society, a society about which she acknowledges that she lacks knowledge and understanding and from which she is debarred from entering. Eva has not only failed in her quest at the National Portrait Gallery where she was unable to discover the true meaning of identity, but she also loses her son, a child who, she hoped would give her some notion of (maternal) identity and therefore a recognisable place in society.[20] That Eva relies upon the presence of Jeremy to provide her with a sense of her own identity is emphasised during her exchange with Miss Applewhite, Jeremy's sculpture teacher. Becoming distraught at the thought of her loss, "Eva, faltering in every part of her body, became afraid […] gradually loosening her fingers, she said between them: 'If he *is* in the past, there is no future. He was to be everything I shall not be' "(*ET*, 199).

Driving around London in the immediate aftermath of Jeremy's disappearance, Eva finds herself ensnared in the streets of the capital, streets that become an analogy for Eva's relationship with society itself, for "the car, trapped in tightening networks it did not recognise, began to convey to Eva its own first exasperation and then terror. So, *she* became trapped, in them and in it. She ran it into an alley that said NO ENTRY, stopped, snatched the keys out and made her escape. Though there was, actually, none." (*ET*, 201).

Whilst Eva might seek answers in the National Portrait Gallery, notions of identity in *Eva Trout* are also bound up with the acquisition and use of language. In their discussion of the novel, Bennett and Royle draw attention to the many references to mouths and language in the novel, referring to these as "mouth events" (1995a, 142). They highlight the frequent references to language from Jeremy's deafness and dumbness, to Mr. Dancey's constant colds which also lead to a speech problem, and suggest that there "is, it would seem, a compulsive scrutiny of oral convulsions in *Eva Trout*. Crucial, in this respect, is the novel's central trope of orality – Jeremy's dumbness" (ibid). Jeremy's "[r]efusal or inability to speak participates in the text's more general questioning of what it is to be a person, to be given a face, a mask, an identity – to become real" (ibid, 145). Lassner makes the further point that

> Bowen's language represents a struggle for autonomy in self-expression, and where her characters express their inability to find a language of self-expression, Bowen's imagery, her own deployment of language, expresses their dilemmas. [...] This is never more acute than in her last novel, *Eva Trout*, where the heroine, who has inherited untold millions, cannot buy, build or make a home in which she feels comfortable and who cannot discover a language of self-expression. Her own aphasia and dispossession are mirrored in the character of her mute son whom she drags from one unsatisfactory place to another. (1990, 162)

Eva's problematic approach to language is noted by Iseult at Lumleigh; there Iseult "proposed to tackle Eva's manner of speaking. What caused the girl to express herself like a displaced person?" (*ET*, 17). Eva's problems with language relate not only to the spoken but also the written word—she suffers from an inability to produce meaningful written work for Iseult. Iseult decides that this stems from a reluctance to "think" and tries to encourage Eva: "[...] I *should* like you to think, though. You have thoughts, I know, and sometimes they're rather startling, but they don't connect yet. [...] But try joining things together: this, then that, then the other. That's thinking; at least that's beginning to think" (*ET*, 62)

However, Eva remains uncomprehending of her problems: it was not "brought home to Eva, the monstrous heiress, that she was unable to speak – talk, be understood, converse" (*ET*, 63). This is, of course, an inability that Jeremy later shares with his adoptive mother. Equally she is unable to understand Henry's colloquialisms—when he asks "Can't you hold your horses till April?", Eva responds questioningly, "My horses, Henry?" (*ET*, 72). Eva's attempt to enter society is emphasised by her return to England after her self-expulsion from the silent world in which she and Jeremy had lived in America. She recognises the effect that the acquisition of language has on her for, "[t]he fact was, since the return to England her mistrust of or objection to verbal intercourse – which she had understood to be fundamental began to be undermined. [...] Incalculable desires had been implanted. An induced appetite grew upon what it fed on" (*ET*, 188).

If Eva's lack of self-expression in her adolescence adds to the lack of knowledge of her own identity, Jeremy's slow acquisition of speech causes even greater disruption in Eva's life. In the past, he had been able to communicate with Eva through an almost "[e]xtra-sensory" perception (*ET*, 158), but, having spent time with Gérard and Thérèse Bonnard, such a form of communication becomes impossible and "Eva noticed chiefly that accustomed communications with Jeremy broke down. He no longer obeyed her, not out of rebelliousness but from genuine lack of knowledge of what was wanted" (*ET*, 215). Eva is concerned that her own desire to participate in "verbal intercourse" has made "her traitorous to the years" with her son (*ET*, 188) and, indeed, their inability to communicate precipitates a further chasm between them, a chasm which is particularly apparent on Jeremy's arrival at Paley's Hotel after his stay with the Bonnards in Fontainebleau and one which marks the end of Jeremy's childhood and his forcible ejection from his own Eden. Eva "had not computed the cost for him of entry into another dimension" (*ET*, 189), a cost which becomes evident when they meet:

> They were seeing each other after their first, their one separation since Jeremy had (virtually) been born to Eva. And what was disconcerting was, not that there was any question of disillusionment, on either side, but rather that the minute was reigned over by a startling, because unavoidable, calmness – a calmness to which there was no alternative. One could have called it, a disinfected one. They were glad to be seeing each other again: anything beyond that, anything primitive, was gone. Who knew when it had breathed its last, or where its grave was? Like as they were, they were *not* of each other's flesh-and-blood, and they both knew it. The dear game was over, the game was up. (*ET*, 254)

Although Jeremy might look at Eva with "a fond, glancing, enticing look, as though to say: 'Both in the same boat, what do we do *now*?' " (ibid), his subsequent actions, although possibly further fuelled by the thought of completely losing his mother to Henry, suggest that he is not altogether reconciled to his growing ability to communicate. Lacan suggests that once a child begins to acquire language it begins to understand separation and lack. Having lost his place in Eden and, perhaps, becoming aware of his apparent impending separation from Eva, Jeremy reaches for the gun (with all its Freudian undertones) which has been placed by Iseult among Eva's belongings. Constantine, however, had predicted that trouble would arise should Jeremy be kept in his silent world; he accuses Eva of keeping Jeremy "in Cellophane" (*ET*, 175), observing that she makes "life too charming for him: an Eden. High time he was cast forth from it" (ibid). It is thus ironic that, having followed Constantine's advice, Jeremy's ejection from his silent Eden has such violent consequences. Such a convoluted twist in the narrative might lead the reader to question whether Iseult is not, in fact, the real murderer, having planted the gun in a place which was accessible to Jeremy, subconsciously, perhaps, laying the seeds for the future and providing Jeremy with the tool with which to carry out the murder. Conversely it could be argued that Jeremy believed the gun to be a toy, a replacement for the toy gun Iseult had bought him during the period of his abduction, and was not aware of his actions on Platform 8, rushing to meet his mother out of pure affection and unaware that he was, in fact, the harbinger of her death. Corcoran suggests that the "complicated plotting which delivers him a gun – that almost risibly phallic appendage – seems to have dropped in from another kind of novel" (2004, 135) and it could be thought that Jeremy's gun is descended from Dinah's gun in *The Little Girls* which is buried and subsequently disappears only, perhaps, to reappear in Eva's room at Paley's Hotel.

Narrative and Manipulation

With its Gothic overtones, the narration of *Eva Trout* could be considered to be a continuation of the style adopted in *The Little Girls*. Christensen particularly notes the Gothic nature of the novel, stating, "[t]he fragmented structure characteristic of much Gothic writing appears in *Eva Trout* in the extraordinary dependence (even more than usual in Bowen's fiction) on extra-narrative features like letters and telegrams, which are used not only to reveal character but also to carry the plot along." (2001, 121).

Certainly, Bowen was keen to emphasise this element of the novel, asking for, and obtaining a dust jacket designed by Philippe Jullian. Writing to William Plomer on 10th May 1968, Bowen asks "Do you think Phillipe Julian (or is it, Philippe?) would ever do a jacket for *Eva Trout* […] I *long* for a P.J. jacket for this book". His subsequent design for the jacket depicts a Gothic castle which closely resembles the "Bavarian fantasy" (*ET*, 11) described by the narrator.[21] However, there are significant differences in the nature of the narrative between Bowen's last two published novels; whereas the narration in the *Little Girls* attempted to present the characters "entirely from the outside" (Curtis Brown, 1975, xxxviii), Bowen returned to a form which includes many instances of free indirect discourse. *Eva Trout* is by no means simply a continuation of Bowen's previous fiction; as Curtis Brown states in his foreword to *Pictures and Conversation*, the novel was:

a complete fulfilment. Here again she was aiming at a method of narration she had not previously attempted. Always before she had shown characters reacting to a situation. In *Eva*, she showed a character creating the situations herself. Elizabeth was relaxed while writing it, and confident that she had succeeded. Neglecting none of the skills she had worked out from her by now long experience of writing, drawing on the emotions accumulated by instinct, by sympathy and by wisdom, she created a book which gave her real satisfaction and gave to many a feeling that this was her most fascinating and effective (1975, xxxix-xl).

Indeed Corcoran goes further, suggesting that the novel is "an absorbingly experimental fiction—even if one has to learn, over the course of several readings, how to be absorbed by it—which both inherits and deviates from Bowen's earlier fictions of motherless children" (2004, 130).

One of the most striking features of the narration of *Eva Trout* is the number of letters and telegrams which, as Christensen suggests, constantly advance the plot. The inclusion of such items has a considerable effect on the epistemological journey of not only the characters in the novel but also the reader since, significantly, whilst the reader may well be aware of the contents of all the letters, these are not always read by the recipient. There are two notable examples of dead letters, Professor Holman's letter and a letter from Henry, neither of which reach Eva. Professor Holman's letter, which occupies a significant part of the novel, both in terms of position and length (it runs to nearly eight pages and is placed centrally within the narration of the novel), provides a philosophical (if somewhat biased) discussion of Eva. His letter immediately raises the question of its delivery. Suggesting that the letter might not reach Eva at the Drake Hotel, Professor Holman ruminates over his emotions, should the letter be returned to him, "[k]nowing for sure that it has missed its mark, what shall I then feel? Chagrin? Relief?" (*ET*, 122). His belief that the letter will not reach Eva is well founded as a parenthetical comment states, "[This unclaimed letter was in due course returned to the sender, Professor Holman, nothing further having been heard of the addressee since she telephoned cancelling her reservation]" (*ET*, 129). Despite his uncertainty about the eventual destination of his letter, Holman is not reticent and proceeds to discuss Eva's character, as he perceives it, in great depth.

The second letter which does not reach its recipient is one from Henry to Eva in which he states his feelings for her. This too goes astray. Realising that her address in France is known (following a visit from Mrs. Dancey), Eva again takes flight, this time to Fontainebleau. Her postcard to Henry advising him of her change of address reaches him too late, and "[i]n the rack of the cross-eyed Paris one, therefore, the letter probably is still, more flyblown with each day." (*ET*, 214)

Superficially therefore, it could be argued that the reader has all the information necessary to completely comprehend the events which occur throughout the novel. However, given its multiple addressees and the varying viewpoints,[22] it can be seen that this is not the case, and indeed the narrative suggests a more sophisticated level of authorial manipulation than in Bowen's previous novels. Steven Connor, in particular, highlights the problems created by multiple addressees within a novel. Connor suggests that the

> uncertainty of address comes to be displaced and dramatised in such forms as the epistolary novel, in which the novel replaces the assumption of direct communication with a structure of oblique or intercepted addresses. Within this the reader must decipher letters written to other addressees (though by no means always delivered to or received by them), installing himself or herself in the crevices between the multiple lines of address set up by the novel. Such a form is the perfect compromise between intimacy and distance, the reliable assumption of known addressee and structures of address, and the uneasy sense of an unknown, inaccessible audience. (1996, 11)

Chapter six discusses the rôle of silence in *The Little Girls*; silence plays a significant rôle too in *Eva Trout* for, although the narrator makes the reader privy to letters that Eva does not receive, there are gaps in the narrative which are not referred to subsequently. As Professor Holman finds himself "prone to abeyances, lacunae" (*ET*, 128), so too is the reader who is unable to discover exactly what happens to Eva in the period between her leaving Lumleigh and arriving at the Arbles. One might assume that she continues with her former nomadic lifestyle but this is not certain and is not supported by the narrative. There is also a significant gap in the narrative between the two sections of the novel. Indeed Part Two starts with the phrase "[e]ight years later" (*ET*, 147), though this lacunae is not complete as some information is given concerning Eva and Jeremy's time in America. A third gap in the narrative occurs in the intervening months between Eric's visit to Eva's house after her escape to Cathay and the meeting between Eva and Iseult in Bleak House later that year. These gaps are further evidence of authorial manipulation, a manipulation which defers the reader's own experience of discovery.

The presence of a third-person omniscient narrator, together with the letters, diary entries and episodes of free indirect discourse should allow the reader greater knowledge and understanding than is sometimes the case with Bowen's novels. However, the reader is often led astray on his or her epistemological journey. This is particularly apparent when, as Iseult misunderstands Eva's proclamation that "[i]n December I shall be having a little child" (*ET*, 121), the reader is also misled. Of course, the more astute reader will realise that as Eva saw Eric some eight or nine months before the meeting with Iseult, it is not possible that Eva will be "having" a child in December, six months later than the date on which this conversation takes place.

Authorial manipulation can also be seen in the multiple viewpoints to be found within the novel. These necessarily affect the reader's understanding of the text as we can never be entirely sure of the reliability of the narrative. This is particularly so in the case of letters and diary entries; although ostensibly part of a coherent narrative, each element provides a necessarily subjective viewpoint. This can be seen from Henry's letters when he tries to describe his feelings for Eva: in the correspondence between Iseult and Constantine and, in particular, in Iseult's long diary entry. Written on the night that Eric goes to visit Eva, the entry explores Iseult's emotions, her fears and her hopes for the future, allowing her to voice these thoughts in a way which would not be possible in any medium other than a diary. In particular, her diary entry expresses her growing dislike of Eva, describing "her will, the patient, abiding, encircling will of a monster [...] She went on wanting to move in; in she moved. She took Larkins over. Those consuming eyes and that shoving Jaguar. Yet she has had her use." (*ET*, 92). Iseult's subjective view thus provides the reader with an alternative view of Eva's character as she becomes a victimiser rather than a victim of circumstances.

The tone of the narrative, too, changes throughout the novel, and this is particularly noticeably in two distinct instances: the first is the shift in narrative tone from the meeting of Eva and Iseult in Bleak House to the analeptic discussion of the relationship between Henry and Mr. Dancey following Henry's attempts to sell Eva's Jaguar. But it is the difference in narrative voice of the second part of the novel in relation to the opening pages which is most striking. The novel begins on a fantastical note that would not be out of place in a novel of romance or a Gothic novel. In contrast, the second part of the novel begins with a piece of reportage: "[e]ight years later, Eva and her little boy, Jeremy, boarded a Pan-American Boeing 707 at O'Hare Airport, Chicago. Destination: London" (*ET*, 147). This is not, of course, the first time that Bowen has diverted her reader in the first few pages of a novel. The opening pages of *The Death of the Heart*, for example, might suggest that Anna, rather than Portia, is the main protagonist. Similarly, attention is initially focused on Louie in the first chapter of *The Heat of the Day,* rather than on Stella. *Eva Trout* too begins with a false premise. The opening sentence " '[t]his is where we were to have spent the honeymoon,' Eva Trout said, suddenly, pointing across the water" suggests a broken engagement; we do not find out whether there was any basis for this assertion. This opening highlights the continuing ambiguity throughout the novel where characters and readers are left in abeyance through the multiple viewpoints and, more importantly, through Eva's apparent inability to tell the truth, an inability highlighted by Constantine when he exclaims " 'I wish you would give up lying like such a trooper!' " (*ET*, 169).

As the reader never fully understands the complexities of Eva's life, Eva too lacks comprehension, and her early death deprives her of the place in society which she had always sought. Although Eva's epistemological journey towards self-knowledge and adulthood apparently culminates in her recognition of Henry's love and her joy at seeing Jeremy at Victoria Station, "unable to take in anything but that this *was* Jeremy" (*ET*, 268), her final words highlight her lack of understanding of the consequences of her actions, asking Constantine " 'what is "concatenation"?" (ibid). Jeremy's actions, whether conscious or subconscious, will presumably have an equally devastating effect on his future as he begins his epistemological journey towards self-knowledge and an understanding of his own identity, a journey which will be placed in jeopardy by his own "[un]favourable concatenation of circumstances".

Notes

[1] This novel will be referred to as *Eva Trout* within the body of the text for the remainder of this chapter and as *ET* when the novel is mentioned in parenthesis.

[2] See letter to William Plomer, 27th February 1968. William Plomer was an author and poet, and was Bowen's editor when she was with Jonathan Cape.

[3] Ritchie's diary entry also notes the annoyance Bowen felt when people "say nostalgically to her, "I did so love *The Death of the Heart*" " (1983, 85).

[4] The first pages of this novel were published posthumously in 1974 in *Pictures and Conversations,* a collection of her work drawn together by her friend and literary executor Spencer Curtis Brown.

[5] Julia Briggs notes Bowen's concerns in *Virginia Woolf: An Inner Life* (Briggs 2005, 394) and I am indebted to her for having brought this point to my attention.

[6] *Love's Civil War* paints a complicated picture of the relationship between Bowen and Ritchie. Consisting of diary entries of Ritchie and letters from Bowen (it is believed that Ritchie burned his letters to Bowen when they were returned to him following her death), we can read of Bowen's love for Ritchie but have no knowledge of the tone of his letters to her. Instead we have his diary entries in which he records his vacillation, sometimes expressing love for Bowen and, at

others, his belief that the love affair is over. It is therefore possible to suggest that Bowen's love for Ritchie was not reciprocated but the last published entry dated 19th November 1973 would indicate otherwise: "I need to know again from her that I was her life. I would give anything I have to give to talk to her again, just for an hour. If she ever thought that she loved me more than I did her, she is revenged." (Bowen and Ritchie, 2008, p.475)

[7] One such case was that of Roberta Cowell who, in her autobiographical account of 1954, wrote about her transition from a male RAF pilot to a woman (Hall 2005, 151).

[8] The Act did not apply to the armed services or the Merchant Navy (Weeks 1990, 11).

[9] See, for example, J Brown's essay, "Poverty in Post-War Britain" in *Understanding Post-War British Society.* (1994 London Routledge, 16-127).

[10] Genesis 2:8-25 and 3:1-24

[11] "Her Table Spread" was first published in 1930 as "A Conversation Piece" in *The Broadsheet Press*, subsequently reprinted in *The Cat Jumps* in 1934, *Look at all the Roses* (1941), *Stories by Elizabeth Bowen* (1959), *A Day in the Dark* (1965) and *Elizabeth Bowen's Irish Stories* (1978) (Sellery and Harris 1981, 35, 48, 80, 91, and 100) and then again in *Collected Stories* (418-424).

[12] "Typhoid Mary" was the name given to Mary Mallon (1869 – 1938), an Irish immigrant to the United States of America. Although Mary appeared healthy and did not show the symptoms of typhoid, she was a carrier who infected many people during her lifetime, mostly through her work as a cook (http://www.crimelibrary.com/criminal_mind/forensics/typhoid_mary). "Sauve qui peut" literally translates as "save who can" but the phrase is usually translated as "let him save himself who can" or "every man for himself".

[13] This isn't of course, the only instance of a humorous telephone conversation and it contains echoes of the conversation between Dinah and Sheikie in *The Little Girls*.

[14] Bowen's use of humour in the novel can also be seen in her choice of Iseult's birthplace. Given her interest in language and literature, the use of Reading as her place of birth seems entirely appropriate. Equally appropriate is the name of the woman looking after Jeremy at Victoria Station as her name (Mrs. Caliber) relates directly to the weapon he is carrying.

[15] Like Eva and Jeremy, the more sophisticated Henry, too, has a place in which he feels secure – his father's parish church in which he is aware of "something pre-natal" (*ET*, 250).

[16] Reprinted in *Collected Stories* pp.21-27.

[17] Bowen's treatment of dying passion within matrimony in relation to the Arbles' marriage is not, of course, a new perspective on marriage, it is one which appears in many novels. Indeed, Maroula Joannou notes a similar theme in Nancy Mitford's novel *The Pursuit of Love*, stating that a "consistent thread running through the novel and through much of Nancy Mitford's fiction is the incompatibility of marriage and passion" (2003, 127).

[18] Eva is twenty-four when she takes the Danceys to the castle, Henry just twelve

(ET, 12 and 14).

[19] In voicing this opinion Eva is echoing Alice's reaction when condemned in the trial at the end of *Alice's Adventures in Wonderland*.

[20] This can be compared with Louie Lewis' satisfaction at having found her place in society when she becomes a mother (*The Heat of the Day*).

[21] See letter to William Plomer, 10th May 1968. A reproduction of the dust jacket can be found in Christensen (2001, 95).

[22] The question of the addressee also occurs in *A House in Paris* where the addressee varies significantly, particularly in regard to the direct addresses to the unborn Leopold (see chapter three).

LAST WORDS

Prior to her death on February 22nd 1973 Bowen started writing a new novel, *The Move-In.*[1] The opening chapter tells the story of three young people as they arrive unannounced at dinnertime at a house they believe to belong to the aunt of a man they met in Spain. In this it would appear that they are mistaken. Of course, it is impossible to predict what trajectory this novel could have taken had Bowen lived but one could surmise that the novel would have continued her examination of the theme of innocence to be found in her earlier novels and it could also be supposed that the narrative of the novel would have been as complex as that of *The Little Girls* or *Eva Trout, or Changing Scenes.* Consideration of this novel would therefore have added to the discussion in this book, throughout which there has been a focus on the notion of innocence and its loss through an examination of the myriad representations of innocence that can be found in Bowen's fiction.

My overriding concern in this book has been the transition from innocence to experience and the epistemological journey for both characters and the reader which accompanies this transition. Moments of recognition (or *anagnôrisis*), the acquisition of knowledge and the understanding of one's identity often provide the impetus for this evolutionary step. Equally, the multivalency of types of innocence in Bowen's fiction—the innocence attributed to childhood, sexual innocence and morality, political innocence and violence as an antithesis to innocence—are all important when considering the rôle innocence has to play in her novels. Emerging from these arguments has been the recognition that the reader's own epistemological journey is also of importance in Bowen's fiction with specific regard to the authorial manipulation of the narrative of later novels which delays the reader's comprehension of the text, a delay which ensures that often both character and reader gain understanding in parallel. It's also important to acknowledge the increasing complexity of her fiction, from the comparatively superficial treatment of both character and narrative of the earlier novels, such as *The Hotel, The Last September* and *Friends and Relations*, to the complexities inherent in Bowen's later fiction; with its tripartite structure *The House in Paris*, arguably, denotes a major development of Bowen's narrative technique, a technique she developed and refined through the remainder of her novels and one that reached its apotheosis in *The Little Girls* and *Eva Trout, or Changing Scenes.*

Bowen stated that "[i]t is not only our fate but our business to lose innocence, and once we have lost that it is futile to attempt to picnic in Eden" (1946:264); however, society also has difficulty contending with the presence of innocence; this is particularly the case in *The Death of the Heart.* Equally, the loss of innocence can be fatal, as in *Eva Trout, or Changing Scenes* or *To the North* but the reader might hope for a more positive outcome for Lois, Louie or Leopold and, perhaps, for Karen Michaelis once she has accepted "the weight of being herself" (*HP*:152). We can therefore reach the conclusion that while the transition from innocence to experience may well be "our fate and our business" it is a journey which is often brutal and painful; nevertheless it is a journey which has to be undertaken so that individuals can function fully in the society in which they live, so that they do not remain "incurable strangers to the world" (*DH*:106).

Notes

[1] Published in Pictures and Conversations, pp.67-76.

APPENDIX

UNPUBLISHED LETTERS
AND AN EXTRACT FROM *ANNA*

This appendix includes transcriptions of letters in the archives of John Rylands Library, Manchester University and Palace Green Library, University of Durham, together with a transcription of a synopsis for *The Death of the Heart.* It also includes transcriptions of part of Bowen's unpublished novel, *Anna*, which is lodged at the Arthur Ransom Centre at the University of Texas at Austin.

Letters from Elizabeth Bowen to Leslie Hartley

All the letters to Leslie Hartley can be found in the L.P. Hartley collection at John Rylands Library, University of Manchester.

Bowen's Court
Kildorrey
Co. Cork

21st October 1952

My dear Leslie

Your understanding is such a comfort and such a stay to me. I don't think anyone has known so clearly what Alan's death has meant – and, believe me, I say this without self-pity. It seems so odd that this is the one experience I cannot talk over with him – I imagine that many people who have been left behind after years of a long, close companionship feel that. I reproach myself, now, for how little I have understood loneliness – and even now, when I have such a letter as yours, I realise that I am still spared what must be worst of all, *friendless* loneliness, a complete exposure to the brutalising indifference of the world.

You understood Alan so well: he did feel always such a great affection for you "What a darling man Leslie is," he said one evening when you were here this spring. I am so awfully glad – more glad than ever, since what has happened – that you were *here* this spring. Not only did your being here give Alan and me such happiness, but I love to think that those days live in your memory, as well in mind.

I'd love to come and see you in England in the later spring: I'm going to America for the mid-winter, then shall be in Italy for the second half of March and beginning of April. In the main, I am going to live on here, if I can.

I do hope the *wretched* business of the drain across your garden has subsided. I hate to think of the worry it must have been. Dear Leslie, I think of you so often. I hope you'll have a good winter, and it will be lovely to see you again after that.

Cynthia tells me you've finished another book.

Thank you again for a letter which meant so much.

> Affectionately
> Elizabeth

> Rome
> April 1st 1953

[…]

As it was, in Venice for two days more or less by myself, except for a few social occasions, I became so melancholy, so much a prey to the feelings of vacancy that I do my best to evade these days, that I wept from a small bridge into one of the small canals. So it was lovely to arrive at Settignaro and find your letter.

[…]

As you know "an establishment" is rather a tie (though I think it's a tie which is worth having) and I cannot expect faithful souls, indoors and out, to keep the place going if I am seldom there.

> 15th September 1954
> Bowen's Court
> Kildorrey
> Co. Cork

[…]

I have loved *The White Wand*, which last week I tried to write about however inadequately for the 'Tatler' […] And as for the *Go-Between*, I nearly wrote to you but hardly knew what to say, you must know, as the rest of the world knows, what a triumph it is – absolutely satisfying on every page. I long to know about your next book. I've finished mine – which J. Cape peevishly complain is rather *short*. But myself I like it.

[…]

Letters from Elizabeth Bowen to William Plomer

These letters can be found in the William Plomer Collection at Palace Green Library, Durham University.

22.9.48
Bowen's Court
Kildorrey
Co. Cork

Dearest William

I'm so desperately sorry to have been, in spite of your telegram, so slow about producing this blurb for *The Heat of the Day*. I've been for weeks in the state of mind equivalent into bursting into tears when one was a child and roaring and wailing "I *cant* …!" And in fact though I appear to have written something, I still can't. Really in fact I think it too much to ask – and that *you* asked it, or I wouldn't say so.

Can you embroider the germs of this that I send in something more concrete + presentable. Or, scrap this entirely and simply summarise the plot?

I ask myself whether the *H. of the D.* needs a blurb – it's so straight forward; nothing about it really needs to be explained. I notice quite lot of novels these days have stopped having blurbs. Of course, from the reviewers' point of view that's a curse …

Well, here it is. I'm sorry to land you up with anything so awful. But I wish you *would* talk Cape's out of having a blurb at all.

Much love
+ I thank you for your lovely letter –
Elizabeth

[Reproduced by permission of Durham University Library: Plomer 19/9]

1st June 1963

WHITE LODGE.
OLD HEADINGTON.
OXFORD.

My dear William,

I can't tell you how happy I was to have your letter about *The Little Girls*. I would have written before, but have been day-and-night at work finishing the book. It *is* now finished, as I have written to Wren Howard by this same post to say. (Am sending the final chapters off to the typist tomorrow, and will send them to Cape's as soon as the copies come back from her (typist.)

It means a lot to me that *you* like The Little G.'s, and see its point. I hope you will like the remaining chapters – which amount to *about* 150 pages more. This book had to have "an end", not just trickle out: that's why, though I foresaw the end, I've been so long in writing it down. It does now please me (impersonally speaking.)

Your query about Suzanne Lenglen is v. important: being (or having been) an exact contemporary of mine, she was a 14-year-old tennis prodigy in 1914. This I could *swear* to. I was myself then, in 1914, fourteen, and how I envied her. The indomitable Sheikie Beaker herself being (or being regarded as being) a child "star" would I think have "collected" the child Lenglen, in spite of Lenglen's being 3 years older than Sheikie. What I must do, I think, is insert into the M.S. "child tennis prodigy Suzanne Lenglen"

I have a horror of anachronisms, real or apparent. This was – I could still swear – apparent; but in so far as it is apparent must be explained. – What I would have more expected to be queried would be the Pauline Chase as Peter Pan photo. Pauline C. created that important role, and remains for many the prototype Peter Pan. She did I think retire from being Peter Pan in about 1910 or 1911; she certainly was not still playing P.P. in 1914. *I* saw her as P.P. in 1908. But it appears to me that Sheikie, though only 5 in 1908, would have been smart enough to accquire [sic] *or* have accquired [sic] on her behalf, a signed Pauline Chase Peter Pan photograph.

The Little Girls as I feel that you saw, though others may not, is not autobiographical. I myself was not one of those 3. But it is what Americans would call "a recall of sensory experience" book. I've taken some liberties with the Folkestone landscape, but as it's called Southstone I suppose that doesn't matter.

       I do wish I could see you.
          Love from
           Elizabeth

27th February 1968

Carbery
Church Hill
Hythe
Kent

Dearest William

I got back from Italy last night and was overjoyed to find your letter. I'd been on tenterhooks to know what you'd think of EVA – what *you'll* think, I mean. Thank you very much, indeed, for writing as you did. One – or I – so easily could begin to believe an entire book has been a hallucination. It means more than I can say to know that you like it, that you have enjoyed it.

Yours affectionately + gratefully
Elizabeth

[Durham University Library: Plomer 19/20]

10th May 1968
Carbery
Church Hill
Hythe
Kent

Dearest William

This is a premature inquiry and a confidential one. Do you think Phillipe Julian (or is it, Philippe?) would ever do a jacket for *Eva Trout*?

And if he would, would Cape's be induced to pay up, or would they shy off, the fee that he could, would and certainly should expect?

I *long* for a P.J. jacket for the book.

Now it's all over, between you and me and the doorpost I did loathe the jacket Cape's gave *The Little Girls*. "A young artist", I was told. I really don't want *Eva* to be used to break in any more young artists. Those 3 little arty monsters on *The Little Girls'* jacket couldn't have been worse. *Neither do I want any more of Miss Joan Cassell.*

I don't want to put you in an awkward position over this. All I wonder is, could you possibly put out feelers?

Longing, as ever, to see you. The Connollys, as you'll have heard, have removed to Eastbourne. Veronica Wedgwood becoming your not-distant neighbour in that house at Alciston they've acquired: I'm going to lunch with them tomorrow week.

I hope *you* are well? I feel it would be egotism to ask for any of your time, but if London, Lewes or Hythe for lunch ever seemed possible, let me know?

> Love from
> Elizabeth

Adastra Avenue must be full of flowering trees. We have many here – it's a pretty month, May, in spite of the tempests.

[Reproduced by permission of Durham University Library: Plomer 19/21]

> 2 Clarence Terrace
> Regent's Park
> N.W.1
> Thursday

My dear William

Here at any rate is my *angle* on the two books [*The Last September* and *The Death of the Heart*]. I do hope the splicing-in of this into whatever more plot summary may be necessary won't give you too much work. You should not of course be doing *any* of this.

> Forgive haste and general squalour
> Much love from
> Elizabeth

THE DEATH OF THE HEART

The scene is London, the time the late 'thirties. Into a group of expensive young–middle–aged people arrives the sixteen-year-old Portia, brought up on the cheap abroad, disconcertingly vulnerable, manifestly trying to understand what this is all about, looking for something that is not there. Were she any living person's child she would not be so trying, but she is an orphan. Involuntarily, innocently, she penetrates everybody's defenses, stumbling upon what it is not good to know. Evident victim, she is also an inadvertent victimiser – most of all in the case of the young man Eddy, whom her impossible lovingness and austere trust break. Eddy, himself of an innocence less deeply corrupted than might appear, has, in his own words, been made a monkey of by the society in which he and

Portia meet: he is a jaded, unwilling playboy who has taken refuge in parodying himself.

Portia's step-brother Thomas Quayne, his wife Anna, their friend St Quentin live in an accomplice world. They never do quite convince themselves or each other. For their lonely acquaintance the outlander Major Brutt the Quaynes stand for a dear illusion: no illusion, however, is entertained by the elderly housemaid Matchett. – For Portia, a break from the Quaynes' London offers itself in the form of an April visit to the seaside: Mrs Heccomb's villa, her step-children and their jovial young set seem a homlier, sturdier proposition. Had Eddy not followed Portia to Seale-on--Sea there might have been tears unshed.

This is a pre-war book: since it was written the urbane gleaming stucco terraces of the Quaynes' Regents Park have been gaunt shells. As for the heart – for it is *not* uniquely the heart of Portia that we contemplate – who shall say? Perhaps it was reanimated just in time.

Note: This letter, although undated, was written after 1945 (the accompanying 'blurb' for *The Death of the Heart* places it after the bombing of London in the Second World War. It is possible that the two 'blurbs' were written by Bowen for the Collected Edition of her work, published on 26th July 1948 (Sellery and Harris, 1981, pp. 26 &42). Both this letter and its accompanying plot outlines for the two novels is reproduced by permission of Durham University Library: Plomer 19/38/1, 19/38/3 and 19/38/4

Anna

Extracts from *Anna*, an unpublished manuscript held by the Harry Ransom Humanities Research Centre, The University of Texas at Austin.

[…] Walking towards Brompton Road, but not meeting St Quentin, Anna now asked herself whom she should go and see next. A good deal of her life was spent in her friends' houses; she went about hopefully, not knowing whom or what she was likely to pick up where. She was on dropping-in terms with a good many people and when not specifically invited often came in and sat.

[…]

"Are you writing a novel?"

"What makes you think that?"

I just wondered

Well yes, St Quentin, as a matter of fact I am. It is not autobiographical; it has not really much plot.

"I hope it will make money?"

"I don't really know" said Anna. "It's my collected impressions"

Then of course it depends a good deal what impressions you have collected. I really should like you, Anna, to have a success. For heaven's sake" he said earnestly "do not not be too subtle.

"Do you think I am subtle?" said Anna, raising her eyes.

"I know a lot about novels" said St Quentin. I read one almost every day. He seated himself abruptly at the other end of the sofa and pulled out his cigarette case but did not smoke, just sat clicking it open and shut. His manner became emphatic. "Be sure and remember" he said "that though you may not be very clever almost everybody who reads you – and still more important, reviews you – will be a good deal stupider than yourself. Intelligence is so rare that it may be taken as negligence. […]

[…] If you must be clever, be clever in such a way as nobody can suspect, in fact be point blank obvious. On days when you don't feel clever be just comfortably muzzy; that will be what they call atmospheric prose."

Harry Ransom Center
The University of Texas at Austin

BIBLIOGRAPHY

Works by Elizabeth Bowen

1927 (1981). *The Hotel*. London: Jonathan Cape Ltd.

1929 (1942). *The Last September.* London: Penguin Books Limited.

1931 (1999). *Friends and Relations*. London: Vintage.

1932 (1999). *To the North*. London: Vintage.

1935 (1976). *The House in Paris*. London: Penguin Books Limited.

1935. "The Mulberry Tree" in *Collected Impressions*, pp.185-194.

1937. "Why I go to the Cinema" in C. Davy (ed) 1937 *Footnotes to the Film*. pp.205-220.

1938 (1962). *The Death of the Heart*. London: Penguin Books.

1939. "Doubtful Subject" in *Collected Impressions*, pp.173-177.

1941. "Virginia Woolf" in *Collected Impressions*, pp.71-75.

1942a (1999). *Bowen's Court & Seven Winters*. London: Vintage.

1942b. *English Novelists*. London: William Collins.

1945a. "Folkestone: July, 1945" in *Collected Impressions*, pp.225-230.

1945b. "Notes on Writing a Novel" in E. Bowen. 1950 *Collected Impressions*, pp.249-263.

1945c. "The Demon Lover" in *Collected Impressions*, pp.47-52.

1946. "Out of a Book" in *Collected Impressions*, pp. 264-269.

1948 (1998). *The Heat of the Day*. London: Vintage.

1948. "Rider Haggard: *She*" in *The Mulberry Tree,* pp.246-250.

1950. *Collected Impressions*. London: Longmans, Green and Co.

c.1950. "London, 1940" in *Collected Impressions*, pp.217-220[1]

1951a. "The Bend Back" in *The Mulberry Tree*, pp.54-60[2]

1951b (2001). *The Shelbourne: A Centre in Dublin Life for more than a Century*. London: Vintage.

1952. "Preface" to *The Last September* in *Afterthought*, pp.95-100.

1955 (1999). *A World of Love*. London: Vintage.

1959. "Stories by Elizabeth Bowen" in *The Mulberry Tree.*

1962. *Afterthought: Pieces about Writing*. London: Longmans, Green and Co Ltd.

1963 (1982). *The Little Girls*. London: Penguin Books.

1965a (1970). *The Good Tiger.* London: Jonathan Cape Ltd.

1965b. "Preface" in *A Day in the Dark and Other Stories*. London: Jonathan Cape Ltd, pp.7-9.

1968 (1982). *Eva Trout, or Changing Scenes*. London: Penguin Books.

1972. "Pictures and Conversations" in *Pictures and Conversations*, pp.3-63.

1973. *The Move-In* in *Pictures and Conversations*, pp.67-76.

1975. *Pictures and Conversations*. London: Allen Lane.

1999a. *Collected Stories*. London: Vintage

1999b. *The Mulberry Tree*. H. Lee (ed) London: Vintage.

2008a. *The Bazaar and Other Stories*. A. Hepburn (ed) Edinburgh: Edinburgh University Press.

2008b. *People, Places, Things: Essays by Elizabeth Bowen*. A. Hepburn (ed) Edinburgh: Edinburgh University Press.

2008c. With Ritchie, C. *Love's Civil War: Love Letters and diaries from the love affair of a lifetime*. V. Glendinning with J Robertson (eds) London: Simon & Schuster UK Ltd.

2010. *Listening In: Broadcasts, Speeches and Interviews*. A. Hepburn (ed) Edinburgh: Edinburgh University Press.

Other works consulted

Arnold, M. 1852. "To Marguerite, in Returning a Volume of the Letters of Ortis" in K. Allott (ed) *The Poems of Matthew Arnold*. London: Longman, Green and Co Ltd, pp.123-125.

Atkins, J. 1977. *Six Novelists Look at Society: An Enquiry into the Social Views of Elizabeth Bowen, L.P. Hartley, Rosamond Lehmann, Christopher Isherwood, Nancy Mitford, C.P. Snow*. London: John Calder (Publishers) Limited.

Austin, A. 1989. *Elizabeth Bowen*. Boston: Twayne Publishers.

Barreca, R. 1994. *Untamed and Unabashed: Essays on Women and Humour in British Literature*. Detroit: Wayne State University Press.

Barry, P. 1995. *Beginning Theory : An Introduction to Literary and Cultural Theory*. Manchester: Manchester University Press.

Baxendale, J. and Pawling, C. 1996. *Narrating the Thirties : A Decade in the Making: 1930 to the Present*. Basingstoke: Macmillan Press Limited

Bellman, The. 1942. "Meet Elizabeth Bowen" in *The Bell*. Volume 4, Number 6 pp.420-427.

Bennett, A. and Royle, N. 1995a. *Elizabeth Bowen and the Dissolution of the Novel*. Basingstoke: Macmillan Press Limited.

—. 1995b. *Introduction to Literature, Criticism and Theory: Second Edition*. Harlow: Pearson Educational Limited.

Bentley, D.M. 1995 "Bliss Carmen's Letters to Margaret Lawrence 1927 - 1925". www.uwo/english/canadianpoetry/confederation/Bliss%Carmen/letters (16.3.04)

Blodgett, H. 1975. *Patterns of Reality : Elizabeth Bowen's Novels*. The Hague: Mouton & Co N.V.

Bluemel, K. 2009a. "Introduction: What is Intermodernism" in K. Bluemel(ed) *Intermodernism: Literary Culture in Mid-Twentieth-Century Britain*. Edinburgh: Edinburgh University Press, pp1-20.

—. 2009b. "Appendix: Who are the Intermodernists?" in K. Bluemel (ed) *Intermodernism: Literary Culture in Mid-Twentieth-Century Britain*. Edinburgh: Edinburgh University Press, pp208-224.

Blythe, R. 1977. "Introduction" in H. James. *The Awkward Age* pp.vii-xx.

Brannigan, J. 2002. *Literature, Culture and Society in Postwar England, 1945-1965*. Lampeter: The Edwin Mellen Press.

Bradshaw, D. 1999. "Hyams Place: *The Years*, the Jews and the British Union of Fascists" in M. Joannou (ed) *Women Writers of the 1930s*, pp.179-191.

Braudy, L. 1998. "The Genre of Nature: Ceremonies of Innocence" in M. Brown (ed). *Refiguring American Film Genres: Theory and History*. Berkeley, L.A. and London: University of California Press, pp.278-309.

Breen, J. 1990. *In Their Own Write: Twentieth Century Women's Fiction*. London: Macmillan Educational Press.

Briggs, J. 2005. *Virginia Woolf: An Inner Life*. London: Allen Lane.

Brittain, V. 1934 "Can the Women of the World Stop War" in P. Deane (ed). 1988 *History in Our Hands : A Critical Anthology of Writings on Literature, Culture and Politics from the 1930s*. London: Leicester University Press, pp.69-73.

Brooke, J. 1952. *Elizabeth Bowen*. London: Longmans Green and Co.

Brooks, P. 1984 (1992). *Reading for the Plot: Design and Intention in Narrative*. Cambridge, Massachusetts: Harvard University Press.

Brown, J. 1994. "Poverty in Post-War Britain" in *Understanding Post-War British Society*. J. Obelkevich and P. Catterall (eds). London: Routledge, pp.16-127.

Buckland, P. 1972. *Irish Unionism 1: The Anglo Irish and the New Ireland 1885 – 1922*. Dublin: Gill and Macmillan Limited.

Burdekin, K. 1937 (1985). *Swastika Night*. New York: The Feminist Press.

Byatt, A.S. 1976. "Introduction" in E. Bowen. *The House in Paris.* London: Penguin Books Limited, pp.7-16.

Calder, R.L. 1994. " "A More Sinister Troth": Elizabeth Bowen's "The Demon Lover" as Allegory" in *Studies in Short Fiction* Volume 31, Winter 1994, No.1, pp.91-97.

Cave, T. 1988 (2002). *Recognitions : A Study in Poetics.* Oxford: Clarendon Press.

Caserio, R.L. 1993. "Narrative in Paul de Man and Elizabeth Bowen" in *Modern Language Quarterly* 1993 54:2 pp.263-284.

Chessman, H. 1983. "Women and Language in the Fiction of Elizabeth Bowen" in *Twentieth Century Literature*. 1983, Volume 29:1, pp.69-85.

Cheyette, B. and Marcus, L. 1998. *Modernity: Culture and 'the Jew'.* Cambridge: Polity Press.

Christensen, L. 2001. *Elizabeth Bowen: The Later Fiction.* Copenhagen: Museum Tusculanum Press.

Clune, M., Day, G. and Maguire, C. 1997. "Decline and Fall? The Course of the Novel" in G. Day (ed.) *Literature and Culture in Modern Britain: Volume Two: 1930 - 1955.* Harlow: Addison Wesley Longman Limited, pp.50-69.

Coates, J. 1990. "Elizabeth Bowen's *The Last September*: The Loss of the Past and the Modern Consciousness" in *The Durham University Journal.* July 1990, Volume 82, No.2, pp.205-216.

—. 1992. "The Tree of Jesse and the Voyage Out : Stability and Disorder in Elizabeth Bowen's *Friends and Relations*". *Durham University Journal*, 84:2, pp.291-302.

—. 1998. *Social Discontinuity in the Novels of Elizabeth Bowen : The Conservative Quest.* Lampeter: The Edwin Mellen Press.

Coles, R. 1974. *Irony in the Mind's Life: Essays on Novels by James Agee, Elizabeth Bowen and George Eliot.* Charlottesville: University Press of Virginia.

Connor, S. 1996. *The English Novel in History 1950 – 1995.* London: Routledge.

Cooney, P. 2001. "The Raj in the Rain" in *The Guardian*, 10 November 2001, pp.28 – 36.

Corcoran, N. 1997. *After Yeats and Joyce: Reading Modern Irish Literature.* Oxford: Oxford University Press.

—. 2003. "A Ghost of Style: The Aftermath of Anglo-Ireland in Elizabeth Bowen's *A World of Love*" in *English: The Journal of the English Association* 2003, Volume 52, Number 203, pp.125-137.

—. 2004. *Elizabeth Bowen: The Enforced Return.* Oxford: Oxford University Press.

Coughlan, P. 1989. "Doubles, Shadows, Sedan-Chairs and the Past: The 'Ghost' stories of J.S. Le Fanu" in M. Allen and A. Wilcox (eds). 1989. *Critical Approaches to Anglo-Irish Literature.* Gerrards Cross: Colin Smythe, pp.17-39.

—. 1997. "Women and Desire in the work of Elizabeth Bowen". In E. Walshe (ed). 1997. *Sex, Nation and Dissent in Irish Writing.* New York: St Martins. Coveney, P. 1967. *The Image of Childhood.* Harmondsworth: Penguin Books Ltd.

Craig, P. 1986. *Elizabeth Bowen.* Harmondsworth: Penguin Books Ltd.

Cronin, M. 2001. *A History of Ireland.* Houndmills: Palgrave.

Crossland, M. 1981. *Beyond the Lighthouse : English Women Novelists in the Twentieth Century.* London: Constable and Company Limited.

Curtis, L. 1994. *The Cause of Ireland from the United Irishmen to Partition.* Belfast: Beyond the Pale Publications.

Curtis Brown, S. 1975. "Foreword" in Bowen, E. 1975. *Pictures and Conversations*, ppvii-xlii.

Darwood, N. 2009. "Empty Boxes, Empty Spaces: Elizabeth Bowen's *The Little Girls*" in A. McNair and J. Ryder (eds) *Further from the Frontiers: Cross-currents in Irish and Scottish Studies.* Aberdeen: AHRC Centre for Irish and Scottish Studies, pp11-20.

Davis, D. 1980. "Introduction" in Traherne, T. *Selected Writings*, pp.7-15.

Davy, C. 1937. "Contributors' Who's Who" in Davy, Charles (ed) 1937 *Footnotes to the Film.* London: Lovat Dickson Ltd, p.334.

Deane, P. 1998. *History in Our Hands : A Critical Anthology of Writings on Literature, Culture and Politics from the 1930s.* London: Leicester University Press.

Deane, S. 1996. *A Short History of Irish Literature.* London: Hutchinson and Co (Publishers) Ltd.

Dostal, R.M. 1964. *Innocence and Knowledge in the Novels of Elizabeth Bowen.* Unpublished thesis.

Ellmann, M. 2003. *Elizabeth Bowen: The Shadow Across the Page.* Edinburgh: Edinburgh University Press.

Fallon, B. 1999. *An Age of Innocence: Irish Culture 1930 – 1960.* Dublin: Gill and Macmillan Ltd.

Farley, D.G. 2010. *Modernist Travel Writing: Intellectuals Abroad.* Columbia and London: University of Missouri Press.

Fisk, R. 1983. *In Time of War: Ireland, Ulster and the price of neutrality 1939 – 1945.* London: André Deutsch Ltd.

Foster, R.F. 1993. *Paddy & Mr Punch : Connections in Irish and English History*. London: Allen Lane, The Penguin Press.

Foster, R.F. 1998. "Introduction" in E. Bowen 1948 (1998). *The Heat of the Day*. London: Vintage, pp.1-6.

Fussell, P. 1980. *Abroad: British Literary Traveling Between the Wars*. Oxford: Oxford University Press.

Genette, G. 1972 (1983). *Narrative Discourse: An Essay in Method*. Trans. Jane Lewin. New York: Cornell University Press.

Gindin, J. 1992. *British Fiction in the 1930s : The Dispiriting Decade*. New York: St Martin's Press Inc.

Glendinning, V. 1977 (1993). *Elizabeth Bowen : Portrait of a Writer*. London: Phoenix.

Hall, J. 1968. *The Lunatic in the Drawing Room : The British and American Novel since 1930*. London: Indiana University Press.

Hall, L. 2005. "Sexuality" in *A Companion to Contemporary Britain*. P. Addison and H. Jones (eds). Malden, Oxford and Carlton: Blackwell Publishing Ltd, pp.145-163.

Hanson, C. 1985. *Short Stories & Short Fictions 1880 – 1980*. London: The Macmillan Press Ltd.

Hartley, J. 1997 *Millions Like Us: British Women's Fiction of the Second World War*. London: Virago Press.

Heath, W. 1961. *Elizabeth Bowen: An Introduction to Her Novels*. Madison: The University of Wisconsin Press.

Hepburn, A. 2005. *Intrigue: Espionage and Culture*: New Haven and London: Yale University Press.

—. 2009. "Trials and Errors: *The Heat of the Day* and Postwar Culpability" in K. Bluemel (ed) *Intermodernism: Literary Culture in Mid-Twentieth-Century Britain*. Edinburgh: Edinburgh University Press, pp131-147.

Hewison, R. 1981 (1988). *In Anger: Culture in the Cold War 1945-1960*. London: Methuen.

Holtby, W. 1934 *Women and a changing civilisation*. London: John Lane The Bodley Head.

Homans, M. 1994. "Feminist Fictions and Feminist Theories of Narrative" in *Narrative*, 1994, Volume 2, pp.3-16.

Hoogland, R.C. 1994 *Elizabeth Bowen : A Reputation in Writing*. New York: New York University Press.

Humble, N. 2001. *The Feminine Middlebrow Novel, 1920s to 1950s: Class, Domesticity and Bohemianism*. Oxford: Oxford University Press

Hynes, S. 1976 *The Auden Generation : Literature and Politics in England in the 1930s*. London: The Bodley Head.

Ingman, H. 1998. *Women's Fiction Between the Wars : Mothers, Daughters and Writing*, Edinburgh: Edinburgh University Press.

James, H. 1899 (1987). *The Awkward Age*. London, Penguin Books Ltd.

—. 1907. "Preface to "The Portrait of a Lady" " in H. James 1907 (1934). *The Art of the Novel*. New York: Charles Scribners' Sons, pp.40-58.

Jameson, S. 1937. "New Documents" in P. Deane (ed) 1998. *History in Our Hands: A Critical Anthology of Writings on Literature, Culture and Politics from the 1930s*, pp.311-318.

Jeffreys, S. 1985. *The Spinster and Her Enemies: Feminism and Sexuality 1880-1930*. London and New York: Pandora.

Joannou, M. 2003. "Nancy Mitford and *The Pursuit of Love*" in J. Dowson (ed) *Women's Writing 1945 –1960: After the Deluge*. Houndmills: Palgrave Macmillan, pp.177-130.

Johnson, E. L. 2004. "Giving up the Ghost: National and Literal Haunting in *Orlando*" in *Modern Fiction Studies*. Volume 50:1, Spring 2004, pp.110-128.

Jordan, H.B. 1992. *How Will the Heart Endure : Elizabeth Bowen and the Landscape of War*. Michegan: University of Michegan Press.

Karl, F.R. 1964. *A Reader's Guide to the Contemporary English Novel*. London: Thames and Hudson.

Kelsall, M. 1993. *The Great Good Place: The Country House and English Literature*. Hemel Hemstead: Harvester Wheatsheaf.

Kenney, E.J. 1975. *Elizabeth Bowen*. New Jersey and London: Associated University Presses.

Kiberd, D. 1992. "Introduction" in J. Joyce 1922 (2000). *Ulysses*. London: Penguin Books Ltd, pp.ix-lxxx.

—. *Inventing Ireland: The Literature of the Modern Nation*. London: Vintage.

Kitchen, M. 1988 (1990). *Europe Between the Wars: A Political History*. Harlow: Longman Group UK Limited.

Kreilkamp, V. 2009. "Bowen: Ascendancy Modernist" in E. Walshe (ed) *Elizabeth Bowen*. Dublin: Irish Academic Press, pp.12-26.

Lane, J. and Clifford, B. 1999. *Elizabeth Bowen: 'Notes on Eire', Espionage Reports to Winston Churchill, 1940-2; With a Review of Irish Neutrality in World War 2*. Aubane: Aubane Historical Society.

Lane, J. 1999a. "Introduction" in *Elizabeth Bowen: 'Notes on Eire', Espionage Reports to Winston Churchill, 1940-2; With a Review of Irish Neutrality in World War 2*, pp.5-10.

—. 1999b. "An Attempt to Discredit" in *Elizabeth Bowen 'Notes on Eire' Espionage Reports to Winston Churchill, 1940-2 with a Review of Irish Neutrality in World War 2*, pp.125-146.

Lanser, S. S. 1992. *Fictions of Authority: Women Writers and Narrative Voice.* Ithaca and London: Cornell University Press.

Larkin, P. 1964. "MCMXIV" in *The Whitsun Weddings.* London: Faber and Faber, p.28.

Lassner, P. 1990. *Elizabeth Bowen.* Houndmills, Basingstoke: Macmillan Education Ltd.

—. 1991. *Elizabeth Bowen: A Study of the Shorter Fiction.* New York: Twayne Publishers.

—. 1998. *British Women Writers of World War II: Battlegrounds of their Own.* Basingstoke: Macmillan Press Ltd.

Lassner, P. and Derdiger, P. 2009. "Domestic Gothic, the Global Primitive, and Gender Relations in Elizabeth Bowen's *The Last September* and *The House in Paris*" in M. McGarrity and C.A. Culleton. (eds) *Irish Modernism and the Global Primitive.* New York: Palgrave Macmillan, pp195-214.

Lawrence, M. 1937. *We Write as Women.* London: Michael Joseph Ltd.

Leavis, F.R. 1930. *Mass Civilisation and Minority Culture* in P. Deane (ed) 1998 *History in Our Hands: A Critical Anthology of Writings on Literature, Culture and Politics from the 1930s*, pp.16-25.

Leavis, Q. D. 1932. *Fiction and the Reading Public.* London: Chatto and Windus.

Lee, H. 1981 (1999). *Elizabeth Bowen.* London: Vintage.

Lyons, F.S.L. 1963 (1985). *Ireland Since the Famine.* London: Fontana Press.

—. 1979 (1989). *Culture and Anarchy in Ireland 1890-1939: From the Fall of Parnell to the Death of W. B. Yeats: The Ford Lectures Delivered in the University of Oxford in the Hilary Term of 1978.* Oxford: Oxford University Press.

Lucas, F.L. 1928 (1946). *Tragedy in Relation to Aristotle's Poetics.* London: The Hogarth Press.

McCormack, W.J. 1994. *From Burke to Beckett: Ascendancy, Tradition and Betrayal in Literary History.* Cork: Cork University Press.

Mackay, J. 1996. *Michael Collins: A Life.* Edinburgh: Mainstream Publishing Company (Edinburgh) Ltd.

Maslen, E. 2001. *Political and Social Issues in British Women's Fiction, 1928-1968.* Houndmills: Palgrave.

May, K. 1977. *Out of the Maelstrom : Psychology and the Novel in the Twentieth Century*, London: Elek Books Limited.

Medoff, J. 1984. " "There is no elsewhere": Elizabeth Bowen's Perceptions of War" in *Modern Fiction Studies* 1984 Spring 30:1, pp.73-81.

Miller, B. 1941 (2000). *Farewell Leicester Square.* London: Persephone Books.

O'Brien, T. 1987. "Light and Enlightenment in Elizabeth Bowen's Irish Novels" in *Ariel,* 1987, Volume 18, April, pp.47-62

O'Faolain, S. 1942. "New Wine in Old Bottles" in *The Bell.* Volume 4:6, pp.381-388.

—. 1956 (1971). *The Vanishing Hero: Studies in Novelists of the Twenties.* Freeport, New York: Books for Libraries Press.

O'Toole, T. 2009. "Angels and Monsters: Embodiment and Desire in *Eva Trout*" in E. Walshe (ed) *Elizabeth Bowen.* Dublin: Irish Academic Press, pp.162-178.

Osborne, S. 2006a. "Reconsidering Bowen" in *Modern Fiction Studies* Spring 2006, Volume 52, Number 1, pp.187-197.

—. 2006b. "Call for Papers: Upcoming Special Issue: Elizabeth Bowen" in *Modern Fiction Studies* Spring 2006, Volume 52, Number 1, p.260.

Parish, P. 1973. "A Loss of Eden': Four Novels of Elizabeth Bowen" in *Critique* 1973 Volume XV, Number 1, pp.86-100.

Parsons, D.L. 1997. "Souls Astray: Elizabeth Bowen's Landscape of War". *Women: A Cultural Review.* Spring 1997, pp.24-32.

Partridge, E. 1966. *Origins: A Short Etymological Dictionary of Modern English.* London: Routledge, Kegan and Paul.

Prince, G. 1973. "Introduction to the Study of the Narrattee" in M.J. Hoffman and P.D. Murphy (eds) 1996 *Essentials of the Theory of Fiction.* London: Leicester University Press, pp.213-233.

Punter, D. 1980. *The Literature of Terror: A History of Gothic Fictions from 1765 to the Present Day.* London: Longman Group Limited.

Radford, J. 1999. "Late Modernism and the Politics of History" in M. Joannou (ed) *Women Writers of the 1930s : Gender, Politics and History.* Edinburgh: Edinburgh University Press, pp.33-45.

—. 1998 "The Woman and the Jew: Sex and Modernity" in B. Cheyette and L. Marcus (eds) *Modernity, Culture and 'the Jew'.* Cambridge: Polity Press, pp.91-104

Richards, J. 1984. *The Age of the Dream Palace: Cinema and Society in Britain 1930-1939.* London: Routledge & Kegan Paul.

—. 1997. "Modernism and the People: the View from the Cinema Stalls" in K. Williams and S. Matthews (editors) *Rewriting the Thirties: Modernism and After.* Harlow: Addison Wesley Longman, pp.182 – 194).

Rimmon-Kenan, S. 1983 (2001). *Narrative Fiction.* London: Routledge.

Ritchie, C. 1974. *The Siren Years: A Canadian Diplomat Abroad: 1937-1945.* Toronto: MacMillan of Canada.

—. 1981. *Diplomatic Passport: More Undiplomatic Diaries 1946 – 1962*. Toronto: McClelland and Stewart Ltd.

—. 1983. *Storm Signals: More Undiplomatic Diaries 1962 – 1971*. Toronto: McClelland and Stewart Ltd.

Rose, J. 2000. "Bizarre Objects: Mary Butts and Elizabeth Bowen" in *Critical Quarterly*, Volume 42, number 1, pp.75-85.

Rowbotham, S. and Weeks, G. 1977. "Introduction" in: S. Rowbotham and G. Weeks (Eds.) *Socialism and the New Life: The Personal and Sexual Politics of Edward Carpenter and Havelock Ellis*. London: Pluto Press Limited.

Rhys, J. 1928 (1969) *Quartet*. London, Andre Deutsch Limited.

Rule, J. 1976. *Lesbian Images*. London: Peter Davies Limited.

Sellery, J.M. and Harris, W.O. 1981. *Elizabeth Bowen: A Bibliography*. Austin: The University of Texas at Austin.

Simon, J., Moloney, T.F., Henry, D.S., Murphy, H.L. 1916. "Report of the Royal Commission on the Arrest on 25th April 1916 and Subsequent Treatment of Mr Francis Sheehy Skeffington, Mr Thomas Dickson and Mr Patrick James McIntyre" in T. Coates (ed) (2000) *The Irish Uprising, 1914-1921: Papers from the British Parliamentary Archive*. London. The Stationery Office, pp.115-152.

Stendhal (M. H. Beyle). 1822a (1986). *De l'Amour*. Paris: G F Flammarion.

—. 1822b. *Love*. Translated G Sale and S Sale. 1986. Harmondsworth: Penguin Books Ltd.

Stewart, J. and Knight, B.C. 1975. "Introduction". in Stendhal, 1822b *Love* pp.9-22.

Thorpe, A. 1992. *Britain in the 1930s: The Deceptive Decade*. Oxford: Blackwell Publishers.

Traherne, T. 1669 (1980). *Selected Writings*. D. Davis (ed). Manchester: Fyfield Books.

Tylee, C. M. 2009. "Hyphenated Identity in the "Woman's Novel": Racisms and Betty Miller's *Farewell Leicester Square*" in R. Hackett, F. Hauser and G. Wachman (eds) *At Home and Abroad in the Empire: British Women Write the 1930s*. Newark: University of Delaware Press, pp.119-136.

Wall, S. 1970. "Aspects of the Novel 1930 – 1936" in B. Bergonzi (ed) *The Twentieth Century*. London: Barnes and Jenkins, pp.222-276.

Walshe, E. 2009. "A Time for Hard Writers" in E. Walshe (ed) *Elizabeth Bowen*. Dublin: Irish Academic Press, pp.95-109.

—. 2009 "A Sort of Lunatic Giant" in E. Walshe (ed) *Elizabeth Bowen*. Dublin: Irish Academic Press, pp.150-161.

Weeks, J. 1990. *Coming Out: Homosexual Politics in Britain from the Nineteenth Century to the Present.* London: Quartet Books.

West, R. 1935. "The Necessity and Grandeur of the International Ideal" in P. Deane (ed) 1988 *History in Our Hands : A Critical Anthology of Writings on Literature, Culture and Politics from the 1930s.* London: Leicester University Press, pp.74-88.

Williams, K. 1996. *British Writers and the Media 1930 – 1945.* Houndmills: Macmillan Press Ltd.

Wills, C. 2007. *That Neutral Island: A History of Ireland During the Second World War.* London: Faber and Faber Limited.

—. 2009. " 'Half Different': The Vanishing Irish in *A World of Love*" in E. Walshe (ed) *Elizabeth Bowen.* Dublin: Irish Academic Press, pp.133-149.

Woolf, V. 1979 *The Sickle of the Moon: The Letters of Virginia Woolf 1932 - 1935.* London: The Hogarth Press Limited.

Wordsworth, A. 1995. "Foreword" in A. Bennett and N. Royle 1995a. *Elizabeth Bowen and the Dissolution of the Novel*, pp.vii-viii.

Wyatt-Brown, A. 1993. "The Liberation of Mourning in Elizabeth Bowen's *The Little Girls* and *Eva Trout*" in A. Wyatt-Brown and J. Rossen (eds) *Aging and Gender in Literature: Studies in Creativity.* Charlottesville and London: University Press of Virginia, pp.164-186.

Yeats, W. B. 1916. "Easter 1916" in W B Yeats. 1990. *Selected Poetry* A Norman Jeffares (editor) London: Pan Books pp.93-95.

Other Internet sources

www.bartleby.com.101/769.html . (28.4.06)

www.collectorspost.com/Actors/pauline_chse.html (6.4.06)

www.crimelibrary.com/criminal_mind/forensics/typhoid_mary (10.11.06)

http://www.tennis.co.uk/player/suzanne-lenglen/index.shtml (27.3.12)

www.explore-biography.com/musicians/L/Lucienne _Boyer.html (9.6.05)

www.george-macdonald.com/Meredith/woods_of_westermain.html (1.5.06)

www.marx-brothers.org (27.3.12)

members.aol.co./wordspage/pr/pr11.html (28.4.06)

pantheon.yale.edu/%7ekd47/What-Is-Epistemology.html (17.11.05)

ppu.ppu.org.uk/ppu/ppu_hisx.html (14.12.04)

TV and Film

BBC. 1998. *Bookmark: Elizabeth Bowen: The Death of the Heart.*
Tartan Video. 1999. *The Last September.* Deborah Warner (Director).

Notes

---

[1] For a discussion of the date of this essay, refer to footnote 12, chapter five.
[2] For a discussion of the date of this essay, refer to footnote 20, chapter six.

INDEX